Biblical EQ

A Christian Handbook For Emotional Transformation

By John Edmiston

ISBN: 1-4196-4913-2

D1096911

Table Of Contents

How to Understand and Use This Book

This is a Christian handbook on emotional transformation. Biblical EQ is about emotional competence, about being able to handle and discern emotions and express them wisely. The emphasis of the book is ongoing growth rather than healing. The book does not assume that the reader has emotional "problems" that need to be "fixed". This is not a book for people with high levels of emotional pain to read in order to get better – though it may achieve that. Biblical EQ is a fitness manual rather than a diagnostic manual. Its focus is strength, health and maturity.

The aim of this book is to equip Christians, especially those in the ministry, by putting them in touch with the basics of their emotional being, getting them to commit to become emotionally mature and Christlike, and helping with the correction of areas of imbalance and immaturity. Our aim is to show them how to express emotions with clarity, integrity and sensitivity in the context they are in. That's a lot for one book, so Biblical EQ starts with some solid foundations and builds upward. We are not tackling one emotion at a time but actually trying to rebuild the Christian's entire understanding of the emotional life of the believer from the ground up.

The first section, Jesus As Our Model, deals with some of the basic overall biblical theology of emotions and is foundational to the rest of the book. It is written from an evangelical viewpoint and at a level that should suit most committed Christians. Its central premise is that Jesus Christ is the model for our emotional life and that the sanctification of our emotions is a work of grace involving the power of the Holy Spirit working in the committed Christian. It pictures the ideal Christian as having grand and powerful emotions that are holy and good and which are wisely and appropriately expressed in God's timing for His glory.

The second section, The Inner Self and Our Emotional World, is the part of the book that perhaps has the most new teaching for many readers. It spends a lot of time looking at how emotions arise in our spirit, in our soul and from our body and how these complex interactions create our emotions and our character. It draws together many counseling techniques and Scriptural insights. It should lead the reader to a deep understanding of self and of how others arrive at the place they are emotionally. It is founded on a very literal and exhaustive treatment of the Scripture and tries to work from the biblical data and carefully build an adequate understanding of the human person. Its central premise is that our inner self is not constant and fixed but is "being renewed day by day" and that we can be co-workers with God in this process of inner renewal.

The practical section is grounded in Proverbs-like general wisdom and common sense. Much will be familiar territory to some readers, however, it is useful to "be stirred up by way of reminder". It deals with our experience of self-mastery, emotions and issues of emotional regulation, how we can read other people's emotions and how to express those emotions appropriately in love. It also deals with how to tap into God's love so we can minister to others. Its central premise is that God links to us through faith, which works through love, that employs specific focused wisdom and knowledge to do good deeds. On our side of the equation we facilitate this process by fixing our minds firmly on Christ and mastering our personal responses.

This book tries to give you both the relationship aspects and the specific focused wisdom and knowledge aspects of biblical EQ. References for further reading, a teachers guide and an exhaustive index has been provided for those who want to dip into the book to research a particular issue. A seminar manual is also available as a separate publication.

PART ONE

JESUS AS OUR MODEL OF HOW OUR EMOTIONS WORK

This first section of the book sets the biblical basis in place. It looks at the emotional life of Jesus and then develops a model for how our emotions work, and how they can be redeemed, so that they end up mirroring the emotional life of Jesus Christ. The change needs a change agent and we look at how the Holy Spirit was behind the emotions of Jesus and how co-operating with Him is a large part of the secret of emotional development. First, we shall look at some common questions about emotions and establish whether or not we should bother about them. Then we shall investigate whether or not we can use Jesus as the model for the emotional life of the Christian. Having established that, we will move on to see how the Holy Spirit empowered His emotional life. At this point a five step model will be put forward for how godly and holy emotions arise. We shall then test this model by seeing if it predicts the results of the emotional life of the apostles, prophets and great Christian leaders. Then we shall test it again to see if it has a kind of "negative prediction" of how the emotional life of carnal Christians will turn out. By the end of this section the importance of the Holy Spirit in the emotional life of the believer will be firmly established. We will have then a biblically based and well tested model of the emotional life, that we will investigate more deeply in the second section of this book.

Commencing the Journey

Keep your heart with all diligence, For out of it spring the issues of life. (Proverbs 4:23 NKJV)

Good emotional management is a highly needed commodity in Christian work. Without it we can unintentionally make a complete mess out of our service for God. One emotional explosion at the wrong moment can be held against us for a long time to come and we are often judged by others on how we handle our emotions. Many very productive Christian workers have had to leave the ministry because they just could not manage their emotions well and this marred all their relationships. So we need to do something – but what can we do? The good secular materials available do not draw on the resources that the Holy Spirit can bring to emotional transformation and few good Christian resources exist that combine biblical insights with good clinical data. This book is an attempt to do that.

In order to do this I have had to start with first principles and work out a biblical paradigm with Jesus at its center and the emotional life of Jesus as our model. The Holy Spirit is seen as the main power behind emotional transformation. Also tips and techniques from secular authors as well as their data has been incorporated where this material is "Christian-compatible" so to speak. So this book is divided into three sections, the biblical basics, discussion of the inner self and our emotions, and practical tips on self-mastery and emotional expression. Each of these sections have five or six chapters. The biblical section discusses some foundational teaching about the Christian emotional life. The "inner self" section looks at how emotions arise in our spirit and soul and are influenced by our body, and how our inner emotional life is formed. Finally, the practical section looks at our experience and understanding of emotions and how they should be best expressed.

What is EQ?
Emotional intelligence is the term we use to describe a complex set of human abilities related to emotional management. The four key aspects of emotional intelligence as described by Mayer and Salovey (the pioneer researchers in the area) are:
1. Emotional identification, perception and expression

2. Emotional facilitation of thought
3. Emotional understanding
4. Emotional management

Various other researchers, most notably Daniel Goleman, have broken these into various sub-factors which are continually being reviewed. Recent findings in neurology have contributed greatly to our understanding of where emotions arise in the brain. The field is fluid and a final decision on what finally constitutes EQ has not been entirely reached yet and there are two or three main schools of thought. However, much is coming out of these studies that are very interesting from a Christian perspective, as we shall see in this study.

What Is Biblical EQ?

This is the biblical perspective on the above four key skill areas. It doesn't neglect the findings of neuroscience but it adds in the transforming power of the Holy Spirit and the wisdom of Proverbs. It has as its model the emotional life of Jesus Christ with His personal presence, self-control, emotional expressiveness and discernment of situations. Thus it has a clear pattern, a master plan that can be used to analyze theories and to determine what is true and false, wise and unwise. Secular theories have no "ideal person" to point to - they merely assemble ideals from their own theories and worldview. In Jesus we have a model, a guide, a point to aim our teaching towards and this is invaluable.

The Christian believer is to aspire to have the emotional life of Christ Jesus for that is very much part of being "in His image". Above all Biblical EQ is *biblical* - founded on faith in the inspired, inerrant and authoritative Scripture.

The Failure Of The Secular Models of EQ

After reading various EQ books you know that emotions are important, that you should handle them better and a lot about how they arose within you, but you are not shown how to conquer them. In fact many of the EQ programs based on this kind of research have had fairly middling results. The corporate sector is pulling back from them, partly because of recession but partly because they are not delivering as expected. Why is this so? Why has the secular approach to emotional intelligence fizzled?

First, they have a philosophical underpinning that has no definite direction. There is nothing intrinsic to the theory that tells them what to aim for when helping a person achieve a higher level of emotional intelligence. Apart from being in touch with ones emotions and being able to express them accurately, appropriately and responsibly there is no "big picture" of what the emotionally intelligent person should be like.

People end up confused and perplexed. Theories seem at variance with each other and the result is that some practitioners are almost Zen Buddhists while others are extremely businesslike, manipulative and pragmatic. Without any agreement on what an ideal person is they cannot make much real progress.

Second, much of the work of Goleman and others involves a model steeped in a medical and neurological framework that sees our responses as entirely conditioned by biology, genetics and environment. Alteration of responses is through medication, education and behavior modification. After a while people start to feel depersonalized by this approach, and react against the diminution of human responsibility that seems to be the outcome. It is so reductionistic and materialistic that after some initial enthusiasm people are repelled.

Third, prayer and spiritual disciplines are marginalized in the literature despite their utility. For instance on page 75 of Goleman's first book, *Emotional Intelligence,* he says, *"Finally, at least some people are able to find relief from their melancholy in turning to a transcendent power. Tice (a researcher into depression) told me "Praying, if you are very religious, works for all moods, especially depression".* Despite this obvious therapeutic value for prayer it is never again referred to in Goleman's book. People know religion works - they are just refusing to admit it much in print.

Should we then throw out their work entirely? Not at all. Truth is truth and measurements are measurements. There is an enormous amount of good work and wise information in the current EQ literature. It can be, and is, very helpful in giving us understanding of how our emotions work. However, it does not give us a whole lot of power to transform them. The power to defeat deep and difficult emotions comes from God and involves the human spirit coming into contact with God's Spirit. So in this book we shall tend to turn to secular sources to explain much of the physiology and the mechanisms of emotion and to Christian sources for the power to deal with them.

Core Concepts

To get answers that genuinely help people we need two things, a clear destination, and the power to get there in a reasonable amount of time. Our destination is the image of Christ Jesus. Our power to get there is the infilling with and transforming work of the Holy Spirit. These are just some of the great advantages of the gospel. We have hope, and we have lots of hope!

Thus the central premise of the book is that Christians can have their emotional life redeemed so that it is transformed to mirror the emotional life of Jesus Christ and that the Holy Spirit's power and grace are the key to this process. This involves renewing seven key aspects which will be discussed in detail as we move along:

1. Renewing our basic perceptions of reality and our perspective on life.
2. Renewing our individual belief system.
3. Renewing the purposes and intents of our heart.
4. Renewing our physical bodies and their influence on our emotions.
5. Renewing our ability to be aware of and to understand our own emotions.
6. Renewing our ability to understand the emotions of other people.
7. Renewing our ability to appropriately express emotion according to the desire of the Holy Spirit.

The first few of these are a very deep work. It takes effort, courage and time to change one's perspective on life or to review and change core beliefs, thoughts and intentions. However, unless this is done the foundations are not strong and any positive emotional changes will be temporary at best. Thus it is important that you work through the foundational chapters and understand them. They are the chapters which will give you the deepest wisdom to assist you with your emotional growth. Before we go much further we need to answer a few of the common questions about emotions and that is the topic of the next chapter.

Discussion Questions

1. What do you want out of this book?

2. Are you prepared to change?

3. How can we combine secular insights with biblical insights?

4. What are some of the reasons that the secular models of EQ have not got the results that everyone hoped they would?

5. What advantages does the revelation of Scripture give us?

6. What advantages do we obtain from having Jesus as our model?

Common Questions About Emotions

A fool vents all his feelings, But a wise man holds them back. (Proverbs 29:11 NKJV)

What Kind of Emotions Should Christians Have?
While God is emotional there are some emotions that God never has. God is never envious, lustful, greedy, bitter with selfish ambition, small-minded, or petty. Neither is he anxious or fretful but dwells in perfect peace. His emotions are positive, holy, noble and appropriate. God is light and in Him there is no darkness at all. Since we are called to be "in the image of God", then whatever else that means, it means that at the end of our Christian maturity, our emotions should in some measure share these divine qualities. We should be "walking in the light".

Thus godliness means forsaking some emotions and embracing others. We should be utterly free from unholy and fleshly emotions and moving toward mature and holy emotional responses. The mature saint of God is filled with love and utterly free from bitter envy and selfish ambition. (James 3:15-18). Petty covetous worldly longings are replaced by the love of the Father (1 John 2:15-17) and perfect love casts out fear so that we dwell in quietness, peace and confidence (1 John 4:18; Isaiah 26:3). Holy people do not easily fly into rages or engage in back-biting and quarrelling, rather they are centered people full of love, joy and peace (Galatians 5:19-23). There is thus a grand and holy emotional authenticity that accompanies maturity in Christ.

Generally speaking, our emotions can be broken down into three classes: **Holy Emotions** – those experienced by God such as compassion, joy, and holy indignation and those that accompany life in the Spirit such as praise, worship and adoration. These emotions are derived from the kingdom of light and the Sprit (Ephesians 5:18-21; Colossians 3:16-17; Galatians 5:22,23) and are in agreement with true wisdom (James 3:17,18) They are the emotions of Christ in us. They are not necessarily religious or pious emotions. Admiring a flower or delighting in beautiful music or focusing on the beautiful and the good can be just as holy as going to church (Philippians 4:8).

Human Emotions – based in our human situation and the created order and shared by Jesus during His time on earth. This includes emotions such as grief, pain, fear, abandonment, sadness and sorrow, anxiety, stress, anguish and vulnerability. These emotions are well chronicled in the Psalms. For the Christian they are temporary and in eternity there shall be no more crying or sadness or pain (Revelation 21:4). While these emotions may feel bad they are not evil or toxic. They can be painful but they are not poisonous.

Fleshly Emotions – are poisonous and destructive and include toxic emotions such as malice, envy, selfish ambition, sensuality, bitterness, overpowering lusts and murderous hatred. They are closely tied to the works of the flesh and with evil deeds. Their outcome is spiritual death. These emotions were not part of mankind at Creation and are not "natural human reactions" (For instance, grief is a natural human reaction but bitterness is fleshly. One can have "good grief" without a trace of bitterness. Bitterness is not natural to the human condition.) Rather these emotions are derived from the kingdom of darkness and have their source in a dark wisdom (James 3:14-16).

This classification helps us see the relative value of our emotional responses and to use the techniques described in the succeeding chapters to assist with our sanctification. It also puts the lie to the old humanist rubric "there are no right or wrong emotions." All emotions are not equal. Some are of much higher value than others and some emotions and impulses are positively wrong. This classification also goes a bit beyond the black and white classification of emotions as "spiritual" or "unspiritual" that causes so much pain in traditional missionary circles. When pain and disappointment are seen as "unspiritual" we simply add to the burden the person is carrying. Hurt, disappointment, pain and frustration are valid human emotions stemming from our creatureliness encountering a fallen world. Human beings were created good but mortal and it is as we explore this mortality that we find out many useful things about ourselves. The above simple classification also saves us from the error of stopping there with our human emotions and being content simply to explore ourselves at that level. It tells us there is something higher, something beyond our mortality and that it is as we focus on our immortality in Christ that we develop the highest and noblest parts of our being.

We are thus called to participate in the holy emotions so that they transcend the human emotions and overcome the fleshly emotions. By this I mean that we must choose our emotional level and which emotions we will be gripped by. When disappointment strikes we can choose to respond with holy emotions and pray through until we trust God and can praise Him as the Psalmist did or we can respond at the human level and sit down disconsolate in human misery and gradually see it through or we can respond from fleshly emotions and lash out in anger, bitterness, distrust and revenge. Consider Paul in jail in Philippi in Acts 16. He praised God, sang psalms and rejoiced thus transcending the human emotions of pain and discomfort and effectively banishing any fleshly emotions such as bitterness or desire for revenge. Thus Paul participated in holy emotions so that they transcended the human emotions and overcame the fleshly emotions. The human emotions are not denied or seen as wrong rather they are acknowledged but not focused on. They are transcended. The saint focuses on and deliberately chooses to move toward the holy emotions. Prayer, fasting, praise and worship, reading Scripture, meditating on good teaching and doing good works are all helpful in this process. However above and beyond these things we need the work of the Holy Spirit.

The Holy Spirit responds differently to each of these three categories of emotion. The Holy Spirit rejoices and assists us when we engage in holy responses. He produces them within us so they can justly be called "the fruit of the Spirit" (Romans chapters 8 & 12, and Galatians 5). On the other hand the Holy Spirit comforts us when the human emotions, such as grief, overwhelm us (see 2 Corinthians 1). Finally He is determined to break the grip of fleshly emotions such as hatred, lust and revenge. In fact the Spirit wars against such impulses so that we cannot fully give way to our worst desires (Galatians 5:16-18). Thus the Holy Spirit produces holy emotions, comforts overwhelming human emotions and wars against fleshly emotions. However, we have a choice in the matter. We can heed the Spirit's promptings or we can discard them in fleshly rebellion. This leads Paul to say that the mind set on the flesh and its fractious emotions "is death" but the mind set on the Spirit with His holy emotions is "life and peace" (Romans 8:5,6).

As we will see in other chapters, the Spirit renews the mind with its personal perspective and belief structure. The renewed mind becomes centered on God and can be validly called "the mind of Christ" (1 Corinthians 2:14-16). Thus as the mind is redeemed, renewed and set on the Spirit, life and peace result. This life and peace that results from a well disciplined and renewed mind is the aim of this book. This simple classification of emotions will be vastly expanded as the complexities and subtleties of the emotional life of the Christian life are explored. Our emotions need redemption if they are to become holy and the focus of all redemption is Jesus Christ who will be our model and pattern for biblical EQ.

Why Do Christians Seem To Stop Changing Emotionally After Few Years?

Massive early transformation followed by accommodation to religious sub-cultural norms is a fairly common pattern among Christians from an emotionally damaged childhood. Church life provides many little nooks and crannies where we can hide from the Holy Spirit and the hard work of emotional transformation. In many cases painful emotions are not understood by the clergy and even by some Christian counselors and damage is done. This book will seek to bring wisdom and balance to the Christian handling of emotions. However all is not the fault of the clergy, church culture or inadequate theological and counseling training. Much is our own fault. Each of us has defense mechanisms against change such as rationalization, projection, and denial. We avoid dealing with God and with change.

I believe one of the greatest obstacles to emotional health in Christian circles is that we simply don't understand our emotions or we lack proper mechanisms for dealing with them. Many Christians are ignorant of Scriptural teaching on emotional life and so are left stranded with a few basic techniques that barely scratch the surface of the problem. In a puzzling, almost paradoxical way, we also take our emotions too seriously and make them the source of our spiritual self-esteem. When we feel holy and good and positive we judge ourselves as being "up" spiritually and when we are feeling distant or depressed we judge ourselves as being "down" spiritually. In fact the connection between emotions and spirituality is fairly loose. Some very happy optimistic people are carnal and worldly, while some serious gloomy types are deeply spiritual - and the reverse applies as well. While it is certainly preferable to feel good and to "rejoice in the Lord always" even the apostle Paul admits to times of intense pressure and discouragement. We see this particularly in his letters to the Corinthians. And, of course, Jesus was known as "a man of sorrows and acquainted with grief...". Even tempting emotions need not be sinful. Jesus was "tempted in all things as we are, yet without sin". Yet there is indeed a deep connection between our emotions and our character.

Are Emotions Important? Do They Build Christian Character And Ethics?
The common observation of philosophers and theologians as diverse as Aristotle and C.S. Lewis has been that right affections and emotions form the basis for right morality. If we love the good and abhor the evil we are far more likely to be good. And if we hate bribes and value integrity we are far more likely to be honest.

Ethics is not a purely intellectual exercise. From antiquity it has involved feeling, thinking and acting rightly. True agape love has emotions that are ethical. *"Love does not rejoice in iniquity but rejoices in the truth"* (1 Corinthians 13:6). Being horrified by certain sins is a good and moral thing. Rejoicing in the truth is a right emotional response for the disciple. Our emotional valuation of life should be in agreement with our ethical stance. In biblical terms the person who is right emotionally loves good and hates evil. In their emotions they value what God values. The emotionally perfected Christian is not just "together" or integrated in the secular sense rather they are righteous, just, holy and perfectly loving. Their emotions agree with their ethics which agree with the Scripture which agree with God.

What we like and dislike gradually shapes the course of our life and character. This is why TV and advertising can have such a profound effect. It teaches us to like a certain lifestyle filled with material things and to value being sexy and attractive. It teaches us, ever so gradually, not to dislike fornication and adultery. Rarely does it blatantly say, "adultery is good" – it just teaches people to like the idea of being attractive to many people and to being quietly thrilled by the notion of perhaps having many sexual partners. Thus, over time their ethical resolve is weakened, the emotions that drive holiness are eroded and thousands of Christians fall into sin they would not have contemplated a few years ago. What we like and dislike, what we value and esteem, is critical to what we will eventually become.

Unfortunately we have divorced emotions from ethics. We see ethics as "our opinion" about things not our reaction to things. At times we even train ourselves to think one way and feel another. We ask people to be righteous and biblical yet feel embarrassed at our fellow Christian who get genuinely angry over sin and moral decay. By doing this we say it's alright to just have notions not emotions. That Christianity is best kept in the head not in the heart. Then we wonder why they do not give and why they do not commit to discipleship! We teach Christian young people to be sexy, sophisticated and emotionally unshockable, then expect them to value chastity. We are asking the impossible.

Our emotions reflect what we value and cherish, admire and love and they also reflect what we dislike, loath and reject. Our emotions undergird our choices and our choices form the foundations for our character and destiny. If our emotions are askew our choices and destiny will surely follow suite. During my university years I often tutored high school students in calculus. The biggest obstacle was nearly always emotional rather than intellectual. It was moving the student past emotional valuations such as "I hate math" and "homework is horrible". Because they had been taught by parents and peers that mathematics was odious and loathsome and homework was dull they were not doing their work. Because they were not doing their work they were failing mathematics. If they failed mathematics they would not get into university in Australia or into a decent career. Their emotional attitude, learned from others, was affecting their entire future.

The ability to delay gratification is fundamental to the development of good character. An experiment was set up where small children were given a choice: one marshmallow now, or two in ten minutes time. To get two marshmallows they had to delay gratification - a basic skill in managing and discipling their emotions. When the children were then followed up in a longitudinal study the difference between the "grabbers" and the "patient" was incredible. The most impatient and impulsive achieved less and got into trouble more while the most patient were more successful in practically every sphere of life. In fact this test proved more predictive of success at school and in life than IQ tests or any other social variable. This simple act of emotional management was a key to later success in life.

Thus right emotions are an important part of right character and right ethics and right emotions undergird right choices and right destiny. To emotionally rejoice in truth, to celebrate justice, to delight in noble actions and to embrace compassion and mercy is to have emotions that complement our faith. On the other hand confused emotions can destabilize us and create conflicts. Finally, the presence of strong lustful and evil emotions can drive us to sin and blind us to truth. Thus sorting ourselves out emotionally is much more than just getting our act together. It is getting our heart in line with our faith and with our God.

But which way is up? How can we know which emotions are right, which are wrong and which are neutral? How can we get an idea of what an emotionally healthy and righteous and holy Christian looks like? As in everything, Jesus is our model and that is the subject of the next chapter.

Discussion Questions

1. What have you learned from this chapter?

2. What are the differences between holy emotions, human emotions and fleshly emotions?

3. How do emotions fit into the Christian life?

4. What would the Christian life be like without emotions?

5. Are people in your church generally threatened by emotional change or generally comfortable with emotional change?

6. Are extroverts more spiritual than introverts, or vice versa or does it matter?

Can Jesus Be Our Model For Biblical EQ?

Therefore we also, since we are surrounded by so great a cloud of witnesses, let us lay aside every weight, and the sin which so easily ensnares us, and let us run with endurance the race that is set before us, (2) looking unto Jesus, the author and finisher of our faith, who for the joy that was set before Him endured the cross, despising the shame, and has sat down at the right hand of the throne of God.
(Hebrews 12:1-2 NKJV)

It is one of the key teachings of Christianity that our Master and Model is Jesus Christ and we are to be conformed into His image and be like Him in all respects. Let's look at two well-known verses in this regard:

> (Romans 8:29 NASB) For whom He foreknew, He also predestined to become conformed to the image of His Son, that He might be the first-born among many brethren.

> (Ephesians 4:15 NASB) But speaking the truth in love, we are to grow up in all aspects into Him, who is the head, even Christ.

God's plan for our lives is that we become conformed to the image of His Son. Now to "grow up in all aspects into Him" includes the emotional aspects of the nature of Jesus Christ. Becoming emotionally mature and skilled is part of our sanctification - but it is only a part. There are many other aspects of sanctification as well such as faith, knowledge and purity. Growing up emotionally is important and it's the part of sanctification that this book focuses on but Biblical EQ is certainly not all there is to sanctification.

Is Jesus Christ an Appropriate Model for Emotional Maturity?
There are a number of objections that people might think of against using Jesus Christ as our Model of EQ:
1. The standard is too high. The idea is terrifying. It gives me a panic attack to think of it. I can never be like that.
2. He was God and sinless; I'm neither. He had an unfair advantage. What's possible for Him is just not possible for me.
3. There isn't enough information in Scripture to make a judgment. It's an argument from silence. You can just make Jesus into whatever you want Him to be to suit your purposes.

4. He was Jewish and lived in the Third World 2000 years ago and just ambled around the place healing lepers. What would He know about the pressures of corporate life and the emotional jungle that my office is? (I'm a woman, He was a man and totally different emotionally. It's just silly to ask me to be like Jesus.)
5. Jesus was a prophet and had the emotions of a prophet. I could never be that confrontational – it's not my spiritual gift.
6. Jesus? High EQ? Kind of lacking in social skills if you ask me! I'm much more tactful and artful that that. Don't ask me to act in ways that get you nailed to a lump of wood.

Well let's look at some ways we can answer those objections and the assumptions that underlie them.

Objection 1: *The Standard Is Too High*
Solution: *Jumping Off Jacob's Ladder - Getting Rid Of Legalism Over Emotions*

Many evangelicals have a "Jacob's Ladder" view of the spiritual life with Jesus at the top, host of angels in-between and Christians climbing up rung by painful rung. The idea is to ascend to perfection – to strive to arrive. One slip and you tumble to the bottom to start all over again. Those that adhere to this view of spirituality are always envying those ahead of them, clinging on to the ladder for dear life, and not having too much to do with those "below" lest they get dragged down.

This view of the Christian life is thoroughly unbiblical. Ephesians 2:6 tells us that all those who are in Christ are already seated with Him in heavenly realms and Hebrews 12 tells us that we *have come* (past tense) to the Heavenly Zion. In Christ we have already arrived in terms of spiritual status. There is no ladder and if there is all born-again Christians are standing shoulder to shoulder on the top rung as brothers of Jesus Christ (Hebrews 2:10-15). We have been saved by grace and not by our own spiritual strivings (Ephesians 2:8-10) and there is no condemnation for those in Christ Jesus (Romans 8:1) including condemnation about our emotional life.

Aspiring to be like Jesus is not a matter of status or spiritual ascent. It's a journey, a destination, a joyous arriving. He is what we were made to be like from all eternity. If we view our emotional life as an indicator of spiritual status then it will be utterly terrifying to think of Jesus as our model. Every emotional insecurity will seem a "sin" and every lustful thought a pathway to Hell. If we judge ourselves and rate our spiritual life by the difference between our emotional life and the emotional life of Christ, by how far we have yet to go on our imaginary Jacob's ladder, then all we will feel is endless guilt and insecurity. By trying to go up, you will go under.

If you recognize yourself as being on an imaginary Jacob's Ladder, it's time to "jump off". You need to let go of striving and relentless self-assessment, and stop comparing yourself to those around you. Let go of the strain of sanctification go and to instead to learn how to receive grace so that you grow far more quickly than you can in your own strength.

When I am saying "let's consider Jesus as our model for the emotional life of the Christian" I am NOT setting a new standard to be "lived up to" by discipline and self-control. Your discipline and self-control will run out long before you reach that standard! Being like Jesus is our vision and our destination. We fix our eyes on Jesus, we seek to grow up into Him, and we pattern ourselves after Him. It becomes an exploration and an adventure, a time of growing and learning, a receiving of grace upon grace as we learn to be like Him. It is a gracious growing - not a terrifying ascent.

Objection 2 - *He was God and that's cheating!*
Solution: *He was also fully human. Jesus was the prototype of the perfect Christian, the elder brother among many brethren. We are of the same kind as Him.*

Jesus was not some aloof divine maharaja floating six inches above the ground, another category of being entirely from you and I. Jesus is God yet He was also fully human and tempted in every point as we are and still retains that humanity in Heaven as our faithful high priest.

> For it was fitting for Him, for whom are all things, and through whom are all things, in bringing many sons to glory, to perfect the author of their salvation through sufferings. (11) For both He who sanctifies and those who are sanctified are all from one Father; for which reason He is not ashamed to call them brethren, (12) saying, "I WILL PROCLAIM THY NAME TO MY BRETHREN, IN THE MIDST OF THE CONGREGATION I WILL SING THY PRAISE." (13) And again, "I WILL PUT MY TRUST IN HIM." And again, "BEHOLD, I AND THE CHILDREN

WHOM GOD HAS GIVEN ME." (14) Since then the children share in flesh and blood, He Himself likewise also partook of the same, that through death He might render powerless him who had the power of death, that is, the devil; (15) and might deliver those who through fear of death were subject to slavery all their lives. (16) For assuredly He does not give help to angels, but He gives help to the descendant of Abraham. (17) Therefore, He had to be made like His brethren in all things, that He might become a merciful and faithful high priest in things pertaining to God, to make propitiation for the sins of the people. (18) For since He Himself was tempted in that which He has suffered, He is able to come to the aid of those who are tempted. (Hebrews 2:10-18 NASB)

This passage and others like it in Hebrews (4:14-16; 5:7-10) emphasize that life or Jesus was difficult. It was so difficult that it was quite rightly described as suffering and had all the emotional hallmarks of suffering. It was no light suffering for it was to have the effect of perfecting Him! It was a suffering that matured His obedience by testing it under very stressful conditions. As we shall see, Jesus was pressed again and again to almost breaking point but He never sinned. Though He was God He laid aside those privileges (Philippians 2:5-11) to become fully human and a servant and was *"made like His brethren in all things that He might become a merciful and faithful High Priest"*.

He was made like us in our experiences of hunger, thirst, tiredness, frustration, misunderstanding, betrayal and even of unjust treatment by others. Even a cursory reading of the gospels will tell you that He did not just cruise through these experiences. He wept, He rebuked, He cried out, He rejoiced, He got angry, He became "troubled in spirit", He groaned in anguish and sweated drops of blood. Life for Jesus was difficult and it was often emotionally intense. This has made Him merciful in His role as high priest for He has fully been where we are.

In fact the reason we can be like Jesus is because He became very much like us. In fact He calls us "brethren"(Hebrew 2:11) which means that we are enough like Him to be considered family and to bear a close "genetic relationship" that has some sort of equality about it. The Scripture also say that we share the heavenly realms with Christ Jesus, and are members of Heavenly Zion (Ephesians 2:6; Hebrews 12:22-24). Therefore, we are literally "in the same realm" as Christ Jesus. Romans 8:29 tells us that we will be conformed to His image almost like someone pressed into a mould. Our shape will be the same as His shape. We will be like Him. There will be a resemblance. We can resemble Him because he chose to resemble us. Finally Ephesians 4:15, which I quote often in this book, says we are to be made like Him "in all respects". That's a very close likeness.

To illustrate this with a touch of humour- imagine I was to compare a trout with a horse using these same criteria. Can a trout occupy the same realm as a horse? No, a trout swims in the river and a horse gallops on land. Can a trout be called a brother of a horse in any genetic likeness? Not at all! Can a trout be made into the image of a horse or expect to be made like a horse in all things? It's ridiculous. In order to occupy the same realms, be brothers and be able to be transformed into the image of Christ Jesus, we must be very much LIKE Jesus. In fact we are like Jesus because we are fully human and He became fully human. He became like us so that we could become like Him. Jesus took on our emotional life so that it may be redeemed and become like His emotional life.

Finally we share a common destiny with Jesus Christ and a common home.

Let not your heart be troubled; you believe in God, believe also in Me. (2) In My Father's house are many mansions; if it were not so, I would have told you. I go to prepare a place for you. (3) And if I go and prepare a place for you, I will come again and receive you to Myself; that where I am, there you may be also. (4) And where I go you know, and the way you know. (John 14:1-4 NKJV)

"That where I am you may be also". This is not just the offer of streets of gold. It's the offer of an elder brother to His younger brethren. It's fellowship, it's love and it's family. We shall be enough like Jesus to be considered family. He as the Son of God and we as sons of God. When we are made in all aspects like Him and conformed to His image we will share His habitations and have meaningful fellowship with our Lord and God. Going back to the trout and horse illustration, there is no possibility of meaningful fellowship there. It is only in likeness and communication that there can be fellowship with God. Jesus is not alien to us but in fellowship with us and we can be like Him. *Our emotions, in the end, will be fitted for life in eternity with God.* The goal of biblical EQ is thus not commercial success or social popularity but fellowship with God and harmony in Heaven.

Objection 3: *There isn't enough information about His emotional life to base an EQ theory on.*
Solution: *There is enough to give us key reference points so we can gain a reasonable impression of what it means to have a redeemed and Christ-like emotional life.*

The information about the emotional life of Jesus is contained both in direct references to His humanity such as "Jesus wept" in John 11 and in broader more theological references that imply His full humanity and complete goodness. For instance, John calls Him "the light of life" and states that darkness had no place in Him and could not overpower Him. To have no "darkness" in one's spirit is to have emotions that are never deceitful, false, envious, spiteful, grumbling or small-minded. All His emotions were "light", not in the sense of light-hearted but as in the sense of positive, true, illuminating, righteous, appropriate and genuine. There was never a snicker or a snarl, never a dark brooding, violent emotion. Whether in tears or triumph the emotions of Jesus were noble, wise, good and perfectly righteous. Then there are the direct references. A survey of any good systematic theology such as Erickson or Grudem will find a wealth of information under the heading "the humanity of Jesus" as well as a good discussion of the complexities this entails (such as how the divine and the human were combined in one person). I will leave these intricacies to the theologians and will just list some of the biblical references which show how complete His humanity and emotional life was: Jesus experienced hunger (Matthew 4:2; 21:18), thirst (John 19:28), fatigue (John 4:6), He rejoiced at the end of the sending out of the seventy (Luke 10:21), marveled at the faith of the centurion (Matthew 8:10) and felt love for the rich, young ruler (Mark 10:21). His most frequent emotion is compassion which is recorded eleven times in the gospels (see Matthew 9:36). Anger was part of life for Jesus such as when He became angry at the Pharisees for their hardened cruelty (Mark 3:5). Zeal for God's honor caused Him to cleanse the temple (John 2:17). He grew in stature and in wisdom and in favor with God and man (Luke 2:52), was subjected to high-powered temptation (Matthew 4:1-11), and learned obedience without sinning (Hebrews 5:8-9). He had some of life's more painful emotions as well. For instance, He wept (Luke 19:41; John 11:35), His soul was troubled (John 12:27) and a while later He was "troubled in spirit" (John 13:21). He underwent extreme emotional distress to the point of death (Matthew 26:36-41) and prayed with loud cries and tears (Hebrews 5:7). Finally, He experienced an agonizing death on a cross (Matthew 27:34-54) with its attendant feelings of abandonment (Matthew 27:46).

The way Jesus processed His emotional life can also be deduced from some of the incidents in His life. For instance, He was extraordinarily calm in the face of storms and authoritative even in the face of arrest. He was an accessible person who was a "friend of sinners" and seemed to enjoy a reasonable social life with stable friendships with His disciples and with the household of Lazarus, Mary and Martha at Bethany. He had an inner circle of Peter, James and John and the apostle John seems to have been a true friend and was known as "the disciple whom Jesus loved". Thus there is sufficient evidence from direct references, incidents in the gospels and proper theological inference to construct a reasonable portrait of the emotional life of Jesus - at least one that can inform our discussion of biblical EQ.

Objection 4: *Jesus is not a culturally relevant or gender relevant model for the emotional life I lead. To ask me to model my emotional life on His is inappropriate.*
Solution: *The cultural details of Jesus life are scant. God seems to have mainly preserved only those details about Jesus that are relevant for all places and times.*

The core message of who Jesus is has been perceived by Jew and Gentile, slave and free, male and female down through the centuries. We will find out that Jesus shows us how to cope with pressure, express anger, set limits and boundaries, participate in grief and feel for the lost, the sick and the downtrodden. No one argues that Jesus shows us how to have compassion and love as our primary emotional realities. These are the sort of principles that survive cultural and gender differences. Each of the EQ skills that Jesus displayed is written into Scripture for our instruction. Much about His personality is left out - even such vital details as His age or His personal preferences. This means that those details that are in there (e.g. He is recorded 9 times as saying thanks at meals) are ones that the Holy Spirit wanted to draw attention to and are largely personality independent. [In the case of "saying grace" it is the value of being thankful and cultivating a life of gratitude for daily provision.] Millions of people in dozens of cultures find the gospel accounts of Jesus highly relevant to their situation. Using Jesus as our model means following what Scripture says not what medieval paintings portray. There is no indication that Jesus had a beard or long hair or was slightly effeminate looking. All these cultural details are absent from the gospels. What is present is the account of a person with a remarkable understanding of humanity and an enormous desire to heal it and redeem it. If we mould our passions on His passions we will be highly relevant people in a very needy world.

Objection 5: *Jesus had a totally different spiritual gifting. I could never be as assertive, confident or confrontational as He comes across as in the gospel narratives.*
Solution: *Becoming like Jesus is not about becoming a clone of a prophet but is a unique journey of self-discovery.*

God does make us each very different and He certainly does not ask us all to be evangelists or prophets. In fact it is quite clear that there is no one "right" Christian personality. Some are like Peter or Paul, while others resemble Moses, Daniel, Barnabas or Elijah. Yet as different as each of these people are or were, each of them was Christlike. There is almost a trick to this. If I imitate another human such as Billy Graham, I end up not being myself in the end yet if I imitate Jesus the reverse happens – I find myself. This is because Jesus is the center of humanity and the crown of humanity and we were all created by Him and for Him and in Him everything holds together, including our personalities (Colossians 1:15-20). Thus becoming like Jesus is like a journey to the center of the universe, full of adventures and surprises where we end up back where we began but marvelously transformed. When the timid person decides to become like Jesus he finds new boldness.

When the sarcastic wit decides to become like Jesus he finds new gentleness and tact. When the messed up and confused person decides to become like Jesus, clarity appears as if from nowhere. The gospels talk about losing yourself in order to find yourself and indeed we do. One person sets out, another returns who is somewhat similar but entirely different. The timid person loses their fear that they have harbored for so long, the sarcastic person loses their cruelty, the disordered person loses their freedom to be foolish. No one becoming like Jesus becomes a clone. It's not a journey to a single point, a "dot" we must all approximate. We don't all end up in Jerusalem wearing sandals. Maybe it's a bit like a spiritual black hole in which we seem to vanish but actually end up on a journey in another universe traveling faster than the speed of light.

Objection 6: *Jesus was tactless and His "high EQ" just got Him crucified. That is not something ordinary people should imitate. They should be tactful and careful.*
Solution: *Jesus was not tactless. He was an effective agent of change and a brilliant communicator who was steadfastly opposed. His EQ skills made Him effective and powerful and thus are worth imitating.*

The ministry of Jesus and His EQ skills seem to have gone through three stages:

Favor: First Jesus grew in favor with God and man (Luke 2:52). Secondly His early ministry was characterized by people being astonished at the gracious words that fell from His lips. (Luke 4:22). At this stage His EQ skills make Him perceptive, gracious and tactful.

Effectiveness: He taught with authority and challenged the teachings of the scribes and the Pharisees. Some opposed Him, many listened and His following grew. His opponents were infuriated by Him, but they were not yet afraid of Him. At this stage His EQ skills make Him authoritative and effective as a public speaker and prophetic teacher.

Power: Jesus eventually became a national political and religious figure that many people wanted to see become King. He was able to challenge the highest authorities in the land and to create genuine fear in His opponents. His enemies were now truly afraid of Him and plotted His death like that of any political enemy. At this stage His EQ skills make Him a skilful leader of a mass movement and also someone able to withstand enormous pressure and persecution.

For Christians the development of a high biblical EQ goes through these same three stages of favor, effectiveness and power. Stage One is "growing in favor" where EQ skills are honed and refined and poor strategies are discarded. Stage Two is effectiveness where EQ skills are honed in one's own home town and district and an effective and authoritative ministry develops. Stage Three is power when EQ skills are used to effect large scale change in one's community such as being a community organizer, politician, writer, moral crusader, preacher or evangelist.

These latter stages generally provoke a reaction from the Evil One who launches his attacks against the now highly effective Christian. Two Scripture are relevant here:

> Yes, and all who desire to live godly in Christ Jesus will suffer persecution. (2 Timothy 3:12 NKJV)

> Then Jesus said to His disciples, "If anyone desires to come after Me, let him deny himself, and take up his cross, and follow Me. (25) For whoever desires to save his life will lose it, but whoever loses his life for My sake will find it. (26) For what profit is it to a man if he gains the whole world, and loses his own soul? Or what will a man give in exchange for his soul? (27) For the Son of Man will come in the glory of His Father with His angels, and then He will reward each according to his works." (Matthew 16:24-28 NKJV)

Godliness will attract the scorn of some and the hatred of a few. If those few occupy places of power then the persecution can be trying indeed. Nevertheless, we are called to be lights in the midst of darkness and sheep in the midst of wolves; as wise as serpents and as innocent as doves. A high EQ will enable you to skillfully handle high level social and political issues and be a real influence for good in your society. However, this will attract attention, envy, rivalry, and in some cases ridicule, scorn and hatred.

The prophet Daniel is a prime example of this. His high biblical EQ, wisdom and maturity made him effective and influential but made others envious and landed him in the lions den amongst other places. But God delivered him! My experience of Christian political involvement is that the persecution is always more than I wanted but always far less than I feared. If you strive to attain the EQ of Jesus Christ you will eventually become so gracious, poised, and authoritative that you will have a real presence that makes a difference at national and international levels. Unfortunately you will also have real enemies opposing the righteous changes that you are seeking to bring about. Then it's time to take up your cross and follow Him!

Conclusion

So we see that Jesus is indeed a very adequate and, in fact, ideal model for the development of the Christian's emotional life. This is a high calling and in some ways a daunting one. How did Jesus cope? What gave Him the strength as His neighbors in Nazareth questioned when He returned from the wilderness, "Where did He get this wisdom?" From the Holy Spirit! And the work of the Holy Spirit in the life of Jesus, particularly in His emotions, soul and spirit, is the subject of the next chapter.

Discussion Questions

1. How scary is it to have Jesus as the model for your emotional life? Is it adventurous, scary or terrifying?

2. How much like Jesus can we hope to be?
3. What is the best thing about having Jesus as our spiritual model?

4. How can we "jump off Jacob's ladder"?

5. Name the three stages Jesus went through in developing His EQ skills?

6. At what stage are you in developing your own EQ skills?

7. Name six emotions that Jesus felt. What do you think it was like for Him?

The Holy Spirit, the Emotional Life of Jesus, and the Emotional Life of the Spirit-Filled Believer.

There shall come forth a Rod from the stem of Jesse, And a Branch shall grow out of his roots. (2) The Spirit of the LORD shall rest upon Him, The Spirit of wisdom and understanding, The Spirit of counsel and might, The Spirit of knowledge and of the fear of the LORD. (Isaiah 11:1-2 NKJV)

The central teaching of this book is that as part of their redemption Christians are to take on the emotional life of their Saviour and that this occurs as a result of the power of the Holy Spirit who transforms us into the image of the Son of God. If the Holy Spirit is indeed the divine dynamic and the agent of deep emotional transformation then we should see some evidence of that in His work in the life of Jesus. Obvious questions arise that we will investigate such as: Did His baptism and empowerment with the Holy Spirit change Him or did He remain just the same? Are there any hints that the Holy Spirit lay behind the impressiveness of His personality? Can we appropriate some of the same power that moved Jesus?

The Baptism of Jesus and His EQ
While Jesus grew in wisdom and stature and in favor with God and man there was also a sudden break in His life, a radical change in His emotions and personal authority so that those who knew Him said "where did He get this wisdom..."

> And when He had come to His own country, He taught them in their synagogue, so that they were astonished and said, "Where did this Man get this wisdom and these mighty works? (55) "Is this not the carpenter's son? Is not His mother called Mary? And His brothers James, Joses, Simon, and Judas? (56) "And His sisters, are they not all with us? Where then did this Man get all these things?" (57) So they were offended at Him. But Jesus said to them, "A prophet is not without honor except in his own country and in his own house." (58) Now He did not do many mighty works there because of their unbelief. (Matthew 13:54-58 NKJV)

He had changed! While Luke shows us that Jesus was a child prodigy (Luke 2:42-50) no one expected Him to turn into a miracle working prophet. The transition from promising youth to powerful prophet seems to have come at His baptism. There was a massive empowering work of the Holy Spirit that changed Jesus just as the Holy Spirit at Pentecost changed the disciples.

The highest level EQ skills such as boldness and courage and skill in healing and proclamation are Holy Spirit endowed. The early church realized this when they prayed for boldness and the room shook! (Acts 4:29-31). EQ change empowered by the Holy Spirit can be remarkable and sudden and leave others astonished. I can testify personally to a remarkable change in one meeting in September 1978 when I went from being a timid and secretive Christian to being as bold as a lion and an ardent evangelist!

The Body of Jesus and the Holy Spirit

As we all know our physical state and our emotional state are closely connected. We are more disposed to get angry when we are tired or hungry. We also seem to inherit certain emotional dispositions from our parents. We are "hard-wired" from birth into a certain emotional disposition. However, this can later be altered as we shall see. This can be as toxic as a problem with rage or as beneficial as the ability to be enraptured by music. The Holy Spirit set Jesus' genetic structure at conception so that He was unusually inclined to love righteousness and hate wickedness (Hebrews 1:9). A passage from Hebrews indicates that His body was prepared for Him by God, so that Jesus would love to do the will of God.

> *Therefore, when He came into the world,* He said: "Sacrifice and offering You did not desire, *But a body You have prepared for Me.* {6} In burnt offerings and sacrifices for sin You had no pleasure. {7} Then I said, *'Behold, I have come*; In the volume of the book it is written of Me; *To do Your will, O God.'"* Hebrews 10:5-7 NKJV. (Author's emphasis)

Here we see that as Jesus came into the world He had a body prepared for Him by the Father and the express intent of His coming into the world was "to do Your will O God." Jesus had a body that was free from sinful genetic predispositions towards rage, alcoholism, drug addiction, or whatever other negative traits that can be passed on genetically. Basically Jesus was born without any sinful dispositions. His body and nervous system were formed to do the will of God by the creative, body-renewing and forming work of the Holy Spirit.

If the creative work of the Holy Spirit was able to make Jesus' body such that it was free from sinful tendencies then obviously that power can go to work in our bodies also. This gives us hope that long standing biological urges can be erased by the healing and renewing ministry of the Holy Spirit. Countless Christian recovery programs attest that this is the case. Alcoholics can and do lose the biological desire to drink, homosexuals can and do have their sexual orientation set right, drug addicts can and do completely lose their cravings, sex addicts can be and are freed from the torment of twenty four hours a day lust. But is this a realistic and a scriptural expectation? Let's look at Romans 8:11:

> But if the Spirit of Him who raised Jesus from the dead dwells in you, He who raised Christ from the dead will also give life to your mortal bodies through His Spirit who dwells in you.

The Holy Spirit can give life to our mortal bodies – not just our resurrection bodies, but the very bodies we have now, our mortal bodies. His renewing life can pulse through us and cleanse us from sins and addictions just as He can heal a person from illness or disease. Like a divine electrician He can fix the fuse box and rewire the house so the circuitry functions as it was always meant to – for the glory of God.

The biological basis of sin is not separate from the spiritual basis of sin. When God delivers you from sin He can deliver you from sin in your spirit, sin in your soul and eventually from the power of sin in your members. He can fix the physical and medical basis of rage, lust, addictions and anti-social behavior. Minimal brain dysfunction, ADHD, post-traumatic stress disorder, and whatever else may be engraved in our neural tissue - can be healed by the Holy Spirit.

Let's see how this happened for the Christians at Corinth:

> Do you not know that the unrighteous will not inherit the kingdom of God? Do not be deceived. Neither fornicators, nor idolaters, nor adulterers, nor homosexuals, nor sodomites, {10} nor thieves, nor covetous, nor drunkards, nor revilers, nor extortioners will inherit the kingdom of God. {11} *And such were some of you. But you were washed, but you were sanctified, but you were justified* in the name of the Lord Jesus and by the Spirit of our God. 1 Corinthians 6:9-11 NKJV. (Author's emphasis)

The Corinthian Christians have come from some terrible backgrounds including fornication and adultery (sexual addiction), homosexuals and sodomites (probably pedophiles in this case), and drunkards (alcoholics). These behaviors are generally acknowledged to have a strong and persistent biological and neurological component.

However, they are now PAST behaviors, they have been repented of and forsaken and the Corinthians are now washed and made holy! "Such WERE some of you" - it's over, dealt with, fixed. And this transformation took place "in the name of the Lord Jesus and by the Spirit of our God". Paul puts it this way:

> For if you live according to the flesh you will die; but if by the Spirit you put to death the deeds of the body, you will live. (Romans 8:13 NKJV)

> I say then: Walk in the Spirit, and you shall not fulfill the lust of the flesh. (17) For the flesh lusts against the Spirit, and the Spirit against the flesh; and these are contrary to one another, so that you do not do the things that you wish. (18) But if you are led by the Spirit, you are not under the law. (Galatians 5:16-18 NKJV)

The Spirit can deal with the flesh in both its spiritual and biological aspects. We are not at the mercy of our genetics or our addictions. The Holy Spirit can set us free! What He did in constructing the body of Jesus so that it was prepared to do God's will can be done for you as well "for nothing is impossible to him who believes".

The Soul and Spirit of Jesus

Listed below are all the direct gospel references to the soul and spirit of Jesus Christ.

> Then He said to them, "My soul is exceedingly sorrowful, even to death. Stay here and watch with Me." (Matthew 26:38 NKJV)

> And Jesus cried out again with a loud voice, and yielded up His spirit. (Matthew 27:50 NKJV)

> But immediately, when Jesus perceived in His spirit that they reasoned thus within themselves, He said to them, "Why do you reason about these things in your hearts? (Mark 2:8 NKJV)

> But He sighed deeply in His spirit, and said, "Why does this generation seek a sign? Assuredly, I say to you, no sign shall be given to this generation." (Mark 8:12 NKJV)

> Then He said to them, "My soul is exceedingly sorrowful, even to death. Stay here and watch." (Mark 14:34 NKJV)

> In that hour Jesus rejoiced in the Spirit and said, "I thank You, Father, Lord of heaven and earth, that You have hidden these things from the wise and prudent and revealed them to babes. Even so, Father, for so it seemed good in Your sight. (Luke 10:21 NKJV)

Jesus called out with a loud voice, "Father, into your hands I commit my spirit." When he had said this, he breathed his last. (Luke 23:46 NIV)

Therefore, when Jesus saw her weeping, and the Jews who came with her weeping, He groaned in the spirit and was troubled. (John 11:33 NKJV)

"Now My soul is troubled, and what shall I say? Father, save Me from this hour'? But for this purpose I came to this hour." (John 12:27 NKJV)

When Jesus had said these things, He was troubled in spirit, and testified and said, "Most assuredly, I say to you, one of you will betray Me." (John 13:21 NKJV)

When he had received the drink, Jesus said, "It is finished." With that, he bowed his head and gave up his spirit. (John 19:30 NIV)

Three things especially stand out:
- ➢ That Jesus perceived life's situations with His Spirit.
- ➢ That Jesus was moved on the basis of those perceptions.
- ➢ That Jesus candidly expressed His emotions to those closest to Him.

Also to be noted are His ability to surrender His spirit to God and that with the surrender of His spirit His life ended. Note the power and depth of Jesus' reactions. He cries out with a loud voice, is troubled unto death, or rejoices greatly. His Spirit-filled emotions were powerful and present. He is no antiseptic, calm beyond belief, purely logical and mental being. The triumphs and tragedies of faith move Him deeply indeed - as they have moved all great men and women of God.

Jesus and Perception

In Mark 2:8 Jesus "perceived in His spirit". The spirit is the true organ for the perception of reality for Jesus as Isaiah declared in one of the best known passages in the Bible:

> There shall come forth a Rod from the stem of Jesse, And a Branch shall grow out of his roots. (2) The Spirit of the LORD shall rest upon Him, The Spirit of wisdom and understanding, The Spirit of counsel and might, The Spirit of knowledge and of the fear of the LORD. (3) His delight is in the fear of the LORD, And He shall not judge by the sight of His eyes, Nor decide by the hearing of His ears; (4) But with righteousness He shall judge the poor, And decide with equity for the meek of the earth; He shall strike the earth with the rod of His mouth, And with the breath of His lips He shall slay the wicked. (5) Righteousness shall be the belt of His loins, And faithfulness the belt of His waist. (Isaiah 11:1-5 NKJV)

The presence of the Holy Spirit upon Jesus gave Him extraordinary knowledge and wisdom so that He judged situations righteously and truthfully and inwardly. He did not judge situations as they appeared to the eyes and ears and to sense perception (verse 3 above). Rather He judged life's situations with a spirit of wisdom and understanding, counsel and knowledge that saw into the heart of things. This special perception that Jesus had shows in many of the gospel encounters and is neatly summarized by the apostle John who writes: *(John 2:24 NKJV) But Jesus did not commit Himself to them, because He knew all men.* (see also Matthew 9:4; 12:25; Mark 5:30; 12:15; Luke 11:17; John 5:6; 6:61, 64; 13:1-3; 18:4)

Jesus' perceptions of situations then led to His emotional reactions to them. On sensing His impending death His soul was troubled unto death. On seeing the grief at Lazarus' tomb He groaned in spirit and was troubled. When the disciples returned victorious He rejoiced. When He perceived the hardness of heart of the Pharisees He became angry. When He sees masses of people coming out after healing and teaching He is moved with compassion. (see "objection 3 in the previous chapter) . Jesus then expressed these emotions powerfully but appropriately. There is always great dignity in the reactions of Jesus Christ. His emotionality was deep and expressive - never trivial, sentimental or chaotic. This then gives us a process for our own emotionality:

1. **Perceive** life spiritually, righteously, truthfully and with a Kingdom perspective.
2. **React** in our soul and spirit. Be moved by life. Not aloof and detached or cold and hard.
3. **Express** those reactions with dignity, power and poise. Be full-hearted emotionally but also be wise in expression.

In the next chapter we will see that the apostles and many great men and women of God over the centuries have done precisely this - bringing their emotions under the control and empowerment of the Spirit of God so they reacted to things no longer from a merely human perspective with its five senses and self-interest but from a divine perspective with spiritual perception and true Kingdom interests. This is what makes a good Christian biography so compelling - we sense a different way of looking at the world - a heart controlled by God and seeing His interests in all things. In that chapter I will argue that a Kingdom perspective is not only good for our sanctification it is also critical for good emotional health and a high EQ. However, I have more to say about the emotional life of Jesus first.

The Beliefs of Jesus Christ

Emotions flow from beliefs. When I was a young boy I was playing by the local creek when I found a huge lump of iron pyrites (Fool's Gold) and it was heavy and soft and looked like gold. I showed my brother Peter and we went home very secretively so nobody could see us with our important find. We then showed Dad and said, "We are rich! We are rich! We found this huge lump of gold and there's more just down by the creek!" Dad just laughed and explained about Fool's Gold. Even though our belief was not a true belief it still made us very happy while it lasted. We were so excited, not by actually finding gold, because we didn't actually find gold, but by the belief that we had found gold. When this belief was corrected, our emotion of joy was unsupported by an adequate belief, and it vanished. We went from very excited to being a bit disappointed. Once the belief vanished, the emotion vanished. Underneath emotions are beliefs, if you take way the belief the emotion vanishes. If you change the belief sufficiently, the emotion changes.

How we believe has a direct affect on how we feel. This applies even in spiritual things. So if, like Jesus, you think that stealing houses from poor widows is wrong, you will react to it with the intensity that Jesus did. The difference between a video camera recording an event and a person seeing the event is that the person has prior beliefs. These prior beliefs cause the person to react to what they see. Let's look at three incidents in the life of Jesus to see how His beliefs informed His emotional reactions and made them different from those of so called "normal people". First we will look at His cleansing of the temple:

> So they came to Jerusalem. Then Jesus went into the temple and began to drive out those who bought and sold in the temple, and overturned the tables of the money changers and the seats of those who sold doves. (16) And He would not allow anyone to carry wares through the temple. (17) Then He taught, saying to them, "Is it not written, 'My house shall be called a house of prayer for all nations'? But you have made it a 'den of thieves.'" (Mark 11:15-17 NKJV)

> Now the Passover of the Jews was at hand, and Jesus went up to Jerusalem. (14) And He found in the temple those who sold oxen and sheep and doves, and the moneychangers doing business. (15) When He had made a whip of cords, He drove them all out of the temple, with the sheep and the oxen, and poured out the changers' money and overturned the tables. (16) And He said to those who sold doves, "Take these things away! Do not make My Father's house a house of

merchandise!" (17) Then His disciples remembered that it was written, "Zeal for Your house has eaten Me up." (John 2:13-17 NKJV)

What beliefs of Jesus lay behind the strength of His reaction here? In Mark's gospel we see that Jesus believed:
a) That the purpose of the Temple was to be a house of prayer for all nations.
b) But that it had become a robbers den.
 In John's gospel Jesus is shown believing that it is:
c) My Father's house.
b) But instead it had become a house of merchandise (with the implication that it was dishonest trade.
[The accounts are not contradictory they just report slightly different examples of Jesus reactions at the time. It is probable that he said many other things as well while He was overturning the tables.]

Let's look at the sequence of events. Jesus believes it should be "A" but perceives it is in fact "B". This leads to emotional reaction "C" which is expressed in verbal and physical behavior D. For Jesus His beliefs included the honor due to His Father, the fact that the right use of the temple was prayer and that all nations should have access to it. They also included the belief that trade, especially dishonest trade, was inappropriate in such a location. These were not widely and strongly held beliefs in His time otherwise the traders would not have been there in the first place. His unique beliefs led to His unique emotional reaction based on His spiritual perception of the nature of the situation.

Let's look at another of Jesus' puzzling reactions - during a fierce storm on the lake of Galilee.

And suddenly a great tempest arose on the sea, so that the boat was covered with the waves. But He was asleep. {25} Then His disciples came to Him and awoke Him, saying, "Lord, save us! We are perishing!" {26} But He said to them, "Why are you fearful, O you of little faith?" Then He arose and rebuked the winds and the sea, and there was a great calm. (Matthew 8:24-26 NKJV)

Here Jesus' belief seems to have been that He was absolutely safe and that nothing could touch Him because His Father was protecting Him and the disciples. His belief also included the fact that it was a sane and reasonable thing for Him to speak to waves and wind and expect that they would obey Him. Furthermore, He seems to believe that the disciples ought to share these beliefs and were quite unjustified in being fearful in the midst of such a storm.

Based on these beliefs Jesus' perception of the situation seems to have been "Not a problem!" It just wasn't a big deal. To say that this is "counter-intuitive" and defies all common sense is no under-statement. Nevertheless, his beliefs were justified for He calmed the storm with a word. It truly wasn't a problem for Him at all.

People of great faith have a tremendous poise in crisis situations. In a later chapter we shall learn how to handle situations we dread from a position of faith and a sense of mastery. Here Jesus' beliefs led to Him having emotions of calm and a sense of mastery in a crisis situation and enabled Him to take effective action to remedy the situation.

For our third illustration of Jesus' belief system we will go a few verses earlier in Matthew 8 to see the only time Jesus is recorded as "marveling" at something...

> And Jesus said to him, "I will come and heal him." (8) The centurion answered and said, "Lord, I am not worthy that You should come under my roof. But only speak a word, and my servant will be healed. (9) "For I also am a man under authority, having soldiers under me. And I say to this one, 'Go,' and he goes; and to another, 'Come,' and he comes; and to my servant, 'Do this,' and he does it." (10) When Jesus heard it, He marveled, and said to those who followed, "Assuredly, I say to you, I have not found such great faith, not even in Israel! (11) And I say to you that many will come from east and west, and sit down with Abraham, Isaac, and Jacob in the kingdom of heaven. (12) But the sons of the kingdom will be cast out into outer darkness. There will be weeping and gnashing of teeth." (13) Then Jesus said to the centurion, "Go your way; and as you have believed, so let it be done for you." And his servant was healed that same hour. (Matthew 8:7-14 NKJV)

Here Jesus is marveling at the "great faith" of the Roman centurion. There are many beliefs of Jesus recorded here such as the hardness of Israel, the salvation of the Gentiles and the power of His commands to heal the sick but none of these beliefs are the mainstay of His marveling at the centurion. Jesus is reacting to the presence of great faith in an unexpected place - a Gentile and a soldier, a man who was outside of the covenant and whose job was killing people and who was in part responsible for the occupation of His nation.

This was the reaction of one belief structure to another belief structure. The centurion expressed His beliefs about a) his unworthiness as a Gentile (though a powerful man) to have Jesus visit him and b) His belief in Jesus' authority and the power of His words of command. As the centurion expressed these beliefs Jesus in turn resonated with them. Just as the hardness of heart of the Pharisees enraged Him, just as the littleness of faith of the disciples disappointed Him, the great faith of the centurion encouraged and astonished Him. It was a "rare find": *Assuredly, I say to you, I have not found such great faith, not even in Israel!*

So we see that belief structures react to one another and evaluate one another. When we find another who is astonishingly full of faith we rejoice. When we find someone hard and cynical and unbelieving we are discouraged or angered. Like Jesus we search out those that resonate with us. They are a rare find and a treasure. The way we interact with others will depend in large measure on what we believe about what they believe. Much inter-denominational misunderstanding revolves around "what we believe about what they believe" and the strong emotional reactions that result. It's a critical area for mental health and is why some types of fundamentalism though very sound in many areas are incredibly damaging psychologically.

Putting It All Together
Earlier we saw that perceptions led to internal emotions which were then expressed appropriately. Later we have seen that our perceptions work with our beliefs to produce astonishing emotional reactions that are unique to the Christlike Spirit-filled believer. In addition, we have a physical predisposition to certain types of emotional reactions and behaviors - covered in the first part of this chapter. Thus we can say that for Jesus and the Spirit-filled believer the steps are:

1. Perception of person or situation – ideally in the Spirit.
2. Interaction of perception with belief system.
3. Internal emotion generated.
4. Interaction of internal emotion with physical predisposition.
5. Expression of emotion outwardly.

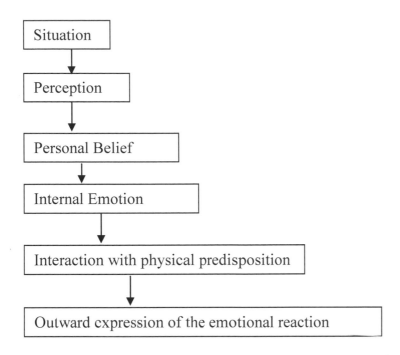

Situation

Perception

Personal Belief

Internal Emotion

Interaction with physical predisposition

Outward expression of the emotional reaction

Let's now look at where the Holy Spirit is in Jesus' beliefs and perceptions!

- **Perception:** Jesus perceives by both His Spirit and the Holy Spirit who brings these realities to Him.
- **Beliefs:** The Holy Spirit writes the law of God on our minds and hearts and forms our beliefs within us as our teacher and the One who shows us the things that God has prepared for those who believe and reveals to us the deep things of God. Here are just a few direct references to His teaching ministry. (John 6:45; 14:26; Galatians 1;11,12; 1 Corinthians 2:9-16; Ephesians 4:21; 1 Thessalonians 4:9; Hebrews 8;10-11; 1 John 2:20,27)
- **Internal Emotions:** Emotions can proceed directly from our spirit under the influence of the Holy Spirit "and Jesus rejoiced in His spirit... " and emotions such as love, joy and peace are called the fruit of the Spirit (Galatians 5:22,23).
- **Interaction With Physical Disposition:** The indwelling Holy Spirit gives life to our mortal bodies that we may be renewed and cry out "Abba Father!" (Romans 8:11-15) to our gracious Heavenly Father. (See also the first section in this chapter on how His powerful work can break the domination of our lives by sin and addictions.)

- **Outward Expression Of The Emotional Reaction:** The spiritual basis for revelation that culminates in teaching is shown in 1 Corinthians.

> But as it is written: "Eye has not seen, nor ear heard, Nor have entered into the heart of man the things which God has prepared for those who love Him." {10} But God has revealed them to us through His Spirit. For the Spirit searches all things, yes, the deep things of God. {11} For what man knows the things of a man except the spirit of the man which is in him? Even so no one knows the things of God except the Spirit of God. {12} Now we have received, not the spirit of the world, but the Spirit who is from God, that we might know the things that have been freely given to us by God. {13} *These things we also speak, not in words which man's wisdom teaches but which the Holy Spirit teaches, comparing spiritual things with spiritual.*
> (1 Corinthians 2:9-13 NKJV) (Author's emphasis)

Thus verse 13 is the culmination of a long sequence. Firstly truth which eye cannot see and ear cannot hear is revealed to us through the Holy Spirit (verses 9-11). Then we receive them through the Holy Spirit who teaches us and works them into our belief system. This is freely and graciously given (verse 12). Finally we speak and we speak not human, but divine wisdom and not in human words and categories but in words the Holy Spirit gives us.

Thus Scripture is not just God's Word in human words; rather it is God's Word in the Spirit's Words. Let's see how this worked for Jesus:

> Then Jesus said to them, "When you lift up the Son of Man, then you will know that I am He, and that I do nothing of Myself; *but as My Father taught Me, I speak these things.* (29) "And He who sent Me is with Me. The Father has not left Me alone, for I always do those things that please Him." (John 8:28 NKJV)

The responses, reactions, words and expressions are taught to us by God and are in spiritual categories "comparing spiritual with spiritual."

That leads on to the last section of this chapter - symbols, metaphors, and archetypes - how the Spirit teaches us to express spiritual things - including our emotions.

The Language of the Spirit and the Emotional Realm - Symbols, Metaphors and Archetypes

As I am writing this "Just As I Am" is playing on the stereo in the background and the choir is singing "O Lamb Of God I come...". This is the language of the Spirit that makes no sense to the carnal man but which abounds in Scripture and in the great moments of the Christian faith including the hymns that lift us to God. To take up where we left off in the passage1 Corinthians:

> These things we also speak, not in words which man's wisdom teaches but which the Holy Spirit teaches, comparing spiritual things with spiritual. (14) But the natural man does not receive the things of the Spirit of God, for they are foolishness to him; nor can he know them, because they are spiritually discerned. (15) But he who is spiritual judges all things, yet he himself is rightly judged by no one. (16) For "who has known the mind of the LORD that he may instruct Him?" But we have the mind of Christ. (1 Corinthians 2:13-16 NKJV)

There is something called "the mind of Christ" which enables the believer to make sense of symbolic language such as "the Lamb of God that takes away the sin of the world" and to quickly grasp the meaning of parables and to feel the wonder of the scenes in Revelation. The Holy Spirit enables us to perceive and believe correctly thus renewing our mind into the mind of Christ. He is our Teacher and instructor and does so in the language of the spiritual realm - dreams, visions, symbols, parables and metaphors - using analogues of the faith to explain it as well as more straightforward language such as that of the book of Romans.

In the language of the Spirit beasts with seven heads and ten horns are juxtaposed with scarlet women and numinous symbols such as the Throne of God. These can be visual as well as verbal symbols and realities. Angels, demons, cherubim and seraphim are seen by the seers and prophets. To the purely material and "scientific" mind this is all quite offensive and many liberal theologians have stumbled over it. The more we think of the power of our own intellect the less we think of God's Word and the more we think of God's Word the less we think of the power of our own intellect!

Jesus was supremely taught of God and a master of the symbolic realm so that He expressed Himself skillfully in parables, aphorisms, sermons and stories. His teaching was unlike that of the scribes and Pharisees for He taught with authority and in such a way that those truly seeking God understood Him while those who were just curious walked away puzzled and frustrated with His teaching. The language of the Spirit is not "plain language" but is strangely numinous and symbolic. If you have seen some of the "New Age advertising" that taps into these common and universal symbols of the emotional world you will know what I mean.

These symbols or archetypes such as a woman dressed in a flowing white robe holding a torch aloft, a dove against a clear blue sky, a rainbow, a man on a white horse dressed for war, a shining sword or a red dragon have universal emotional content almost independent of culture. The psychologist Carl Jung spent His life exploring them and Hitler was a master at exploiting them. Transpersonal psychology and various schools of psychoanalysis take them very seriously indeed. Myth, saga, music, song and poetry all tap into this treasure trove of emotional and spiritual symbols as do fables and stories and most national anthems.

We interact with spiritual language either totally or not at all. The phrase "the Lamb of God" either has immense meaning or is a total enigma. It is an almost binary form of communication that literally "separates the sheep from the goats" and believers from unbelievers.

> Jesus answered them, "I told you, and you do not believe. The works that I do in My Father's name, they bear witness of Me. (26) But you do not believe, because you are not of My sheep, as I said to you. (27) My sheep hear My voice, and I know them, and they follow Me." (John 10:25-27 NKJV)

In a startling statement Jesus said "but you do not believe because you are not of my sheep". In other words you have to be one of God's people to understand His teaching! It's the other side of the more usual "because you do not believe you are not God's". Here it's "because you are not God's - you do not believe." Some eagerly believe and can understand the language of the Spirit while others are just further hardened by it. (John 12:40).

Thus the spiritual person understands the things of the Spirit including symbols, parables and dreams. He is taught spiritual things by God and has a deep emotional response to them which in turn finds its deepest expression in the language of the Spirit, speaking spiritual truths in words taught by God comparing spiritual with spiritual.

Summary

For Jesus and ideally for the Christlike Spirit-filled believer the model of
the process for the development of the emotional life is as follows:

1. Things are perceived in and by the spirit by believers with the mind of
   Christ and a lucid grasp of symbol and metaphor. These believers see
   life as being in a Kingdom framework.
2. This perception is then passed through a grid of beliefs taught to the
   believer by God.
3. This results in a godly internal emotional state in the believer of
   rejoicing, awe, wonder, repentance, burdens for the lost, etc.
4. This is then mediated through the renewed life-filled temple of the
   Holy Spirit that is the believer's body and translated through his
   natural God-given temperament.
5. Finally, the emotional response is expressed in words taught by the
   Spirit bringing edification to the body of Christ and reflecting the
   mind of Christ on the matter.

This should result in a deep, powerful resonant emotional life that is
totally in tune with Kingdom realities and which can express matters of
justice and truth as well as care and compassion. This Holy Spirit
produced emotional life should weep for the lost, ache for the poor and
celebrate the repentance of a single sinner. Like Jesus we should have a
Holy Spirit given courage that enables us to speak God's truth in God's
words at God's moment. Like Jesus the Holy Spirit in us should make us
radiant with a healing and gracious personality so that people sense the
love and peace that is in us and know that in our earthen vessels dwells a
priceless treasure.

The next two chapters will test the above five-step theory before we put
it into practice on ourselves. First, we will look at the emotional life of
apostles, prophets and great Christian leaders. Next we shall examine the
dreadful emotional life of carnal Christians. Finally, we shall see if the
model we have developed works.

Discussion Questions

1. What are the steps in the five-step model?

2. What was special about the body of Jesus Christ?

3. What difference did the Holy Spirit make in the life of Jesus?

4. How did Jesus perceive reality differently from others?

5. How did the beliefs of Jesus Christ affect or determine His behavior?

6. How is symbolic language often quite different from the language we normally use? Why is it useful?

The Emotional Life of the Apostles, Prophets and Great Christian Leaders

"... 'I have found David the son of Jesse, a man after My own heart, who will do all My will.'(Acts 13:22 NKJV)

If the previous chapter summary of the emotional life of the Christlike Christian is correct, then it will predict the lives of the most Christlike people and will also predict, in a negative way, the lives of the most carnal people.

In this chapter we will check to see if the theory of biblical EQ has predictive validity when applied to the lives of the great Christian leaders. In the next chapter we will check to see if it also predicts the emotional lives of carnal Christians.

According to our model the following twelve things should be true of the apostles, prophets and great Christian leaders.

Perception
1. They should see the world differently from the rest of us. For them the Kingdom perspective will be the only true perspective.
2. They should be able from time to time to see into the hearts of men and women and to speak accurately to their condition.
3. They should be conversant with dreams, visions and symbolic language. They should readily grasp the prophetic and be excited by the Scripture.

Beliefs
4. They should have beliefs that the surrounding culture has not taught them or which it opposes vehemently; beliefs that only God can have taught them.
5. Those beliefs should give them a sense of what is righteous and what is unrighteous, like Jesus had when He cleansed the temple. These should create an unusual zeal within that consumes them.
6. Those beliefs should give them unusual poise and power in crisis situations, like Jesus in the storm.

7. As a result of those beliefs they should resonate with and be emotionally drawn to others who are of great faith, like Jesus resonated with the Roman centurion.

Emotions

8. They should have deep and vivid emotions like those of Jesus Christ.
9. They should have a sense of their emotions being God's emotions and be aware of what they are feeling and able to name it clearly as Jesus did with His emotions. They should be people of authentic and powerful emotional expression - groans, tears, crying, and rejoicing.

Physical Nature

10. They should demonstrate victory over addictions and sexual temptations and have a renewed physical nature whereby they were able to express their emotions in godly ways through their physical bodies.

Emotional Expression

11. These righteous emotions should lead to righteous actions such as when Jesus' compassion moved Him to act. Their emotionality should be an integral part of being a righteous person, not detached from life like the emotions of an actor or a hypocrite.
12. The course of their lives should demonstrate an ever-increasing wisdom in emotional expression as if they were being taught by God in how to say things.

Do these twelve predictions pass the test of Scripture and of the testimony of the saints down through the ages? Are great men and women of God people of deep and vivid emotionality? Do they demonstrate an unusual sense of righteousness? Do they indeed see life differently? Do they hold counter-cultural beliefs or have an unusual power and poise in crisis situations? The answer is Yes! In fact great men and women of God are so vivid emotionally that they are often accused of being overly emotional - from Jeremiah with his tears to John Wesley with his preaching. Luther saw life so differently that he threw his ink-pot at the devil! Isaiah was so counter-cultural that he went around for three years with his buttocks uncovered! (Isaiah 20:1-3).

Let's test our predictions on the spiritual heroes of Hebrews 11. I will go paragraph by paragraph commenting on how these heroes perceived, believed, felt and reacted differently.

> Now faith is the substance of things hoped for, the evidence of things not seen. (2) For by it the elders obtained a good testimony. (3) By faith we understand that the worlds were framed by the word of God, so that the things which are seen were not made of things which are visible. (Hebrews 11 NKJV)

These heroes of faith saw a different reality than others. They had evidence of things not seen and they understood that the visible world was predicated on perception of an invisible spiritual world.

> (4) By faith Abel offered to God a more excellent sacrifice than Cain, through which he obtained witness that he was righteous, God testifying of his gifts; and through it he being dead still speaks. (5) By faith Enoch was taken away so that he did not see death, "and was not found, because God had taken him"; for before he was taken he had this testimony, that he pleased God. (6) But without faith it is impossible to please Him, for he who comes to God must believe that He is, and that He is a rewarder of those who diligently seek Him.

The belief system of these people was different from and more excellent than that of their contemporaries and was grounded in the invisible spiritual reality that they perceived.

> (7) By faith Noah, being divinely warned of things not yet seen, moved with godly fear, prepared an ark for the saving of his household, by which he condemned the world and became heir of the righteousness which is according to faith.
> (8) By faith Abraham obeyed when he was called to go out to the place which he would receive as an inheritance. And he went out, not knowing where he was going.
> (9) By faith he dwelt in the land of promise as in a foreign country, dwelling in tents with Isaac and Jacob, the heirs with him of the same promise; (10) for he waited for the city which has foundations, whose builder and maker is God. (11) By faith Sarah herself also received strength to conceive seed, and she bore a child when she was past the age, because she judged Him faithful who had promised. (12) Therefore from one man, and him as good as dead, were born as many as the stars of the sky in multitude; innumerable as the sand which is by the seashore.
> (13) These all died in faith, not having received the promises, but having seen them afar off were assured of them, embraced them and confessed that they were strangers and pilgrims on the earth. (14) For those who say such things declare plainly that they seek a homeland. (15) And truly if they had called to mind that country from which they had come out, they would have had opportunity to return. (16) But now they desire a better, that is, a heavenly country. Therefore God is not ashamed to be called their God, for He has prepared a city for them.

These great men and women of God had beliefs that gave them an unusual sense of righteousness which condemned their generation e.g. Noah. Their beliefs gave them the courage to be counter-cultural to seek a heavenly country and to see life from a Kingdom perspective.

> (17) By faith Abraham, when he was tested, offered up Isaac, and he who had received the promises offered up his only begotten son, (18) of whom it was said, "In Isaac your seed shall be called," (19) concluding that God was able to raise him up, even from the dead, from which he also received him in a figurative sense. (20) By faith Isaac blessed Jacob and Esau concerning things to come. (21) By faith Jacob, when he was dying, blessed each of the sons of Joseph, and worshiped, leaning on the top of his staff. (22) By faith Joseph, when he was dying, made mention of the departure of the children of Israel, and gave instructions concerning his bones. (23) By faith Moses, when he was born, was hidden three months by his parents, because they saw he was a beautiful child; and they were not afraid of the king's command. (24) By faith Moses, when he became of age, refused to be called the son of Pharaoh's daughter, (25) choosing rather to suffer affliction with the people of God than to enjoy the passing pleasures of sin, (26) esteeming the reproach of Christ greater riches than the treasures in Egypt; for he looked to the reward. (27) By faith he forsook Egypt, not fearing the wrath of the king; for he endured as seeing Him who is invisible. (28) By faith he kept the Passover and the sprinkling of blood, lest he who destroyed the firstborn should touch them. (29) By faith they passed through the Red Sea as by dry land, whereas the Egyptians, attempting to do so, were drowned.

Their unique beliefs led to godly emotions such as Jacob worshipping on the top of his staff. It led to unusual poise and courage in the face of enraged Pharaoh. It led to the ability to go against normal human emotions in the case of Abraham sacrificing Isaac.

> (30) By faith the walls of Jericho fell down after they were encircled for seven days. (31) By faith the harlot Rahab did not perish with those who did not believe, when she had received the spies with peace. (32) And what more shall I say? For the time would fail me to tell of Gideon and Barak and Samson and Jephthah, also of David and Samuel and the prophets: (33) who through faith subdued kingdoms, worked righteousness, obtained promises, stopped the mouths of lions, (34) quenched the violence of fire, escaped the edge of the sword, out of weakness were made strong, became valiant in battle, turned to flight the armies of the aliens. (35) Women received their dead raised to life again. And others were tortured, not accepting deliverance, that they might obtain a better resurrection. (36) Still others had trial of mockings and scourgings, yes, and of chains and imprisonment. (37) They were stoned, they were sawn in two, were tempted, were slain with the sword. They wandered about in sheepskins and goatskins, being destitute, afflicted, tormented; (38) of whom the world was not worthy. They wandered in deserts and mountains, in dens and caves of the earth. (39) And all these, having obtained a good testimony through faith, did not receive the promise, (40) God having provided something better for us, that they should not be made perfect apart from us.

Finally, we see such great emotional mastery and Kingdom perspective that men and women of faith were enduring torture in the hope of a better resurrection! Poise, power and peace and a most unusual set of emotions characterized these heroes of faith. Their emotions moved them to righteous lives and actions. They were not subject to cravings or addictions or impulses of the flesh, rather they had the steady strong enduring emotions that were part of the life of Jesus Christ.

What's the Difference Between Overly-Emotional People and the Vivid Emotions of Jesus and the Prophets?

Let's start this investigation by taking a look at that chronicler of the emotional life of David the Psalmist. I have chosen a Psalm "at random" - Psalm 30.

> I will **extol** You, O LORD, for You have lifted me up, And have not let my foes rejoice over me. {2} O LORD my God, **I cried out** to You, And You healed me. (3) O LORD, You brought my soul up from the grave; You have kept me alive, that I should not go down to the pit. (4) **Sing praise** to the LORD, You saints of His, And **give thanks** at the remembrance of His holy name. (5) For His anger is but for a moment, His favor is for life; **Weeping** may endure for a night, **But joy** comes in the morning. (6) Now in my prosperity I said, "I shall never be moved." (7) LORD, by Your favor You have made my mountain stand strong; You hid Your face, and I was **troubled.** (8) **I cried out to** You, O LORD; And to the LORD **I made supplication:** (9) "What profit is there in my blood, When I go down to the pit? Will the dust praise You? Will it declare Your truth? {10} Hear, O LORD, and have mercy on me; LORD, be my helper!" (11) You have turned for me my **mourning** into **dancing**; You have put off my sackcloth and clothed me with **gladness,** (12) To the end that my glory may sing **praise to** You and **not be silent.** O LORD my God, I will **give thanks** to You forever. (Psalms 30 NKJV) (author's emphasis)

These twelve short verses give us a good example of David's emotional life. What is the difference between David's emotional life and the emotional roller coaster of some Christians?

- The negative emotions are temporary, "weeping may last for a night but joy comes in the morning".
- There is a righteous resolution of the emotions, a giving of thanks in the end.
- The emotions are primarily directed towards God in a private and appropriate fashion.
- There is a wide range of appropriate emotions from joy to a troubled spirit. The emotional thermostat is not stuck in just one position e.g. deep gloom or constant happiness.
- There is an ability to see good in God in the midst of it all - to

sing praise and give thanks. The spiritual perspective is not lost.

- There is no stifling of emotions, they are expressed in spiritual terms, "that my glory may sing praise to You and not be silent".
- There is repentance of false perspectives and beliefs. "Now in my prosperity I said 'I shall not be moved.'". When God challenges this David repents of his self-sufficiency. People who are out of balance emotionally do the opposite and cling to their self-defeating perspectives.
- In the expression of emotions there is genuine dignity and beauty. This psalm is poetry!

[If this area interests you why not take some more of the Psalms and explore their emotional content. The men and women of God down through the centuries have valued them for the insights they give into the emotional life of the believer.]

So we see there is a vast difference between the deep, powerful and godly emotions of the saints and the clanging, shrill emotions of Christian neurotics. The emotions of the saints have God at the center. The emotions of neurotics have self at the center.

What About the Different Temperaments?
The question "which Bible character are you most like?" is an interesting one. I am a miniature "clone" of Paul the apostle sharing much of his impatience and his intellectual approach to the faith. Others say they are like Peter or Moses or David or Jeremiah or Amos. Tim La Haye made an important contribution with his book, Transformed Temperaments, which identified four personality types - Sanguine, Choleric, Melancholy and Phlegmatic. Those of you familiar with Myers-Briggs personality tests will know it also has four basic categories divided into sixteen sub-types. Whatever your schema, one thing is obvious, there is a wide range of personality types! God uses people of all temperaments in His Kingdom and designs ministries and places for each of them. He called complex Thomas as well as straightforward Peter, Simon the Zealot and the sons of Thunder as well as Matthew the pragmatic tax-collector. Sophisticated Daniel was sent to minister to Nebuchadnezzar while Amos the farmer went to bluntly prophesy to the northern kingdom. Having a high biblical EQ does not mean that you are the same as everyone else or that you

become a cute, saccharine sweet, always smiling, never-a-hair-out-of-place believer. There is a vast range for individuality and even for eccentricity within the Kingdom of God!

Eccentricity? Well the prophets were hardly "normal"! John the Baptist wearing camel's hair clothes and eating locusts may be viewed as "eccentric" along with Elijah, Ezekiel and characters such as Samson. These people were culturally distinct but not the least bit mentally ill - they just lived by a different and higher reality which consumed them.

Different temperaments have different uses within the Kingdom of God. Barnabas was a great encourager of the brethren, while Peter's high emotionality made him a master preacher and evangelist. Paul's razor sharp mind made him a great one for attending to the operational details and theology of church life. John's mystical temperament pointed to the deep abiding spiritual realities and resulted in wonderful teaching on prayer. Titus seems to have been a born trouble-shooter while Timothy was the sensitive and caring pastor par excellence.

God will use your basic temperament that He has built into you - and even some of your weaknesses, for when you are weak then you are strong! Your basic God-created and renewed self is OK! God can and will use it and has accepted it in Christ Jesus (Romans 14:7).

Being accepted does not mean being unchanged. The Holy Spirit will take certain parts of your basic emotional temperament and refine them into the image of Christ Jesus. Paul matured in tolerance and love and Peter became stable and reliable. Timothy had to overcome his timidity and learn to suffer hardship as a good soldier of Christ Jesus. As the Holy Spirit convicts you, teaches you and ministers to you a slow but sure transformation will take place that will increase your maturity in Christ and your usefulness to the Master. I find Hebrews especially encouraging by the fact that I have a merciful and faithful High Priest in heaven who understands my weakness and intercedes for me and I have a throne of grace to go to for strength and help in time of need (Hebrews 4:12-16).

Emotions In Times of Revival
If the Holy Spirit acts to redeem our emotions into those of Christ Jesus what causes the emotional excesses during times of revival? Does the Holy Spirit, who so desires balance, holiness, wisdom and truth cause these bizarre manifestations? This is an often discussed question and in

recent years this has become a controversial topic. Therefore, I will try to offer some comment and resolution.

Firstly, emotions DO run high when God moves mightily in times of genuine revival. I recommend the book "The Nature of Revival" a collection of writings from the journals of John Wesley, Charles Wesley and George Whitfield abridged and put into modern English by my friend Clare G. Weakley Jr. and published by Bethany House Publishers. These journal entries give great insight into the emotionality of these great men of God and the extraordinary events of their times. Here are a few random extracts:

P 84. John Wesley.. "On Friday all Newgate rang with the cries of those whom the word of God had cut to the heart. Two of these were filled with joy in a moment, to the astonishment of those who watched them."

P 85. John Wesley regarding one who opposed the revival: "While reading the last page he changed color, fell off his chair, and began screaming terribly as he beat himself against the ground... between one and two in the morning I came in and found him on the floor. The room was full of people who his wife tried to keep out. He cried aloud "No let them all come! Let all the world see the just judgment of God!" Two or three men were trying to hold him down. He immediately fixed his eyes on me, stretched out his hand and said "Aye this is he who I said was a deceiver of the people! But God has overtaken me! I said it was all a delusion, but this is no delusion!" ...(He is eventually released from torment.)

P 87. "While I was enforcing these words "Be still and know that I am God" (Ps 46:10), God began to bare His arm, not in private but in the open air and before more than two thousand witnesses. One then another, and yet another was struck to the earth, greatly trembling at the presence of God's power. Others loudly and bitterly cried "What must we do to be saved?"

Few revivals have been without great emotion and the revivalist Jonathan Edwards wrote a famous treatise on "Religious Affections." which established that the emotions were a by-product of grace not its chief aim. The aim of the godly evangelist is not an emotional audience but a repentant and believing audience.

If the emotions expressed so powerfully indicate that repentance is taking place and that people are meeting with God and having their souls transformed then that emotion is a good thing. However, if it is simply emotionality, hype, manipulated sentimentality and the like and no work of God is taking place and people are not truly turning from darkness to light then it is unprofitable.

A revival in which there is no great emotion would be like a wedding without joy. Such a momentous thing is happening to so many people that surely some great expression of emotion must accompany it. However, when the emphasis is on the manifestations - the tears, the laughter, the falling, etc., then it has gone off track. The wedding should focus on the bride and groom and the revival on Christ and on the believer's transformation. The emotions are just part and parcel of the process and not ends in themselves. In a later chapter on handling our strong emotions I go into the issue of discernment at quite some length. However, I think we should conclude this brief section by saying that the powerful and bizarre emotions of revival are a temporary excess that God permits, but does not encourage. After the emotions and the changes the person so powerfully affected should go on to lead a normal, balanced, wise, godly and sanctified life. They should not keep on having bizarre emotional experiences. That is immature. Mature people display resonant love, deep wisdom and emotional control.

Christian Maturity and Emotion

I soon got the impression as a new Christian that my enthusiasm was expected to wear off and that when I "became mature" I would have rather dull and respectable emotions that resembled cold porridge poured into a grey flannel suit. Is this the sort of emotional maturity that Scripture speaks of in Ephesians?

> Till we all come to the unity of the faith and of the knowledge of the Son of God, to a perfect man, to the measure of the stature of the fullness of Christ; (14) that we should no longer be children, tossed to and fro and carried about with every wind of doctrine, by the trickery of men, in the cunning craftiness of deceitful plotting, (15) but, speaking the truth in love, may grow up in all things into Him who is the head; Christ. (Ephesians 4:13-15 NKJV)

Christian emotional maturity does involve emotional stability - we are not "tossed to and fro... by every wind of doctrine". It also involves "growing up" in all things and becoming a person participating in the stature and fullness of Christ. While it involves the stability of Christ it also involves the passion and zeal of Christ (John 2:17; Titus 2:14) and His ability to bless and to care. In fact part of the purpose of our redemption is to become a people "zealous for good deeds".

> Who gave Himself for us, that He might redeem us from every lawless deed and purify for Himself a people for His own possession, zealous for good deeds. (Titus 2:14 NASB)

Maturity is not the loss of emotions but the educating of emotions so they are like those of Jesus Christ and the mature person is both stable and zealous.

Childish emotions are OUT for the mature Christian but Christ-like emotions are IN. In the next chapter we will see what carnal emotions look like, how they are the reverse of the biblical EQ process and how we can move beyond them and start the process of "growing up in all things into Him who is the head - even Christ".

Discussion Questions

1. Do you think that King David was overly emotional? If not, why not?

2. What is different about the emotions of the great Christian leaders?

3. What about revival? How should we cope with strong emotions in Christian gatherings?

4. Go back over the twelve predictions at the beginning of this chapter. How do you feel as you read them and what picture do they paint for you about how the Christian life should be lived?

5. How do our different characters and temperaments fit in with a view of emotions that is centered around one person – Jesus Christ?

6. What do you think Christian maturity looks like?

The Emotional Life of The Carnal Christian

And I, brethren, could not speak to you as to spiritual people but as to carnal, as to babes in Christ. (2) I fed you with milk and not with solid food; for until now you were not able to receive it, and even now you are still not able; (3) for you are still carnal. For where there are envy, strife, and divisions among you, are you not carnal and behaving like mere men? (4) For when one says, "I am of Paul," and another, "I am of Apollos," are you not carnal? (1 Corinthians 3:1-5 NKJV)

We just saw how the five-step model of emotions quite accurately predicted the emotional life of Spirit-filled men and women of God. Now the model has as its central theme that emotional maturity is arrived at by focusing on Jesus, and modeling our emotions after Him in the power of the Holy Spirit. It is the Holy Spirit who renews our perceptions, beliefs, emotions, and physical bodies and who gives us wisdom in how to express our emotions in ways that are "taught of God". We saw a positive correlation between what the theory predicted about the great saints of God, who cooperated with the Holy Spirit, and how they turned out emotionally, becoming beings of emotional grandeur. If our model stands the test, then those who resist the Holy Spirit, those who are unspiritual, should not be beings of emotional grandeur. Rather they should be emotionally unformed and immature. If, as our theory predicts, the Holy Spirit is essential for full emotional formation, then unspiritual Christians should be emotional wrecks, or at the least quite shallow and indifferent emotionally. These unspiritual Christians are termed "carnal Christians" and in this chapter we will see if our model can predict how they will turn out and what lessons we can learn from that.

The carnal Christian is characterized by an astonishing lack of spiritual maturity to the point where they cannot be addressed as spiritual people. Carnal Christians behave like "mere men" and are indistinguishable from the surrounding culture with their actions and reactions. Using our model we can again make certain predictions about the emotional life of those who do not give the Holy Spirit full lordship of their lives. We will just reverse the predictions in the previous chapter.

Perception

1. They will see the world in much the same terms as the surrounding culture. For them the Kingdom perspective will be rare and they will be mainly self-centered.
2. They will be unable to see into the hearts of men and women and even empathy will be rare. They will not speak accurately to the human condition.
3. They will be baffled by dreams, visions and symbolic language. They will be bored by the prophetic and struggle with understanding the Scripture.

Beliefs

4. They will mainly have beliefs that the surrounding culture has taught them. They will not hold beliefs that the culture opposes vehemently, and will have few beliefs that only God could have taught them.
5. They will have a very weak sense of what is righteous and what is unrighteous and rarely react to social evil. They would tolerate the selling of doves in the Temple. Zeal will be unusual for them and even undesirable. They will not be consumed by Kingdom interests.
6. They will not have unusual poise and power in crisis situations, like Jesus in the storm, but rather will be prone to anxiety.
7. They will not resonate with and be emotionally drawn to those who are of great faith. Rather they will feel more at home with the world and with other carnal Christians.

Emotions

8. They will not have deep, vivid and stable emotions like those of Jesus Christ. They will instead be characterized by shallow sentimental spiritual feelings that vary with every wind of doctrine.
9. They will have little sense of their emotions being God's emotions. They will often be unaware of what they are feeling and will be unable to name their emotions clearly. They will not be people of authentic emotional expression.

Physical Nature

10. They will not demonstrate victory over addictions and sexual temptations. They will fail to express their emotions in godly ways

through their physical bodies.

Emotional Expression

11. Their spiritual emotions will rarely lead to righteous actions. Compassion for the lost or the poor will rarely be felt and will not move them to action. Their emotionality will be detached from real life and be like the emotions of an actor or a hypocrite.
12. The course of their lives will not demonstrate an ever-increasing wisdom in emotional expression. They will go from bad to worse and become increasingly discordant like "a clanging gong and a clashing cymbal" if they should continue as carnal Christians.

How does this tally with your experience of carnal Christians? Unfortunately, the tally indicates they are not growing and in fact they are often going backwards spiritually. Let's see what the New Testament says about them:

In the quote that opened this chapter we find Paul referring to the church in 1 Corinthians as "carnal", so what was it like? The carnality of the church is reflected in a long list of very serious sins. The first four chapters detail division, intellectual and spiritual pride, factions, and infighting. Chapters five and six show they were visiting prostitutes, and engaging in sexual immorality, and incest. Chapter seven discusses marriage, divorce and the basics of sexually appropriate behavior. Chapters eight through eleven correct gross disorder such as being drunk at the Lord's Supper, not waiting for one another so one goes hungry while another is full, and participation in feasts in pagan temples and eating food sacrificed to idols. Chapters twelve to fourteen reveal a paganization of the spiritual gifts and their use in competitive, unloving and chaotic ways. Chapter fifteen finds them denying the resurrection and being in major error over basic doctrines. The church was a mess but it was still considered a Christian church. The church James wrote to may have even been worse! There they murdered one another (James 4:2) and treated the poor with contempt (James 2). Both these churches were considered Christian churches and the recipients were addressed as believers and referred to as saints or holy ones (1 Corinthians 1:2).

Several epistles are addressed to churches with a good percentage of carnal Christians these are: Galatians, 1 & 2 Corinthians, Titus,

Hebrews and James. In these epistles the language is extremely plain and there are many stern warnings about the consequences of sin and the judgment of God (Galatians 5, Hebrews 6, 1 Corinthians 5, 2 Corinthians 12 & 13). In the first six or so chapters of his epistle the writer to the Hebrews says of his audience that they were sluggish, unfruitful, dull of hearing, immature, like children, neglectful of their salvation, in danger of drifting away from the faith, hardening their hearts to God's Word and at the point of having "evil, unbelieving, hearts" (Hebrews 3:12). In chapter ten the writer goes on to say they are neglecting meeting together and on the verge of giving up the faith, returning to sin and being judged by the living God. This is a terrifying picture indeed!

Carnal Christian's lifestyles are almost indistinguishable from that of unbelievers. Such Christians are characterized by apathy, division, ongoing strife and a very low EQ! Carnal Christians "bite and devour one another" (Galatians 5:15). The carnal Christians needed lengthy instructions on the basics of human relationships and fortunately the apostolic response to this need has given rise to some of the finest literature on relationships in the world including the famous "love chapter" in 1 Corinthians 13. This is in direct contrast with other more Spirit-filled churches like the one at Thessalonica of whom Paul said:

> But concerning brotherly love you have no need that I should write to you, for you yourselves are taught by God to love one another. (1 Thessalonians 4:9 NKJV)

Where Then Is the Holy Spirit?
All truly born-again Christians receive the Holy Spirit as part of the dynamics of conversion and the formation of the new man in them, which is Christ in them the hope of glory. So all these Christians in Corinth, called "saints" by Paul, presumably had the Holy Spirit. Yet they were a mess. Something was dreadfully wrong. There seems to be a breakdown in their sanctification process. The Holy Spirit in them was not producing maturity. The fruit of the Spirit was not evident. Was this God's fault? Had God given up on them? Surely not! These people were doing something that was stopping the Holy Spirit from having His way in their lives. They were sinning against the Spirit's presence in their lives.

This raises a question. What then happens to the Holy Spirit in born-again Christians who have become carnal? In tribal cultures they often think that the Holy Spirit vanishes from you if you sin. That is not New Testament teaching. The Holy Spirit remains within the believer but is sinned against. Several terms are used such as: grieved (Ephesians 4:30), quenched (1 Thessalonians 5:18-21) lied to (Acts 5:4), put to the test (Acts 5:9), insulted / outraged (Hebrews 10:29), made jealous (James 4:4,5), blasphemed (Matthew 12:31) and resisted (Acts 7:51). In Jude the divisive people are said to be "devoid of the Spirit" (Jude 1:19). We will very briefly look at each of these terms to gain some understanding of the spiritual dynamics of sinning against the Holy Spirit and its effects on the emotional life.

Grieved (Ephesians 4:30) - by unnecessary and immature interpersonal conflict such as bitterness, wrath, slander and malice. The Holy Spirit is a Spirit of love and is grieved by that which is opposed to love. Carnal behavior such as divisiveness and quarreling is anti-love, and causes grief to the Holy Spirit who is constantly trying to mature us in love.

Quenched (1 Thessalonians 5:18-21) - by despising the gifts of the Spirit, especially prophesy. It implies that His fire - His inspirational activity in prophecy and revival is resisted - perhaps in the name of order, and "cold water" is thrown on attempts to minister in spiritual power.

Lied To (Acts 5:4) - Ananias and Sapphira conspired in an act of financial deception of the apostles. This was seen as not deceiving men but God and lying to the Holy Spirit (Acts 5:4) and resulted in them being carried out dead.

Put To The Test (Acts 5:9) - Again refers to Ananias and Sapphira and refers to their testing the omniscience of the Holy Spirit by thinking they could deceive those He had filled with power and anointed.

Insulted/Outraged/Do Despite Unto (Hebrews 10:29) - refers to someone who turns back from Christianity to Judaism (or to any other religion) and thus says that the work of the Spirit of grace in his or her life was of no value to them. These are apostates.

Made Jealous (James 4:4,5) - Adulterers and adulteresses! Do you not know that friendship with the world is enmity with God? Whoever therefore wants to be a friend of the world makes himself an enemy of

God. Or do you think that the Scripture says in vain, "The Spirit who dwells in us yearns jealously"?

Blasphemed (Matthew 12:31) - is used of those unbelieving Jews who so deeply resisted the Holy Spirit that they saw the miraculous ministry of Jesus Christ as the work of the devil and attributed His power to Satan. Again it is never used of Christians.

Resisted (Acts 7:51) - refers to the unbelieving Jews who were stoning Stephen and resisting the clear testimony of the Holy Spirit. Later God said to one of those resistant Jews "Saul, Saul, it must be hard for you to kick against the goads..." This term is not used of believers.

Devoid Of The Spirit (Jude 1:19) - refers to false teachers who joined into Christian groups and created division leading people away to their own groups. These are probably not even believers to start with.

This is difficult verse to translate. It refers to friendship with the world, which is seen as spiritual adultery and makes the Spirit jealous. The world system and the Kingdom are opposites. To love one is to make the other jealous and if we love the world (as in worldliness, not as in John 3:16) we enrage the Holy Spirit. Worldliness is often characteristic of carnal Christians and does great damage to their relationship with God.

The emotional consequences of sinning against the Holy Spirit are dire indeed. The more people sin against the Holy Spirit the nastier they become. In the above verses we see them pilfering, murdering, lying, fighting and quarreling. As the Holy Spirit is quenched, grieved and resisted His love departs and hatred enters in.

How does this come about? A love of worldly things, a growing resentment, anger and malice, a dislike of prophecy and revivals, a little dishonesty with finances here and there and after a while the activity of the Holy Spirit in the believer's life is reduced to a whisper. As they head out the back door of the faith they deliver the final insult by rejecting the value of Jesus whom the Spirit bears witness to.

In answer to our question, "What is the relationship between the Holy Spirit and the carnal Christian?" the relationship is one of struggle and pain. The Spirit is grieved, made jealous, quenched and resisted. He seeks to bring the carnal believer to a point of repentance and to cooperation with God. However, in the words of the famous Campus Crusade booklet "How to Be Filled With The Holy Spirit" (which I thoroughly recommend), "self is on the throne". The carnal Christian is a "me first" Christian led by their own desires, and seeking their own interests and having their own agenda. Christ may be in their life but He is not being allowed to fully direct their lives. The struggle with the Holy Spirit will only end for them when they abdicate from their throne, and instead decide to place Christ on the throne, obey His commandments and be led by the Spirit, not by their own desires. If you think that this may apply to you why don't you consider praying a prayer somewhat like the following:

"Lord, I am sorry that I have put self on the throne and run my life according to my own desires rather than according to Your will. I repent of this and ask that Christ may be on the throne and in the control room of my life, and that I may be ruled by His desires, and by the Holy Spirit. I ask that You may fill me with the Holy Spirit and produce in me a soft and obedient heart. In Jesus name. Amen".

The Low Biblical EQ Of Carnal Christians
The poor control carnal Christians have over their emotional life is due to their lack of co-operation with the Holy Spirit and can be seen in:

Poor Impulse Control: Giving in to sexual immorality, drunkenness and even in the disorder of their worship.

Poor Anger Management: Most notably the congregation that James wrote to which were murdering each other (James 4:2) and the Galatians which were "biting and devouring" each other (Galatians 5:15).

Disintegrating Relationships: Envying, factions, strife and contentions (1 Corinthians 3:3).

Low Levels of Personal Motivation: They are variously described as evil beasts and lazy gluttons (Titus 1:12-14) , neglectful, dull of hearing, and in danger of drifting.

Instability: Following after "the latest" false teachers particularly if they were good talkers and emotionally persuasive

(2 Corinthians 11) and being tossed around by every wind of doctrine.

Lack of Basic Empathy and Compassion: Such as saying to a person who was without food or shelter "be warm and filled" and not doing anything to help or dishonoring the poor by making them sit in lowly places in church (James 2).

A Toxic Tongue: Gossip, slander, and the like that proceeds from out of control emotions (James 3).

A Poisonous Personality: Such people are described as a "root of bitterness that defiles many" or like the emotionally rigid Diotrephes who "like to put himself first" and controlled the church (3 John).

The Obvious Conclusion
So we see that our model for Biblical EQ predicts accurately the disastrous perceptions, beliefs, actions and reactions of people who are carnal Christians. We see that the process we have outlined accurately predicts good and holy emotions for those filled with the Spirit and negative and hateful emotions for those who resist and grieve the Spirit. This leads to two conclusions. Firstly, that our model seems to fit the biblical data and probably does describe the process of emotional development and expression. More importantly it leads to the conclusion that the single most important factor in a high biblical EQ is the work of the Holy Spirit in the life of the cooperating and Spirit-filled believer. Those most full of the Spirit are grand beings of deep emotional authenticity. Christians that grieve the Spirit are emotional wrecks.

However, believers do not neatly fall into two camps, one with wonderful emotions and the other with sharp, brittle and unstable emotions. That is because we start at different points. Some Spirit-filled believers from emotionally difficult backgrounds may have a lot of learning and growing to do with respect to their emotions, but they are going in the right direction. In time, providing they remain close to God, they will learn and grow and become more Christlike in their emotions. This seems to have been very much the case with Paul who went from being very abrasive in his early years to very gracious in later life. On the other hand some very worldly and carnal Christians are squandering a wonderful emotional inheritance from a loving Christian family. They seem emotionally together but in time, slowly but surely, emotional disintegration sets in and generally becomes obvious by late middle age.

What About Non-Believers?
What does our model say about non-believers? Generally, non-believers are neither cooperating with nor resisting the work of the Holy Spirit. Thus the emotional life of non-believers should be normally distributed (that is "on a bell curve") around a central mean that is less than the emotional mean of Spirit-filled Christians but perhaps not as low as that of truly carnal Christians. Since the Spirit does not indwell unbelievers, the great inner work of the Spirit is not there and the upper reaches of the Christian life are unavailable to them. For instance, they are generally not able to love their enemies. While they may be very decent and loving people they will generally not have the tremendous power and life that being like Christ produces. This deep pulsating joy is almost exclusively a work of God in the regenerate believer. Thus our model is not destroyed by the fact of the occasional good non-Christian.

> It needs to be also said that God has His prevenient and common grace and the Holy Spirit will give some external aid to anyone who seeks to live a good, decent and loving life and encourages Jews, Buddhists, humanists and existentialists alike to be decent human beings. In such people many Christian values will be found in the belief system that undergirds their emotional life. Such people who are seeking good, but have not yet found Christ may well be emotionally together as they are cooperating with God in a stumbling sort of way. However the deep transformational power of the Holy Spirit may well be lacking.

The Conclusion
1. The five-step model accurately predicts the emotional state of both saintly Christians and carnal Christians.
2. Emotional authenticity is entirely a work of the Holy Spirit . However, it can occur to some extent in non-believers who seek it as a work of common grace. More commonly it is found in Spirit-filled believers who are walking in holiness.
3. Emotional functionality and authenticity come about through the person cooperating with the Holy Spirit as He forms spiritual perspectives and a Christlike belief system in the person.
4. Resisting this work of the Holy Spirit results in emotional catastrophe.

5. Emotionally undeveloped Christians who remain close to God can grow into emotionally adept people just as it seems Paul did.

6. Cooperating with God means not grieving or quenching the Holy Spirit and being careful to avoid worldliness.

Is There a Fast Track To a High Biblical EQ?

Obviously being Spirit-filled and obedient is a great place to start for emotional growth. However, Christians can also directly work on their emotions. Information on how to do this has been provided in three ways. Firstly, God has given His Son to show us what holy and true emotions look like. Secondly, He has given us the special revelation in Scripture and their precise description of the emotional life and the inner man. Thirdly, He has given His natural revelation to scientists who so assiduously seek the truth about emotional growth. Combining these together we will find out how to directly achieve emotional growth and a high biblical EQ. That takes us to the next section of this book, the section on the inner self which deals with how emotions are formed within us, and what we can do about it. This section will give us the knowledge and tools we need to work on our perceptions of reality and our belief systems. We will also learn how to renew them and to produce Christlike outcomes and godly emotions.

Discussion Questions

1. What are the emotional consequences for a Christian if they choose not to cooperate with the work of the Holy Spirit?

2. What are the sins against the Holy Spirit?

3. What sort of descriptions does the Bible give of carnal Christians, e.g. "sluggish"?

4. Read the twelve predictions at the start of the chapter. What impression do they make on you? What does it say about why some churches experience problems?

5. How important is the Holy Spirit in developing the emotional life of Christians?

6. Why can some non-Christians be in a better emotional state than some Christians? Can emotionally clumsy Christians ever improve?

PART TWO

OUR INNER SELF AND OUR EMOTIONAL WORLD

(2 Corinthians 4:16 NASB) Therefore we do not lose heart, but though our outer man is decaying, yet our inner man is being renewed day by day.

Our "inner man" is not constant, but for the Spirit-filled Christian it is being renewed day by day. This section is about how we can understand and cooperate with that process of inner renewal. We will look at how emotions arise within the inner being of the Christian, in our spirit, soul and body. We will look at what forms our emotions and what affects them and how we can introduce constructive change into those processes. We will primarily do this by considering their functions such as perception, belief, and will. Any explanation of the inner self and our emotions, that comes anywhere near being comprehensive, sane and balanced, will be complex. After all, we are complex and somewhat incomprehensible beings made in the image of a complex and totally incomprehensible God (Romans 11:28-30). Emotions arise from the depths of our spirit, from our body being over-tired or the affects of illness or medication, and yet others arise from our beliefs and the determinations of our will. We can even have conflicting emotions. The process the Holy Spirit takes within us as He transforms us emotionally is both profoundly simple and infinitely complex. I hope you will consider both realities in the following chapters.

Perception

For we walk by faith, not by sight. **(2 Corinthians 5:7 NKJV)**

Perception is the first of the five stages of Biblical EQ and by far the most complex, which is why we will spend two chapters looking at it. In this chapter we will look at perception as it flows from our stance toward life, our life perspective, how we see things and how we explain the world to ourselves. These perceptions and explanations later become that from which we form our beliefs, and out of those beliefs will flow our emotions. In the next chapter we will look at perception at its deepest level, in the human spirit, and how it forms the foundations and framework for our personality. In logical order that chapter should precede this chapter but I have chosen to put the simple material first and move you to the more difficult as a better teaching strategy.

How do you suppose the people of Jesus' day would have seen Jerusalem? A tourist may have just seen a dusty city with a beautiful temple in the middle of it. A trader may have seen an economic opportunity. A priest most likely would have seen the religious community and a chance for prominence in the Temple service. An anxious mother would possibly see it as "the big smoke" where her son had gone to find work. Rome saw it as a trouble spot to be kept under tight control. The disciples at this time saw Jerusalem as a dangerous city with Herod and others intent on killing them (Luke 13:30; John 11:16). Jesus saw Jerusalem in terms of its long hostility towards messengers of God:

> "O Jerusalem, Jerusalem, the one who kills the prophets and stones those who are sent to her! How often I wanted to gather your children together, as a hen gathers her brood under her wings, but you were not willing! (35) "See! Your house is left to you desolate; and assuredly, I say to you, you shall not see Me until the time comes when you say, 'Blessed is He who comes in the name of the LORD!'"O Jerusalem, Jerusalem, the one who kills the prophets and stones those who are sent to her! (Luke 13:34-35 NKJV)

His unique perspective was one that viewed cities in terms of their spiritual responsiveness and their attitude to the light that they received. Jesus, the apostles and the prophets all had a unique perspective on people, places and events. They saw things differently and viewed reality in spiritual terms. Instead of the world being a chaotic jumble of almost random events it is a place planned by a sovereign and just God. For Jesus the primary reality was not economic but spiritual - how a person, or even a city relates to God. Spiritual people see life differently. They have deep abiding spiritual perspectives. They perceive reality through an entirely different set of glasses. They see the world "right side up".

When our perceptions about life are wrong soon all else goes wrong. If we perceive life to be utterly random we will be without hope. If we perceive ourselves to be unlovable we will live alone in the land. If we perceive others to be hostile, when in fact they are friendly, we will needlessly create enemies. In this chapter we shall first look at secular material that explains how our perspective on life is formed. We will also look at some proven secular techniques for correcting common errors and becoming optimistic and functional. Then once we have achieved that we shall then look at how to gain a biblical heavenly perspective and know life and peace.

The correct perspective on life can calm fears, break us out of depression, give us peace and stability, bring joy and hope, give us empathy and compassion and give us the ability to plan wisely and well for our future. First we have to understand how our perspective is created, then we can look at how it can be fully redeemed.

Explaining Reality to Ourselves
A key element in the creation of our perspective is how we explain reality to ourselves. Bit by bit these explanations become our story about the world and how it came to be and why it is the way it is. Soon we start seeing the world the way we have imagined it to be, through the story we have constructed from our explanations of the world. The psychologist Martin E. P. Seligman has done much research on people's "explanatory style" and his book, "Learned Optimism", is excellent. Here is my twelve point summary of its basic teachings:

1. Optimism and power-fulness are the opposites of pessimism and Helpless-ness.
2. Optimism and pessimism are learned by experiences in life.
3. Experiences form beliefs. These beliefs then combine to produce outlooks on life.
4. The beliefs which we draw from experiences can be well-founded

or poorly founded depending on how we explained the experience to ourselves.

5. We can explain things Personally (it's always our fault) or Externally (it's something outside)
6. We can explain things Pervasively (it's in everything, everywhere) or Specifically (this is just one instance).
7. We can explain things Permanently (it will always be this way) or Temporarily (it's just a glitch).
8. Personal, Pervasive and Permanent explanatory styles produce self-defeating beliefs and a negative outlook.
9. The negative outlook is reflected in negative self-talk.
10. The self-defeating beliefs we have formed can be reasoned with and our negative thoughts can be disputed.
11. Marshalling evidence against self-defeating beliefs and attacking them logically can slowly but surely lead to a more optimistic outlook.
12. Sometimes you can "externalize" the belief by writing the thought down on paper or talking it over with a friend.

Martin Seligman then goes on to show how we can dispute our wrong perspective and learn to be optimistic by writing down our thoughts and looking at them logically and in the light of the three P's - Personal, Pervasive and Permanent. According to Seligman's research, optimists are healthier and have better lives than pessimists. But oddly enough pessimists tend to be more accurate! Pessimists are right in their conclusions but wrong in their living. They are unhappy, unsuccessful and unhealthy. The three key ways pessimists defeat themselves is through their explanatory style - see points 5-8 above. For instance the way we explain things to ourselves will determine how quickly we recover from minor incidents. If I have an argument with a friend and then think "I am terrible at relationships, I will always have arguments with everyone I meet, I'm just a total loser" then I will be unhappy and I may stay unhappy for a while. On the other hand if after the argument I say, "I think I was overtired, I'll get over this and have a better day tomorrow, I don't always blow up at people" then I will be much happier and recover more quickly.

Faith Application

Christians have explanatory styles too that determine their faith level, their happiness and their joy. Explanations can vary from "God is punishing me and will always punish me because I am so wicked" to "The devil made me do it." We have a habitual faith perspective on life and just like the pessimists in Seligman's research we can be re-educated to a more functional and liberating explanatory style and faith perspective. This is a three-stage process:

Stage One: Acknowledging that our spiritual explanatory style is in need of major repair.

Stage Two: Finding out exactly where it needs to be corrected and

Stage Three: The job of repairing it.

Is Your Explanatory Style In Need of Repair?

Try the following consciousness raising quiz. It's not a psychological test, just a series of questions to help you become aware of the way you explain events to yourself. It is just a simple diagnostic tool to help you realize what you are thinking so you can correct it. Please be honest. Answer the following questions by putting the numbers 0 to 4 in the corresponding lines as follows:

0 - I never think that way.

1 - I sometimes think that way.

2 - I think that way a fair amount of time but not often.

3 - I frequently think that way.

4 - I always think that way.

There are fifty questions in two sections Personal Explanations (20) & Spiritual Explanations (30) and unlike many tests they are deliberately arranged so as to make the patterns obvious so you can see how you are thinking. The areas being examined include the three P's - Permanent, Personal and Pervasive and a factor called "locus of control" which looks at who or what you see as being in control - yourself, God, other people, luck or the devil. The theological section also looks at these but adds questions testing our trust in God and our belief in His goodness and our faith in His Word as part of our spiritual explanatory style.

Personal Explanations

Permanence

____   After making a mistake I tend to think "this is the end".

____   I feel as if I will never change.

____   If you are a success you stay successful. If you are a failure you are always a loser.

____   Nothing can be done about society, it is bound to go downhill forever.

____   You never recover from bankruptcy.

Locus Of Control

____ I believe you need a lot of luck to succeed in life. Success is mainly random.

____ The world is unpredictable, chaotic and confusing so it's not worth trying too hard to do anything big. It will probably just be messed up.

____ Other people make me react. My emotions are not under my control.

____ I can't do anything about the Government.

____ If I win at anything it is because the other people do not try hard.

Pervasive

____ Evil is everywhere and here to stay. All people and systems are ruined by it.

____ My entire personality is dysfunctional.

____ I am basically bad and if people really got to know me they would despise me or hate me.

____ I am frequently suspicious of other people and their evil motives.

____ All politicians are corrupt.

Personal

____ I find failure depressing because it reflects on who I am.

____ The reason I make mistakes is because I cannot do anything right.

____ When people are late for an appointment and say it was the traffic they are just lying to me. It actually means that I am unimportant to them.

____ When someone fails to return a phone call I think they are rejecting me.

____ If I fail an exam it means that I am stupid.

Now add up your score in each section:

Permanence _____   Locus of Control_____

Pervasive _____   Personal   _____

Did you notice any patterns emerging? Where were your highest scores?

Spiritual Explanations

Permanence

   ____   My habitual sins are there for life.

   ____   You can't change the world. It will always be this way.

   ____   It is easy to sin or mistakenly miss God's will and the results are life-long.

   ____   I am what God has made me to be and I cannot change.

   ____   It's all over, I'm washed up, I've totally failed God. This is the end.

Locus of Control

   ____   Things go wrong because God is not really in charge of my life.

   ____   Satan is very powerful and in charge of this physical world and much of my circumstances.

   ____   I must save the world, the job just cannot be done without me.

   ____   I am not responsible for my actions. The devil makes me sin.

   ____   Of course I have to panic in a crisis. Someone has to do the work and the worrying - namely me!

Pervasive

   ____   The universe is totally polluted by sin and cannot be enjoyed.

   ____   Even my prayers are an abomination to God.

   ____   My life is riddled with inconsistencies. I am hopeless.

   ____   All denominations are filled with greedy clergy.

   ____   Theological error is everywhere.

Personal

   ____   My failure to memorize Bible verses means that I am totally unspiritual.

   ____   I haven't led anyone to Jesus so my life has been a total failure.

   ____   Good events happen to good people and bad events happen to bad people. When bad things happen to me it must be my fault.

   ____   I experience temptation because I am sinful and wicked.

____ The reason my family isn't saved is because I have been a poor witness.

Transcendent Spiritual Focus

____ Emotional security and happiness is almost impossible if I cannot pay the bills.

____ When I talk about blessing I mainly mean something tangible in this life such as a salary increase or a new car.

____ For me God's approval of me and the pastor's / Christian community's approval of me is almost identical.

____ I am easily devastated by criticism at church.

____ It is a long while since I have prayed fervently and truly expected a major answer.

Goodness of God

____ Bad people get all the good things.

____ Prayer is for prayer warriors, average people don't get their prayers answered.

____ My life is miserable and difficult but I must not strive to change it, I must accept it as character-building punishment for my sins.

____ I fear that if I obey God to the maximum He will make me a poverty-stricken missionary in outer Uzbekistan (or similar).

____ The safest thing to do as a Christian is not to expect too much from God.

Now add up your scores in each section:

Permanence ____   Locus of Control ____ Pervasive ____
Personal ____   Transcendent Spiritual Focus ____
Goodness of God ____

Did you notice any patterns emerging? Where were your highest scores?

NOTE: *This is NOT a clinical test and should not be used as such or employed as a selection tool. This is a consciousness-raising instrument designed to help individuals become aware of their explanatory style and to help them surface a few issues regarding it.*

Interpreting the Results

If you get 10 or more in any one section then you may have a problem in that area. This does NOT mean that you are crazy or dysfunctional. It does mean that like many people it may be worth your while spending some time looking at that perspective on life and working out what emotions it is bringing to you. Does your perspective cause you to feel out of control? Do you have trouble believing in a consistently good God? Just use the results from the test to alert you to areas you may need to work on. Right perspectives and beliefs provide a firm foundation for emotional health. We will see much more on this in the section on beliefs that follows.

A Dose of Perspective Restorer

When I was in Balimo in the remote Western Province of Papua New Guinea the missionary doctor there, Dr. Kath Donovan, used to talk about "taking a dose of perspective restorer" when things got out of sorts with someone in the mission station. A dose of perspective restorer was often a provocative question or statement that got us to rethink our miseries. In a similar vein here are a few provocative statements and questions that can help you to challenge the dysfunctional perspectives that you have identified as having some influence in your life. I am sure you will quickly get the idea.

Challenging Ideas of Permanence

- Are your negative circumstances really permanent or do they just feel permanent?
- How impossible is impossible? Is anything impossible with God?
- Haven't you gotten out of difficult situations before? Can't you do it again?
- Haven't you changed and learned before? Can't you do it again?
- Hopelessness is never from God. It is a lie and a deception. He is the God of hope.

Challenging Ideas of Low Locus of Control

- Is there one single thing you CAN do to change things? .
- Who is in charge, you, other people, the devil or God?
- Luck is preparation meeting opportunity. Make your luck by preparing your skills and seeking opportunities.

- The devil is not in control. Resist the devil and he will flee. (James 4:7)
- You are not God so you don't have to be responsible for everything. However, you do have some responsibilities - fulfill those and let God handle the rest of the universe.

Challenging Ideas of Pervasive Evil

- You are not totally sinful if you are worried about sinning. Totally sinful people are unconcerned about sinning.
- Are all politicians corrupt? Was Ghandi corrupt? Was Abraham Lincoln corrupt? Are there really no good churches - not even one? Is absolutely everyone wrong in their theology?
- Has the redeeming work of Christ accomplished nothing in 2000 years? Has He not created some good in some corner of the world?
- Is the devil so powerful that he can ruin everything? Cannot God preserve some things that are good and beautiful? Cannot one wildflower be excellent in beauty?
- Cannot God make all things beautiful in their time? (Ecclesiastes 3:11) Can He not make you a wonder and a glory? (Romans 8:28-31)

Challenging Ideas That Everything That Goes Wrong Is Your Personal Fault

- Have you noticed that sometimes you think people are rejecting you when in fact they are just busy or having a bad day? Might you be exaggerating the degree of rejection? Maybe it's not that bad.
- Is it really you at fault? Could it just be the circumstances or the other people?
- When thinking about yourself stop using "absolute" terminology including words such as: must, have to, always, never, and totally. They are rarely true. One mistake does not make you a "total failure".
- When there is a problem, list those factors you can control and also list those factors that you cannot control. Leave those outside your control to other people or even to God. Do not feel personally responsible for things you cannot control. Then feel free to responsibly and wisely tackle those things you can do.

- Cease seeing yourself as being at the center of the universe with so many things spinning around you. Be content to just be one of God's creatures, a son or daughter with a few assigned tasks to do.

Renewing Transcendent Spiritual Focus

- We walk by faith, not by sight. Do not let visible things such as bills and criticism be the only reality.
- Expect great things from God. Attempt great things for God (Carey). Read Hebrews 11 and Matthew 6

- Faith is often "more caught than taught" so hang around people who are full of faith.
- Have you drifted away from faith? Have you been deeply disappointed with God? Would it help to talk to a good pastor or Christian counselor?
- Are there genuine concerns about the canon of Scripture, miracles, evolution, etc? Get some material and investigate your doubts and find answers to your genuine intellectual questions.

Believing In the Goodness of God

- Look at the goodness of God and how He provides for the birds. As a friend of mine says she has "never seen a skinny sparrow". If God is good to sparrows, then how much more good will He do for you!
- Remember all the Lord has done for you. Make a list of His goodness and remind yourself of the things He has done. Bring to mind His past love of you and remember He never changes! He is faithful!
- Spend some time in Psalm 23 and Romans 8. Sing hymns, play Christian music.
- Examine your background for things like deprivation, cruelty and disappointment. Are you projecting your experiences, particularly of your father/parents, onto God? Try and separate the two so that you can see God for all He truly is in His constant lovingkindness and faithfulness. Stand against those lurking feelings from your past and rebuke them in the name of Jesus. Maybe even seek counseling.

- Move self off center stage. Sometimes we doubt God's goodness because we are demanding a certain thing - a partner, wealth, the return of a divorced spouse, etc. and He has not answered us yet and we are furious that God is not meeting our agenda in our time. The goodness of God is bigger than His meeting a single important demand of yours. Your focus is too narrow. While you wait for your answer to prayer notice how He sends you beautiful days and good friends and daily bread. Cultivate thankfulness for what you DO have instead of focusing on what you do not have.

Coming Up With Your Own Bottle of Perspective Restorer
Cognitive therapists have come up with a general process for giving yourself a dose of perspective restorer. They believe that underneath our difficult emotions are thoughts that fuel those emotions. With every painful incident there is a thought that makes it painful that keeps the pain ongoing, such as "I'll never get over this, my life is ruined forever". When those thoughts are corrected the emotions lose their power and can be brought under control. People vary greatly in their underlying thoughts. That is why one person can just laugh something off and another takes it to heart. Underneath person A is the thought 'Oh that was nothing…", underneath person B is the thought "that's so unjust, unfair and horrible…" Our thoughts are under our control and as we change them we can also change the emotions that they produce. For instance, if you change your thoughts from "I'll never get over this" to "One day I'll be able to look back on this and laugh" then you create optimism and give power to your life. Most of the thoughts that hurt us deeply are simply not true. In fact if we take a hard look at them they are nearly always illogical. Self-talk such as "Everybody hates me" is generally not true at all. It's painful, it's untrue and it needs to be challenged. Your perspective is your thought on the situation and like any thought you can change it. As you change it you change the emotions that result. So you can heal yourself of many painful emotions just by working out a more truthful, balanced and biblical perspective on life. How can we do this? The five step process below is summarized from the book, "Feeling Good - A New Mood Therapy", by David. M. Burns.

1. Find a recent incident that caused you some emotional discomfort.
2. Look at the feeling - name and write down the feeling.

3. Try to find the underlying thought that produced that feeling, e.g. "I am always stupid".
4. Dispute the thought with facts, Scripture, logic and common sense until you come up with a more functional perspective on the event.
5. Write down the new feeling that comes with the new explanation.

Let's apply this process to a common Christian situation - rejection at the door of the church:

Incident: Rob goes to shake the hand of the pastor after church but the pastor abruptly turns away because he has just caught sight of the church treasurer who wants a check signed. The pastor gives one of those insincere "fake smiles" as he does so. Rob feels discounted and hurt and is depressed and angry. However, Rob realizes he may be over-reacting and thinks maybe a dose of perspective restorer is needed so he gets out his spiritual journal and starts scribbling...

Name the Feeling: Rob writes in his journal - "I feel rejected, hurt, discounted, yes that's the word discounted - like I didn't count, like I don't matter and I have been at that church for five years!"

Find the Underlying Thought: He deliberately discounted me and despite the fact that I have been at that church for five years I was treated like a nobody.

Dispute the Thought: Yes it was inconsiderate and fake but it wasn't that bad. Most of the time he is polite to me and I need not take things so personally. It was a mistake by him but it doesn't make me valueless or unimportant. I am important whether or not the pastor pays attention to me. God thinks I am important enough to love, save and die for - that's enough for me. I'll go back and try again next week.

Write Down the New Feeling: I feel much more calm and balanced and I am surprised that I over reacted! Boy can I be overly sensitive sometimes. Glad I gave myself a dose of perspective restorer! I will try again next week.

Well that's about as far as the best secular approaches can take us. Cognitive psychotherapy, like the work of Beck, Seligman, Burns, Ellis and many others, is very good and is generally quite compatible with a biblical approach. It offers real relief from emotional pain however it only "goes so far". It cannot open our eyes to spiritual realities nor can it produce the sudden whole-of -person perspective changes that the Holy Spirit and Scripture can. To go deeper still in changing our perspective we must turn to that which is uniquely spiritual and biblical.

The Perspective of Your Soul

There are three "places" in the inner man that can have a perspective on life. Firstly, there is the mind, the rational part of us that we have just discussed and which can be addressed logically. Secondly, there is the perspective of the spirit, how we perceive life in and with the spirit and how prophets see the world. That will be discussed in the next chapter. Thirdly, there is the soul. The soul is the place of life, joy, personhood, subjective judgments, and valuations. Our soul quickened by the spirit is what makes us a living being. The soul is also a place of unruly and temporary emotions of daily frustrations, of falling in love, of the joy of a good meal, a wonderful sunset, the smile at a catchy tune, the sentiments at a movie. It can be a place of tempestuous emotional storms that need to be stilled. The soul can be up one minute and down the next. [In contrast the spirit is a place of grand and timeless emotions, of great joys and piercing sorrows. We shall discuss this in the next chapter.]

Bringing the stormy world of the soul under control is one of the great tasks of the Christian life and results in what the Bible calls peace. Peace is when the soul is in the state that God wants it to be in. Peace can be brought to the soul, which is subjective, through things such as a sunset or music of which William Congreve said, "Music has charms to sooth the savage breast" and which seemed to work for King Saul. However, such methods are morally neutral and do not form character or do anything much for us in the long run. We need something better. Pure logic does not quite work with the soul to the extent that it does with the mind. For the heart has reasons that the mind never knows.

The law of the soul is the law of likeness. Our souls become like the souls of people we love, admire or emulate or people we respect, see as authoritative, and obey. That is why children become like parents and disciples like their masters. Adoration and authority mold the soul. We become like Jesus through loving and obeying Jesus. Thus I have found four methods to work in bringing peace to the soul and giving it a dose of perspective restorer. Christo-Centric Worship, Self-Exhortation, Positive Confession Of Scripture (in its proper context), and Scripture Memory.

Christo-Centric Worship

Worship, praise and adoration of Jesus mold the soul into a Christ-like shape. Just like a married couple that adore each other become like each other, just like a young lad that adores his father walks like his Dad and talks like his Dad and wants to grow up like his Dad, just like faithful pooch and the grouch owner sometimes look alike, so worship that is focused on Jesus gradually makes us like Him. Worship can also help get our soul's perspective on life back into line. Here are some extracts from Psalm 73.

> Truly God is good to Israel, To such as are pure in heart. (2) But as for me, my feet had almost stumbled; My steps had nearly slipped. (3) For I was envious of the boastful, When I saw the prosperity of the wicked... (12) Behold, these are the ungodly, Who are always at ease; They increase in riches. (13) Surely I have cleansed my heart in vain, And washed my hands in innocence...(16) When I thought how to understand this, It was too painful for me; (17) Until I went into the sanctuary of God; Then I understood their end. (18) Surely You set them in slippery places; You cast them down to destruction. (19) Oh, how they are brought to desolation, as in a moment! They are utterly consumed with terrors... (21) Thus my heart was grieved, And I was vexed in my mind. (22) I was so foolish and ignorant; I was like a beast before You.....(27) For indeed, those who are far from You shall perish; You have destroyed all those who desert You for harlotry. (28) But it is good for me to draw near to God; I have put my trust in the Lord GOD, That I may declare all Your works. (Psalms 73 NKJV)

This Psalm reflects a time of instability and spiritual crisis. The Psalmist says "my feet had almost slipped", "it was too painful for me", "my heart was grieved", "I was like a brute beast before you". He had lost his spiritual perspective, he was in deep emotional pain, he was envying the wealth and success of the wicked and he thought it was futile to be righteous. He was on the verge of giving up.

The turning point comes when he enters the temple and in God's presence sees the fate of the wicked as it truly is - precarious. After this the Psalmist confesses his folly and rejoices in God saying "it is good to draw near to God". The act of worship was the critical turning point in the spiritual crisis. By fixing his mind on God, adoring Him and coming into contact with spiritual realities his soul and spirit were healed of the turmoil within and a proper perspective on life returned.

By worshipping God, his own perception of reality was changed in three areas. He changed his perceptions about the world, himself and

God. Instead of perceiving the wicked as prospering he now saw them as on the brink of destruction. Instead of seeing his behavior as rational and justified he now saw it as wrong and foolish. Instead of seeing God as not rewarding him he turns and says "surely it is good to draw near to God". True worship restored the Psalmist to a right perspective on his faith.

True worship works. Idolatry does not work. Idolatry creates emotional catastrophe and the soul becomes darkened, limited, superstitious and unstable. If we worship an idol our soul is lowered to the level of the thing we adore be it a statue, a rock, a tree or a fast car. So our worship must be of the Living God, in and through Jesus Christ, in the power of the Holy Spirit. Worship in Spirit and in truth works because we are designed right from Creation to experience life and peace when our mind is stayed on God and we behold the true God in adoration and become like our Father in Heaven.

Prayer and worship do not need to be in a certain building on a certain day but they do need to be in Spirit and in truth. Certain practices can help us to cultivate an atmosphere of true worship in our daily life. I do not wish to be too prescriptive or legalistic as we do have a great deal of freedom in Christ but no matter how free we are we do need to be stayed on God. My personal practice is to have times of prayer and meditation in the morning and in the evening. I also take "saying grace" quite seriously. I always pray with meals and refocus myself on God. As I work I may have some Christian music playing in the background. I also find great assistance from reading carefully selected high quality Christian books. There are other helpful practices as well but the key is to keep your focus on God. The constant cultivation of the presence of God based on fixing one's mind on the truth of God and adoring His glorious nature is one of life's secrets for maintaining a sweet perspective and right perception of life.

I believe there needs to be a greater focus on Jesus Christ not just on doctrine, nor on ethics or even on good Christian psychology. Those ministering from the pulpit in particular should preach Christ crucified and regularly take the congregation to behold Jesus in His life, ministry and inner nature. This is the most powerfully transformational of all preaching because it portrays Christ to our souls most clearly.

Self-Exhortation

The following section is based on an excellent sermon of Dr. Daniel Tappeiner that I had the privilege of hearing while attending the Union Church of Manila. His surprising claim was that you can interact with your soul and instruct it to take on certain emotional states. His text was Psalm 42 where the Psalmist, a son of Korah, became aware of his emotional state and eventually used self-exhortation to conquer his despondent mood.

A two-stage process is used of a.) Questioning the value of the emotion b) then commanding it to change. First the Psalmist questions the value of his present emotional state that was hindering his ability to lead the throng in the worship procession. "Why are you downcast O my soul". After that the Psalmist gives his soul a repeated command to change mood and perspective "hope in God... for I shall yet praise Him" . This eventually causes him to triumph and function again in ministry. In other words, the Psalmist did not just accept his dysfunctional emotional state but corrected it by speaking to his soul quite firmly and bringing it to a functional and biblical resolution.

As speaking to yourself or addressing one's soul sounds rather strange and building a whole therapy on one Psalm is a bit tenuous I searched to see if there is any further scriptural validation. I located a number of Bible references where people interact directly with their soul. These interactions include speaking to one's soul or commanding the soul to do something. Seven direct references are listed below and there are many more in a similar vein especially in Psalms (quite a few on the familiar theme "bless the Lord O my soul...").

... O my soul, march on in strength! (Judges 5:21 NKJV)

To You, O LORD, I lift up my soul. (Psalm 25:1 NKJV)

When I remember these things, I pour out my soul within me. For I used to go with the multitude; I went with them to the house of God, With the voice of joy and praise, With a multitude that kept a pilgrim feast. (5) Why are you cast down, O my soul? And why are you disquieted within me? Hope in God, for I shall yet praise Him For the help of His countenance. (6) O my God, my soul is cast down within me; Therefore I will remember You from the land of the Jordan, And from the heights of Hermon, From the Hill Mizar... Why are you cast down, O my soul? And why are you disquieted within me? Hope in God; For I shall yet praise Him, The help of my countenance and my God. (Psalm 42:4-6 NKJV)

My soul, wait silently for God alone, For my expectation is from Him. (Psalm 62:5 NKJV)

In the day of my trouble I sought the Lord; My hand was stretched out in the night without ceasing; My soul refused to be comforted. (implies an attempt to speak to the soul to comfort it and some interaction with the soul... author's thought) (Psalm 77:2 NKJV)

Bless the LORD, O my soul; And all that is within me, bless His holy name! (2) Bless the LORD, O my soul, And forget not all His benefits: (Psalm 103:1-2 NKJV)

'And I will say to my soul, "Soul, you have many goods laid up for many years; take your ease; eat, drink, and be merry."'(Luke 12:19 NKJV)

So we see that here the soul/self is being commanded to: be strong, be lifted up to God, hope in God, wait silently for God, be comforted, bless God and lastly (by the rich fool) to take it easy. We are all familiar with talking to ourselves and even with telling ourselves to cheer up. However, Scripture-based self-exhortation is much more powerful.

With Scripture-based self-exhortation you empower yourself to take charge of your emotional state and to command it to change by divine authority. You use authority to mold your soul. When Deborah the prophetess, in Judges 5:21 above, says "O my soul, march on in strength!..." she is not just giving herself a pep talk! She is celebrating a divine victory over Sisera and is maintaining a faith position that the God who gave her victory then will continue to give her victory in the future so that she can progress and "march on" with a confident expectation of God's help and deliverance. Underneath these exhortations lies a deep relationship with God.

Here is the process for changing your perspective by biblically-based self-exhortation:

1. **Awareness:** Become aware of the state of your soul ("why are you downcast").
2. **Questioning:** Decide whether it is godly and functional. If it is not godly and functional then don't accept it. Decide that it must be firmly corrected and brought into alignment with the Word of God.

3. **Go Upstairs:** Take your soul before the throne of God either directly or in prayer and worship.
4. **Firmly Command the Change:** Command your soul to change to a more biblical perspective within the framework of God's will and covenant purposes.
5. **Repeat As Necessary.**

Let's take an everyday case. *You feel depressed for no good reason. You just feel lonely and blue and you start questioning the goodness of God. You find yourself becoming out of sorts spiritually and losing your true perspective.*

> **Awareness:** "I'm feeling a bit depressed and blue and I'm questioning God".
> **Questioning:** Is this useful and spiritual? No! It's useless and thinking this way is damaging my relationship with God.
> **Go Upstairs:** Lord, I come before your throne and I admit that I am out of sorts and depressed and that my soul is not fixed on You as it should be.
> **Firmly Command the Change:** "Soul, why are you this way? Stop it! Turn and focus on God. Rejoice in the Lord always! That's an order!"

That may seem a little strange and dramatic but believe it or not- it works. Painful emotion that is off-center and inappropriate, that does not flow from peace, is often an indicator that our soul is not properly tuned into God, not fixed on the Spirit as it should be. This process is just taking your soul back to its right position – that of being stayed on God. Once it is stayed on God then life and peace will flow in accordance with the promises of God in Romans 8:11 and Isaiah 26:3. Let's take another example, this time with the common and very painful problem of feelings of inferiority:

> **Awareness:** "I am feeling inferior and the pain is intense".
> **Questioning:** "Why am I feeling inferior?" There is no good reason in the here and now for me to feel inferior, it's just messing up my emotions and spilling over into my relationships. I can see that it's just a hangover from the past. I can also see that it is not relevant today, it is not true today and it is not functional today".
> **Go Upstairs:** O Lord I come before You now. I know that this inferiority is a lie and that you love me but just now it feels very,

very true. Bring to mind Your Word and Your truth so I can stay my mind on You. There is no condemnation for those who are in Christ Jesus (Romans 8:1). God does not condemn me and He is the only true judge. In fact He regards me as His son! Some people may think that I am inferior to them and I may even be not as good looking or important or powerful as they are but that does not make me inferior in my soul, in my inner self, in my true self. I have received the grace of God, I am seated in heavenly realms with Christ Jesus. God has chosen to display me as a trophy of grace (Matthew 11:11-13; Ephesians 2:6; 1:20; 1 Corinthians 6:1-3). I am not inferior! I am in the Kingdom of God! I will rule with Jesus (Revelation 2). Praise the Lord.

Firmly Command the Change: Now listen to God, O my soul! Listen to His word and stop your lying and grumbling. Stop telling me I am unworthy. It's not true. Soul I instruct you to believe the truth of the gospel and to hope in God and I instruct you to believe in the righteousness you have received. Because you have received righteousness you are righteous and since you are righteous you are not inferior! Believe in God and rejoice!

This is not just a mental exercise it's spiritually taking hold of one's self and changing one's orientation in life. The person stands outside themselves and their pain and their circumstances and makes a faith decision about what they will believe and how they will feel. They then decide to enforce their faith decision by referring to God's Word and applying the full strength of their will. Thus the above process moves the person from pain to peace by almost forcing their soul to accept the truth of God's Word. Dr. Daniel Tappeiner recommends walking around as you do this, saying it out loud and with energy. It seems to take energy to move an out-of-balance soul back into balance.

Now I know that this may sounds a bit weird but all I ask is that you try it in private and see how it goes for you. It does work, even if it is unconventional. Taking yourself in hand (in a scriptural way) is good for you.

Positive Confession of Scripture In Its Proper Context
With this method we correct an out-of-balance perspective by again using the authority of the Scripture. In this case we vigorously and

repeatedly assert out loud the truth of Scripture in context. As we do this we are fixing our mind on God and bringing peace to our soul. Unfortunately, some have taken this practice to foolish and materialistic extremes. They confess Scripture like a magic amulet to bring good fortune. Let's leave that version of this practice well behind and focus on how to use positive confession in a way that brings emotional transformation.

So here is how to engage in Bible based positive confession:
- Acknowledge the problem.
- Search the Bible and find appropriate and in context Scripture.
- Repeat them out loud declaring them to be true.

Let's just look at how we can use the positive confession of Scripture to deal with an inappropriate and overly anxious life perspective - that of the chronic worrier.

Stage One: Acknowledge the problem. "Lord, I have a problem with worrying, I worry over every little thing."

Stage Two: Do your research and find out what the Scripture say about worrying:

Rest in the LORD, and wait patiently for Him; Do not fret because of him who prospers in his way, Because of the man who brings wicked schemes to pass. (8) Cease from anger, and forsake wrath; Do not fret; it only causes harm. (Psalms 37:7-8 NKJV)

Anxiety in the heart of man causes depression, But a good word makes it glad. (Proverbs 12:25 NKJV)

"Therefore I say to you, do not worry about your life, what you will eat or what you will drink; nor about your body, what you will put on. Is not life more than food and the body more than clothing? ... "Which of you by worrying can add one cubit to his stature? "So why do you worry about clothing? Consider the lilies of the field, how they grow: they neither toil nor spin;... "Therefore do not worry, saying, 'What shall we eat?' or 'What shall we drink?' or 'What shall we wear?' ... "Therefore do not worry about tomorrow, for tomorrow will worry about its own things. Sufficient for the day is its own trouble. (Matthew 6:25-34 NKJV)

But He said to them, "Why are you fearful, O you of little faith?" Then He arose and rebuked the winds and the sea, and there was a great calm. (Matthew 8:26

NKJV)

"But when they deliver you up, do not worry about how or what you should speak. For it will be given to you in that hour what you should speak. (Matthew 10:19 NKJV)

And Jesus answered and said to her, "Martha, Martha, you are worried and troubled about many things. (Luke 10:41 NKJV)

Be anxious for nothing, but in everything by prayer and supplication, with thanksgiving, let your requests be made known to God. (Philippians 4:6 NKJV)

Stage Three: Turn this into a positive confession or self-exhortation by quoting the Scripture or rephrasing it in your own words and applying it directly to your life and circumstances:

- Fretting is ineffective and cannot make one of my hairs white or black or add a cubit to my height. It's useless and I must stop it now (Matthew 5:36; 6:27).
- Jesus has commanded me saying "Do not worry". It's a serious command from Jesus and I must obey it (Matthew 6:31).
- I will relax and live one day at a time as Jesus told me to. (Matthew 6:34)
- God has promised to take care of me if I seek His kingdom and His righteousness (1 Peter 5:7; Hebrews 13:8-10; Matthew 6:33).
- Fretting only leads to sin. I will not do anything that leads to sin. I will stop fretting now (Psalm 37).
- Repeat actual Scripture such as I Peter 5:7; Philippians 4:6,7 and Matthew 6:33,34.

Repetition and will-power are the keys to positive confession as it is with the following technique of Scripture Memory. You are deliberately willing your self to grasp the truths of God and "dinning it into yourself". In a way it is a humble thing to do because you are acknowledging your own unruly nature and the necessity of taking hold of it almost "by force" and submitting it to the truth of God's Word. This acknowledgement of a problem, the biblical research, the humility and wisdom to take one's nature in hand and the power of being focused on the truths of God make in-context confession of

Scripture a very powerful tool for correction of our perspective and renewal of our perceptions.

Scripture Memory
Scripture memory is a way we can fix our minds on the truths of God's Word until it "sticks" and is memorized. In the process it develops personal discipline! Scripture memory can make a very useful contribution to having a renewed mind, an informed soul and a more stable emotional life. It is also a valuable perspective restorer and well-memorized verses can be helpful all through one's lifetime. Navigators and other organizations produce Scripture memory flash cards that are quite helpful.

Concluding the Chapter
We have seen that our perceptions of reality and our perspective on life have a lot to do with how we react emotionally. We can restore a more functional and godly perspective through changing the explanatory style that builds up our view of events and how life works. We can also change the way we perceive life by correcting the wrong beliefs that underlie painful emotions. On a deeper level we can change the perception of our soul and its stance on life by bringing it into line so it is fixed on God through Bible based self-exhortation, Christo-centric worship, positive confession and Scripture memory. As we do these things we will find that our emotions are more constant and more godly and that we experience more and more life and peace and less and less depression and anxiety. We will be stayed on God with our mind set on the Spirit with all the blessings this brings. But there is a deeper perception - spiritual perception - and we will deal with that in the next chapter.

Discussion Questions

1. What was Jesus' perspective on Jerusalem? How did it differ from that of other people?

2. How important is having the right perceptions and the right perspective on life?

3. What are the "three P's" of our explanatory style and how do they affect us emotionally?

4. How can we get the biblical and the eternal to be part of our life perspective so that it even changes the way we view reality (as it did for Jesus)?

5. Do you sometimes find yourself challenging the goodness of God? What happens to you emotionally when you do that?

6. List three techniques for fixing your perspective on life? Which one do you like the most?

Perception – In and By the Spirit

But immediately, when Jesus perceived in His spirit that they reasoned thus within themselves, He said to them, "Why do you reason about these things in your hearts? (Mark 2:8 NKJV)

Now while Paul waited for them at Athens, his spirit was provoked within him when he saw that the city was given over to idols. (Acts 17:16 NKJV)

The spirit is the place of intuition, dreams, visions and revelation and of the deepest intimacy and the most direct kind of knowledge. It is the deepest part of our humanity and it is the place where we "know that we know". The primary functions of the spirit are wisdom, perception, and knowledge.

The Bible often talks about our spiritual eyes and ears and of people's ability or inability to perceive spiritual things. The spiritual man of "1 Corinthians 2:10-16" is the person who is most at home perceiving things spiritually and accurately. In a few places the New Testament makes the seemingly strange assertion that it would be a good idea if all Christians were prophets. What it most probably means is that all Christians are to become people of accurate spiritual perception and have a deep intuition of spiritual reality.

[This includes sensing what is God's will in the immediate situation like the New Testament prophet Agabus did (Acts 11:28; 21:11,12). The considerable difference between OT prophets and NT prophets is well brought out by the systematic theologian Wayne Grudem in his book, "The Gift Of Prophecy". Again, I will just refer the interested reader to this work and move on.]

What is clear is that Christians are to move from a place of very obscure spiritual perception prior to conversion to a place of abundant and accurate spiritual perception.

Prior to conversion – darkness:
> But the natural man does not receive the things of the Spirit of God, for they are foolishness to him; nor can he know them, because they are spiritually discerned. (1 Corinthians 2:14 NKJV)

Unlike Moses, who put a veil over his face so that the children of Israel could not look steadily at the end of what was passing away. (14) But their minds were blinded. For until this day the same veil remains unlifted in the reading of the Old Testament, because the veil is taken away in Christ. (15) But even to this day, when Moses is read, a veil lies on their heart. (16) Nevertheless when one turns to the Lord, the veil is taken away. (2 Corinthians 3:13-16 NKJV)

But even if our gospel is veiled, it is veiled to those who are perishing, (4) whose minds the god of this age has blinded, who do not believe, lest the light of the gospel of the glory of Christ, who is the image of God, should shine on them. (2 Corinthians 4:3-4 NKJV)

Having their understanding darkened, being alienated from the life of God, because of the ignorance that is in them, because of the blindness of their heart. (Ephesians 4:18 NKJV)

After conversion - universal and abundant spiritual revelation:

"For this is the covenant that I will make with the house of Israel after those days, says the LORD: I will put My laws in their mind and write them on their hearts; and I will be their God, and they shall be My people. (11) "None of them shall teach his neighbor, and none his brother, saying, 'Know the LORD,' for all shall know Me, from the least of them to the greatest of them. (12) "For I will be merciful to their unrighteousness, and their sins and their lawless deeds I will remember no more." (Hebrews 8:10-12 NKJV)

But you have an anointing from the Holy One, and you know all things. (1 John 2:20 NKJV)

But the anointing which you have received from Him abides in you, and you do not need that anyone teach you; but as the same anointing teaches you concerning all things, and is true, and is not a lie, and just as it has taught you, you will abide in Him. (1 John 2:27 NKJV)

"But this is what was spoken by the prophet Joel: (17) 'And it shall come to pass in the last days, says God, That I will pour out of My Spirit on all flesh; Your sons and your daughters shall prophesy, Your young men shall see visions, Your old men shall dream dreams. (18) And on My menservants and on My maidservants I will pour out My Spirit in those days; And they shall prophesy. (Acts 2:16-18 NKJV)

For you can all prophesy one by one, that all may learn and all may be encouraged. (1 Corinthians 14:31 NKJV)

This is truly a vast transition in our nature. We go from being spiritually blind and without understanding, to being able to sense spiritual realities and both understand and enjoy them. We may even sense them so keenly that we are able to edify the Church. A whole new way of seeing things is opened up. This is variously called "being quickened in spirit", "having the eyes of your heart enlightened" or having one's spiritual eyes and ears "opened" to spiritual reality. This work of the Holy Spirit is independent of human intellect (see 1 Corinthians chapters 1-4). Some very intelligent people are spiritually blind while some simple folk grasp the things of the Kingdom. Jesus rejoiced in seeing simple people grasping great spiritual realities by faith alone and being obviously taught by God.

> At that time Jesus answered and said, "I thank You, Father, Lord of heaven and earth, that You have hidden these things from the wise and prudent and have revealed them to babes." (Matthew 11:25 NKJV)

> Jesus answered and said to him, "Blessed are you, Simon Bar-Jonah, for flesh and blood has not revealed this to you, but My Father who is in heaven." (Matthew 16:17 NKJV)

Thus true spiritual perception which gives poise and balance to life and underlies true emotional stability is a gift of God. While spiritual perception is a sovereign work of God it can also be gained through prayer (James 1:5-8) and Paul prays for spiritual insight to be granted to Christians in many of the famous prayers in his epistles.

> The eyes of your understanding being enlightened; that you may know what is the hope of His calling, what are the riches of the glory of His inheritance in the saints. (Ephesians 1:18 NKJV)

> And this I pray, that your love may abound still more and more in knowledge and all discernment. (Philippians 1:9 NKJV)

> For this reason we also, since the day we heard it, do not cease to pray for you, and to ask that you may be filled with the knowledge of His will in all wisdom and spiritual understanding. (Colossians 1:9 NKJV)

> that their hearts may be encouraged, being knit together in love, and attaining to all riches of the full assurance of understanding, to the knowledge of the mystery of God, both of the Father and of Christ. (Colossians 2:2 NKJV)

Paul prays asks for "all wisdom and spiritual understanding" for the Colossians. The first place the biblical exegete must start is in prayer, asking the Lord to break open the Word of God in all wisdom and spiritual understanding. Commentaries have their place but they are ineffective if the ability to perceive spiritual things is not there to start with.

Spiritual Sensitivity and EQ

What does spiritual sensitivity have to do with our emotions and our biblical EQ?

1. Spiritual sensitivity opens our eyes to God's love and thus allows us to be solidly grounded as persons:

    > That He would grant you, according to the riches of His glory, to be strengthened with might through His Spirit in the inner man, (17) that Christ may dwell in your hearts through faith; that you, being rooted and grounded in love, (18) may be able to comprehend with all the saints what is the width and length and depth and height; (19) to know the love of Christ which passes knowledge; that you may be filled with all the fullness of God. (Ephesians 3:16-19 NKJV)

    To be so able to perceive the love of Christ that we are rooted and grounded in love and even filled up to all the fullness of God must be the ultimate in emotional stability.

2. Spiritual perception gives us the right spiritual passions such as Jesus beholding Jerusalem and seeing it with his spirit, and reacting with compassion. With right spiritual perception we see the lost, our church, our city, and our nation through the eyes of Jesus Christ. We will experience the vast range of spiritual emotions from weeping over the lost to indignation over cruelty and hardness of heart. Whatever our emotion, it will be the Spirit's emotion based on the Spirit's perception of that situation.

3. Spiritual sensitivity allows us to be grounded in faith and in the spiritual realm not on sight, human reason and sentiment alone (For we walk by faith not by sight). Moses was able to be steadfast in the face of threats from a tyrannical Pharaoh because of his special spiritual perception:
    "By faith he forsook Egypt, **not fearing the wrath of the king; for he endured as seeing Him who is invisible**" (Hebrews 11:27 NKJV) (author's emphasis).
    Just as Moses did not fear the Pharaoh and all the pursuing chariots of Egypt because he could "see Him who is invisible" so spiritual perception allows us to discern situations so that fear and anxiety are removed. Under pressure and trials we still see the Presence of an all-loving God; a God who is working all things together for our good (Romans 8:28).

4. Occasionally people of high spiritual sensitivity will be granted a revelation that turns the whole situation around and has an effect not just on their emotions but the emotions of all involved. For instance, Paul's revelation from God during the storm at sea:

> On the third day we threw the ship's tackle overboard with our own hands. (20) Now when neither sun nor stars appeared for many days, and no small tempest beat on us, all hope that we would be saved was finally given up...(22) "And now I urge you to take heart, for there will be no loss of life among you, but only of the ship. (23) For there stood by me this night an angel of the God to whom I belong and whom I serve, (24) saying, 'Do not be afraid, Paul; you must be brought before Caesar; and indeed God has granted you all those who sail with you.' (25) "Therefore take heart, men, for I believe God that it will be just as it was told me. (26) However, we must run aground on a certain island."...(Acts 27:33-36 NKJV) And as day was about to dawn, Paul implored them all to take food, saying, "Today is the fourteenth day you have waited and continued without food, and eaten nothing. {34} Therefore I urge you to take nourishment, for this is for your survival, since not a hair will fall from the head of any of you." {35} And when he had said these things, he took bread and gave thanks to God in the presence of them all; and when he had broken it he began to eat. {36} Then they were all encouraged, and also took food themselves. (Acts 27:19-26 NKJV)

The situation in verses 19 and 20 is such utter despair that "all hope that we would be saved was given up". Then in verse 22 an angel appears with a revelation from God to spiritually sensitive Paul. Paul's faith in this revelation caused him to be able to encourage others so they ate, acted appropriately during the crisis and had hope. Thus Paul's openness to the spiritual realm made him able to receive a revelation that had a profound effect on the lives of all aboard.

Errors in Spiritual Perception and Their Effect On a Christian's Emotional Life

In discussing errors in perception, I am not talking about errors in doctrine. That subject will be covered in the chapter on beliefs. This chapter is on perception, viewpoints, world-view and perspectives that underlie our beliefs. For instance, errors in spiritual perception include blindness but the resultant beliefs of such blindness are varied. If you are blind to God and His salvation through Christ, then many false beliefs can arise in the darkness within you. Thus the disorder of perception lays the foundation for the disorder in belief. In this section we will deal with what happens when our human spirit goes awry and how this distorts our whole perspective on life.

Inability To Perceive the Obvious: This is called "a spirit of stupor" and implies that the hearers are dull to the point of senselessness to spiritual things. Those addressed in the epistle to the Hebrews were called "dull of hearing" and the synagogue Jews were warned by Paul:

> "The Holy Spirit spoke rightly through Isaiah the prophet to our fathers, (26) "saying, 'Go to this people and say: "Hearing you will hear, and shall not understand; And seeing you will see, and not perceive; (27) For the hearts of this people have grown dull. Their ears are hard of hearing, And their eyes they have closed, Lest they should see with their eyes and hear with their ears, Lest they should understand with their hearts and turn, So that I should heal them."' (28) "Therefore let it be known to you that the salvation of God has been sent to the Gentiles, and they will hear it!" (Acts 28:25-28 NKJV)

> Just as it is written: "God has given them a spirit of stupor, Eyes that they should not see And ears that they should not hear, To this very day." (Romans 11:8 NKJV)

People in the "spirit of stupor" fail to "get it". They live life with practically no true spiritual awareness though they may be outwardly religious. If they are religious they tend to be stubborn and quite rejecting of anyone who has genuine spiritual experience. Emotionally they are at ground zero with a purely human perspective on life.

Paying Attention To Deceptive Spirits: Just as the Holy Spirit is our Teacher, Satan is our deceiver! Demonic spirits can and do tell lies and Christians who pay attention to them can become unstable both spiritually and emotionally and be drawn away from the faith.

> Now the Spirit expressly says that in latter times some will depart from the faith, giving heed to deceiving spirits and doctrines of demons, (2) speaking lies in hypocrisy, having their own conscience seared with a hot iron. (1 Timothy 4:1-2 NKJV)

> For if he who comes preaches another Jesus whom we have not preached, or if you receive a different spirit which you have not received, or a different gospel which you have not accepted; you may well put up with it! (2 Corinthians 11:4 NKJV)

> And Jesus answered and said to them: "Take heed that no one deceives you. (5) For many will come in My name, saying, 'I am the Christ,' and will deceive many ... (11) Then many false prophets will rise up and deceive many. (12) "And because lawlessness will abound, the love of many will

grow cold. (13) But he who endures to the end shall be saved. (Matthew 24:4-5; 11-13 NKJV)

Let no one deceive you by any means; for that Day will not come unless the falling away comes first, and the man of sin is revealed, the son of perdition, (4) who opposes and exalts himself above all that is called God or that is worshiped, so that he sits as God in the temple of God, showing himself that he is God...(9) The coming of the lawless one is according to the working of Satan, with all power, signs, and lying wonders, (10) and with all unrighteous deception among those who perish, because they did not receive the love of the truth, that they might be saved. (11) And for this reason God will send them strong delusion, that they should believe the lie, (12) that they all may be condemned who did not believe the truth but had pleasure in unrighteousness. (2 Thessalonians 2:3-4; 9-12 NKJV)

And I saw three unclean spirits like frogs coming out of the mouth of the dragon, out of the mouth of the beast, and out of the mouth of the false prophet. (14) For they are spirits of demons, performing signs, which go out to the kings of the earth and of the whole world, to gather them to the battle of that great day of God Almighty. (Revelation 16:13-14 NKJV)

Spiritual deception involves an opposite kind of error to hardness of heart. Those who are hard of heart miss seeing the good while those who are spiritually deceived miss seeing the evil. The carnal nature of false teachers, their lies, immorality and lust for money is overlooked. The deceived person does not love the truth and does not really seek it (2 Thessalonians 2:10,11) but instead they pursue signs and wonders and good feelings. The promises of wealth and freedom to do as they please mean more to them than finding out the truth about God and His Son Jesus Christ. They do not stop and look at the leader's character or the fruit on the tree, but instead they follow wolves in sheep's clothing (see Matthew 7; John 10; Acts 20 and 2 Peter). Those who are deceived in turn deceive others becoming increasingly unstable. They are described as "clouds" and "tossed to and fro" even downright bad "with eyes full of adultery..." (see 2 Peter 2:12 and following for some colorful descriptions). The cure for spiritual deception is to know and love God's Word, pursue truth, check basic doctrine and character and to test the spirits as in 1 John 4:1-5.

Spiritual Inflation
This term "spiritual inflation" was coined by Carl Jung but has good biblical antecedents. It describes the overpowering effect of suddenly encountering the spiritual realm on certain individuals who had generally not encountered much of the spiritual realm previously. Lacking a proper

grounding in their inner being for spiritual things they become totally carried away with notions of spirituality. They almost seem to blow up like balloon, becoming overly obsessed with "being spiritual", and are often grandiose, clamorous, and frequently pompous. Their utterances, which they esteem as being of great value, are generally of dubious worth. An elegant and brief description is found in Colossians of people who are *"puffed up"* (In other words "inflated"!). They are wordy but powerless. Saying they know more of Christ, they are actually completely out of touch with Him. They place their faith in "what they know" about spiritual things – which, according to Paul, indicates they actually know nothing at all. For it is not knowledge that justifies but faith working through love. Not infrequently they are also licentious in their morality. The Corinthians also seem to have had a problem with spiritual inflation and were overly confident in their knowledge of spiritual things.

> Let no one cheat you of your reward, taking delight in false humility and worship of angels, intruding into those things which he has not seen, vainly puffed up by his fleshly mind, (19) and not holding fast to the Head, from whom all the body, nourished and knit together by joints and ligaments, grows with the increase that is from God. (Colossians 2:18-19 NKJV)

> But I will come to you shortly, if the Lord wills, and I will know, not the word of those who are puffed up, but the power. (20) For the kingdom of God is not in word but in power. (1 Corinthians 4:19-20 NKJV)

> It is actually reported that there is sexual immorality among you, and such sexual immorality as is not even named among the Gentiles; that a man has his father's wife! (2) And you are puffed up, and have not rather mourned, that he who has done this deed might be taken away from among you. (1 Corinthians 5:1-2 NKJV)

> Now concerning things offered to idols: We know that we all have knowledge. Knowledge puffs up, but love edifies. (2) And if anyone thinks that he knows anything, he knows nothing yet as he ought to know. (1 Corinthians 8:1-2 NKJV)

Being Spiritually Enslaved to Rules and Regulations:
This is known as a *spirit of bondage* and slavery:

> For you did not receive the spirit of bondage again to fear, but you received the Spirit of adoption by whom we cry out, "Abba, Father." (Romans 8:15 NKJV)

> And because you are sons, God has sent forth the Spirit of His Son into your hearts, crying out, "Abba, Father!" (7) Therefore you are no longer a slave but a son, and if a son, then an heir of God through Christ. (8) But then, indeed, when you did not know God, you served those which by nature are not gods. (9) But now after you have known God, or rather are known by God, how is it that you turn again to the weak and beggarly elements, to which you desire again to be in bondage? (10) You observe days and months and seasons and years. (11) I am afraid for you, lest I have labored for you in vain. (Galatians 4:6-11 NKJV)

The spirit of bondage is characterized by a desire to observe "days and months and seasons and years" to take on aspects of the Law such as circumcision and to be much concerned with dietary regulations and minor laws such as the Sabbath. (Also see Colossians 2 and 1 Timothy 4 as well as all of Galatians). This produces a sanctimonious rigidity. It also produces fear, "the spirit of bondage again to fear..." and a terror of trespassing in even quite minor matters. This fear can be tremendously destabilizing and in my experience full-blown phobias are not uncommon in children from legalistic backgrounds. It is seen at its worst in victims of mind-control cults where flashbacks occur. In people recovering from spiritual abuse and coming out of the "spirit of bondage" quite biblical levels of freedom may feel sinful at first. They nearly always have bouts of fear over "breaking a rule" no matter how innocent - such as going to a G-rated family movie if all movies were previously "of the devil".

A Spirit That Lacks Courage and Assertiveness: Paul calls this a *"spirit of fear"* and it is counteracted by stirring up the Spirit within you and praying for boldness as the church did in Acts 4. It seems to be most common when there is real danger and persecution and the temptation is to go easy on preaching the gospel. Emotionally it produces the desire to back out of God's clear calling on one's life and is a perspective of "safety first".

> For God has not given us a spirit of fear, but of power and of love and of a sound mind. (2 Timothy 1:7 NKJV)

> "Now, Lord, look on their threats, and grant to Your servants that with all boldness they may speak Your word, (30) by stretching out Your hand to heal, and that signs and wonders may be done through the name of Your holy Servant Jesus." (31) And when they had prayed, the place where they were assembled together was shaken; and they were all filled with the Holy Spirit, and they spoke the word of God with boldness. (Acts 4:29-31 NKJV)

Timidity seems to have been Timothy's affliction and he is told at various times to "stir up" the gift that was in him, not to let people despise him, not to be fearful, to suffer hardship as a good soldier of Christ Jesus and so forth. This exhortation seems to have worked because Timothy was there through the last, and according to Hebrews even endured a bout of imprisonment himself.

Other Spiritual Errors

Below are twenty two references to the human spirit going "out of true". In each of them the person's perspective on life is deeply affected by their spiritual affliction. In some cases a spirit of jealousy, in others of ill-will. Others feel that they are poisoned in their spirit and bitterness colors their world. Some references seem to be what we would call "moods" and some would hesitate to attribute them to a spiritual cause. But the ancient Greeks - who invented the term "mood" thought of moods as inspired and as the work of the spiritual realm. They would even call on certain spirits when certain moods were desired (see Theocritus "Idylls"). Moods resemble spirits in that moods tend to come over us unbidden, dominate us for a while then leave. There is thus some spiritual connection between the human spirit and moods, and that connection sometimes comes across in these verses. The human spirit is complex and interacts with the person, with God and with the various entities in the whole spiritual realm. [I will again duck and weave around the verses below that mention the Lord sending an evil spirit on someone and just say, "Go look up a commentary!".]The point I want you to get is that our emotions can flow from our human spirit which can go out of balance due to a wide variety of factors (we will see four main ones) and that many of these discordant emotions are grounded in our spiritual perspectives and out-of-balance perceptions.

1. **A Spirit of Jealousy:** (Numbers 5:14 NKJV) 'if the spirit of jealousy comes upon him and he becomes jealous of his wife, who has defiled herself; or if the spirit of jealousy comes upon him and he becomes jealous of his wife, although she has not defiled herself.

2. **A Hardened And Obstinate Spirit:** (Deuteronomy 2:30 NKJV) "But Sihon king of Heshbon would not let us pass through, for the LORD your God hardened his spirit and made his heart obstinate, that He might deliver him into your hand, as it is this day.

3. **A Spirit Of Ill-Will:** (Judges 9:23 NKJV) God sent a spirit of ill will between Abimelech and the men of Shechem; and the men of Shechem dealt treacherously with Abimelech.

4. **A Sorrowful Spirit:** (1 Samuel 1:15 NKJV) And Hannah answered and said, "No, my lord, I am a woman of sorrowful spirit. I have drunk neither wine nor intoxicating drink, but have poured out my soul before the LORD.

5. **A Distressing Spirit :** (1 Samuel 16:14-16 NKJV) But the Spirit of the LORD departed from Saul, and a distressing spirit from the LORD troubled him. {15} And Saul's servants said to him, "Surely, a distressing spirit from God is troubling you. {16} Let our master now command your servants, who are before you, to seek out a man who is a skillful player on the harp; and it shall be that he will play it with his hand when the distressing spirit from God is upon you, and you shall be well."... And so it was, whenever the spirit from God was upon Saul, that David would take a harp and play it with his hand. Then Saul would become refreshed and well, and the distressing spirit would depart from him.

6. **A Sullen Spirit:** (1 Kings 21:5 NKJV) But Jezebel his wife came to him, and said to him, "Why is your spirit so sullen that you eat no food?"

7. **A Poisoned Spirit :** (Job 6:4 NKJV) For the arrows of the Almighty are within me; My spirit drinks in their poison; The terrors of God are arrayed against me.

8. **An Anguished Spirit:** (Job 7:11 NKJV) "Therefore I will not restrain my mouth; I will speak in the anguish of my spirit; I will complain in the bitterness of my soul.

9. **A Spirit Turned Against God:** (Job 15:13 NKJV) That you turn your spirit against God, And let such words go out of your mouth?

10. **A Broken Spirit:** (Job 17:1 NKJV) "My spirit is broken, My days are extinguished, The grave is ready for me.

11. **A Hasty And Compelling Spirit:** (Job 32:18 NKJV) For I am full of words; The spirit within me compels me.

12. **An Unfaithful Spirit:** (Psalms 78:8 NKJV) And may not be like their fathers, A stubborn and rebellious generation, A generation that did not set its heart aright, And whose spirit was not faithful to God.

13. **A Spirit That Is Overwhelmed By Troubles:** (Psalms 142:3 NKJV) When my spirit was overwhelmed within me, Then You knew my path. In the way in which I walk They have secretly set a snare for me.

14. **A Failing Spirit:** (Psalms 143:7 NKJV) Answer me speedily, O LORD; My spirit fails! Do not hide Your face from me, Lest I be like those who go down into the pit.

15. **A Haughty Spirit:** (Proverbs 16:18 NKJV) Pride goes before destruction, And a haughty spirit before a fall.

16. **An Uncontrolled Spirit:** (Proverbs 25:28 NKJV) Whoever has no rule over his own spirit Is like a city broken down, without walls.

17. **A Perverse Spirit:** (Isaiah 19:14 NKJV) The LORD has mingled a perverse spirit in her midst; And they have caused Egypt to err in all her work, As a drunken man staggers in his vomit.

18. **A Spirit of Deep Sleep:** (Isaiah 29:10 NKJV) For the LORD has poured out on you The spirit of deep sleep, And has closed your eyes, namely, the prophets; And He has covered your heads, namely, the seers.

19. **An Errant Spirit:** (Isaiah 29:24 NKJV) These also who erred in spirit will come to understanding, And those who complained will learn doctrine.

20. **A Spirit of Heaviness:** (Isaiah 61:3 NKJV) To console those who mourn in Zion, To give them beauty for ashes, The oil of joy for mourning, The garment of praise for the spirit of heaviness; That they may be called trees of righteousness, The planting of the LORD, that He may be glorified.

21. **A Grieved Spirit:** (Isaiah 65:14 NKJV) Behold, My servants shall sing for joy of heart, But you shall cry for sorrow of heart, and wail for grief of spirit.

22. **A Merely Human Spirit:** (Ezekiel 13:3 NKJV) Thus says the Lord GOD: "Woe to the foolish prophets, who follow their own spirit and have seen nothing!

This biblical data may be uncomfortable for many from overly rational backgrounds. However, the realm of the human spirit needs to be explored if we are to understand the human person. After all, our spirit is the deepest part of us. Without getting lost in all the details let's see if we can draw out some general principles:

- The human spirit has a vast emotional range. It is not an analytical, emotionless part of the human person. In fact the spirit generates the deepest and most powerful emotions we know.
- A person's fundamental outlook on life flows from their spirit and when the spirit is affected this affects the actions of the whole person.
- The spirit is vulnerable and can be damaged. Traumatic life circumstances and intense suffering can break the spirit or cause it to be overwhelmed.
- The person has some degree of control over their spirit, and this is a good and desirable thing. A person who lacks control over their spirit has trouble with maintaining proper boundaries (Proverbs 25:28).
- The human spiritual realm is subject to change. Moods seem to be linked to a temporary state of the human spirit.

- God can cause both positive and negative changes in the human spirit. In Isaiah a spirit of heaviness is changed into a garment of praise. In the case of King Saul he moves from being anointed with the Holy Spirit to being tormented by a distressing spirit.

The Four Main Causes of Problems With the Human Spirit
I have found the above list of spiritual problems can be put into four fundamental categories based on what causes them. The four main causes of problems with the human spirit are – sin, folly, trauma and spiritual attack. Each of these can affect our most basic perceptions of ourselves, life, others and God and lead to emotional discordance. By understanding these four causes we will be able to frame a wise and appropriate response as we minister the grace of God.

1. **Problems Caused By Sin**
Firstly, there are those spiritual problems based on *sin* - such as the "haughty spirit" described above which flows from the sin of pride, and affects our perceptions of others. The others in this category is "a spirit turned against God" which flows from the sin of rebellion, and affects our perception of God.

All of us sin but this is different. This is much deeper. Here the sin has got right down to the deepest level of the personality and gained a stronghold. In these cases the human spirit itself has been captured or defiled by a particular sin. Pride or rebellion has become deeply ingrained in the person's nature and now affects their entire outlook on life. When our own inner spirit has become allied with either of these sins the only cure is deep repentance, confession and restoration. God repeatedly engineers painful circumstances in our lives until we realize the great hold such sins can have on us.

A third and special case of this is where the sin is the sin of unbelief concerning Christ in which case repentance and faith leads to conversion. Christian approaches that are repentance based and helpful here include Jay E. Adams' Nouthetic Counseling, and Alcoholics Anonymous.

Indications of When Sin Has Deeply Affected the Human Spirit :
- Where there is a deep love of, or blindness to, clear and obvious sinful behavior such as that in the sin lists in Paul's epistles.
- Celebration of lawlessness, defiance of rules and authority. Rebellion (1 John 3:4).

- Glorying in unrighteous scheming (Prov 24:9).
- A deep spiritual obstinacy. Consistently knowing the right thing to do and refusing to do it (James 4:17).
- A faithless and violated conscience. Habitually doing things contrary to one's faith (Romans 14:23).

Dealing With Sins of the Spirit:
The course here is fairly well known. Awaken the person to their sin, then ask them to repent from their sin and to confess it to God and to make restoration where practical. Repentance involves a turning around from the wrong behavior or attitude to the right behavior or attitude.

> Let the wicked forsake his way, And the unrighteous man his thoughts; Let him return to the LORD, And He will have mercy on him; And to our God, For He will abundantly pardon. (Isaiah 55:7 NKJV)

Wrong ways are to be forsaken and an unrighteous thought life is to be put aside. Sin is not just confessed, it is also left behind. Awakening the person to their sin may be a difficult process and may even require some confrontation by the elders of the church. This should not be done lightly and the proper procedure is outlined in Matthew 18:15-20. The seriousness with which the apostle Paul took church discipline and its severity is almost unknown in the modern church (see 1 Corinthians 5 and 2 Corinthians 12 & 13). Above all pray that the Holy Spirit will enable you to help the sinner and will provide both the conviction of sin and the grace and power for change.

2. Problems Caused By Folly
Secondly, there are those spiritual problems based on *folly* in the human spirit. This is an abiding disposition of foolishness rather than just a one-off mistake. People characterized by folly in their human spirit demonstrate a nature lacking in personal insight and basic wisdom. They are unbalanced and unwise and unable to rightly judge themselves or others. A foolish person lacks wisdom in one or more key areas of their life and makes the same mistakes over and over again. They are frequently stubborn and unteachable and education is of little avail until the errant spirit is fixed.

They seem to need discipline combined with a sudden transforming work of God that corrects the spiritual damage at the root of their folly. Once the error in their spirit is corrected and wisdom flows a whole major aspect of their character can instantly change. There is frequently a moment of realization when light dawns and they say, "how could I have been so dumb!". Among them are those having an errant spirit, a perverse spirit, a hasty spirit, a sullen spirit, and an inappropriate spirit of jealousy as described in the Bible passages above.

Proverbs describes a range of foolish people such as the naïve, the young men seduced by a harlot, the unteachable fool, the lazy sluggard, the scoffer, the person wise in their own eyes and the boorish fool. For these people loving discipline, fervent believing prayer for wisdom (James 1:5), good scriptural teaching and high quality ongoing discipleship may help correct the error in their spirit. Christian approaches that have proved helpful here include Neil T. Anderson's truth encounters and various discipleship strategies, church discipline and accountability groups. Many men's ministries specialize in this approach.

Indications of When Folly Has Overtaken the Human Spirit:
- When the person consistently makes unwise choices that are not so much "bad" as "just real dumb", they are characterized by an
- total lack of insight about themselves, their lifestyle and other people.
- Where they are naïve, credulous, gullible or always falling in love.
- A deeply derisive attitude to education, knowledge and learning and wisdom.
- They constantly show off their knowledge but do not listen to others and are quite unteachable.
- Foolish habits, erratic behavior, impulsiveness, wild schemes, dreaming, loud inappropriate and boorish behavior, lack of insight, poor decisions.
- The person does not set out to be immoral but finds themselves being easily caught up in immoral relationships or they seem unable to avoid bad company.
- Where a person is chronically lazy, slack and disorganized and their life drifts from job to job and failure to failure, when there is a great sense of wasted potential.
- Poor and very inappropriate communication such as boastfulness, an inability to listen or be corrected, hasty speech, quick displays of anger and provocation and little idea of how to be socially appropriate.

Dealing With Folly In the Human Spirit

As we saw in previous chapters wisdom is closely associated with the presence and teaching ministry of the Holy Spirit. Wisdom can be prayed for and is prayed for by Paul. James is quite specific in saying that a Christian can receive wisdom from God directly through prayer (James 1:5) This wisdom can be in ordinary daily things where wisdom may be lacking. An interesting passage that illustrates this is found in Isaiah 28:

> Give ear and hear my voice, Listen and hear my speech. (24) Does the plowman keep plowing all day to sow? Does he keep turning his soil and breaking the clods? (25) When he has leveled its surface, Does he not sow the black cummin And scatter the cummin, Plant the wheat in rows, The barley in the appointed place, And the spelt in its place? (26) For He instructs him in right judgment, His God teaches him. (27) For the black cummin is not threshed with a threshing sledge, Nor is a cartwheel rolled over the cummin; But the black cummin is beaten out with a stick, And the cummin with a rod. (28) Bread flour must be ground; Therefore he does not thresh it forever, Break it with his cartwheel, Or crush it with his horsemen. (29) This also comes from the LORD of hosts, Who is wonderful in counsel and excellent in guidance. (Isaiah 28:23-29 NKJV)

God guides and instructs the farmer in the humble daily routines of farming! God is thus concerned with our work as well as with our religion. It is His will for us to have wisdom in all aspects of our lives. This confidence that God loves to instruct His people should give us great hope when dealing with foolish Christians. It gives us a solid basis for prayer when we ask Him to give wisdom to those who lack it. He delights to do this and James says He gives "without reproach" (James 1:5-8).

Foolish Christians first need to realize they have been foolish. Once the light dawns they need to be encouraged to seek wisdom from God. Finally they need to learn the basic disciplines that will enable them to correct their folly in the light of their new wisdom. This process takes place best in a Christian community where accountability and discipleship are lovingly practiced without harshness or legalism. [See the chapter on Learning Organizations later in this book]. In such communities personal change is normal and others around them are also working on aspects of their character. Support groups, Bible study groups, one to one discipleship sessions, counseling and Christian communities all provide good contexts for the correction of folly in the life of the Christian.

However, awakening a person to the fact that their behavior is foolish is not easy. Pain is the great awakener as well as honest and true Christian friends who speak the truth in love. One method that can work is to get a person to write out in a journal the consequences of the behavior you are trying to get them to correct. Then get them to do a cost-benefit analysis. This has awakened many gamblers once they have honestly done a calculation of the cost of their habit.

Some people know they are foolish but have no idea how to change. If you want to lead someone from folly to wisdom be prepared to provide careful, detailed step by step instruction and modeling. Going from folly to wisdom involves learning and learning requires a good and patient teacher. Do not dump a whole heap of demands and ideas on people. Give them bite-sized bits of counseling homework and encourage every step of improvement. As I mentioned earlier sometimes wisdom can arrive from God in answer to godly believing prayer. When it does it sometimes comes in a rush, in a huge "Aha" moment the person sees what they should have seen all along and suddenly changes. This is good, but a good structure of discipleship and the careful systematic teaching of biblical truth can help those moments to occur with greater frequency.

3. Problems Caused By Trauma

Thirdly, there are those spiritual problems based on the effects of **suffering or trauma**. For such people the trauma of life has been so deep and so overwhelming that it has affected their human spirit. These people literally have a damaged spirit, which is in need of healing or comfort. The spirit of such people can be described as broken, failing, poisoned, overwhelmed, grieved or anguished.

This damage to the human spirit is far beyond the normal upsets of life and is a deep and personal wound such as those inflicted by rape, violent crime, death, divorce, deep injustice, cult involvement and torture. For these people there needs to be prayer ministry and an atmosphere of gentle encouragement. In some cases the damage may be so profound that the person has an "uncontrolled spirit" and is like a city with broken down walls - easily exploited, and easily manipulated. Such people will need much rebuilding of the walls and instructions in setting appropriate personal boundaries. For many damaged people the biblical truths that give hope and grace may need to be repeated often in an atmosphere of love, encouragement and healing prayer. Counselors operating in this area have to be especially gentle and caring and able to spend hours in healing prayer with a single client. Christian and Christian-compatible approaches that have proved helpful here include healing of the memories, inner healing, Theophostic counseling, many retreat centers and prayer ministries, Bradshaws' book Championing the Inner Child, etc.

Indications of Trauma Having Affected the Human spirit:
- A distinct event that precipitated the problem.
- Painful emotions such as grief, bitterness and sorrow.
- Flashbacks, problems with memory.
- The person is overwhelmed by life, fearful, or consumed with anxiety.
- The person indicates they feel they are emotionally crippled and "lame".
- The person communicates that they are broken or damaged inside.
- The person pulls away from life and indicates a deep need for comfort and healing, space and privacy, gentleness and restoration.
- As you talk to someone you get the sense that you are dealing with both an adult and a damaged child in the same person.
- Unusual reactions to normal stimuli. A sense that the person is reacting inappropriately because some wound is being touched.

Dealing With People Whose Spirit Has Been Affected By Trauma
Go slowly and go gently. Traumatized people need care and comfort and support because life has already overwhelmed them. *Dealing with severely traumatized people should be left to trained professionals.* However, many people can be helped and many ordinary Christians restored by appropriate and gentle prayer ministry and healing of the memories. One of the better Christian approaches is Theophostics (it's not as New Age as the name sounds) by Dr. Ed Smith of Kentucky. David Seamands has also done good work with his books "Healing Of The Memories" and "Healing For Damaged Emotions". Of secular approaches John Bradshaw's "Championing the Inner Child" is among the better ones and is worth a read by those involved in ministry. A lot of research is now

being done on Post-Traumatic Stress Disorder and on Multiple Personality Disorder which I believe are extreme forms of having a damaged and broken spirit. So you can see that this is a huge and specialized area in which a great deal of research is currently being undertaken and which is quite impossible to cover in a few hundred words in this chapter. What can we do then?

1. Be supportive, understanding, loving and caring. Give the person lots of freedom. Let them be angry but don't let them dwell too long on it.

2. Be extremely patient, do not condemn, do not censure. They are bruised and hurting. Remember "a bruised reed He will not break and a sputtering wick He will not extinguish."

3. Avoid strong emotion. A gentle quiet retreat atmosphere is generally far more healing for trauma than a hyped up evangelistic meeting. There is so much strong emotion inside them that they are already overloaded emotionally. Part of healing is to decrease this overloaded emotional level.

4. Above all do not suggest to them how they may have been abused or attempt to recover memories. False memory syndrome induced by zealous counselors is very real and very damaging.

5. Where necessary help them seek justice. Empower them to go to the police and through the court system. Many Christians are uncomfortable with this but people need to feel supported and protected and that there is justice in the world. If the offender is hardened and unrepentant and a continuing risk to the community then that offender should not be protected by "gracious" Christians. I faced this dilemma when I knew that a schoolteacher was a serial pedophile, lacked insight into his condition and was still around young children. He went to jail for eight years. The victims agreed with this course of action and were benefited by it.

6. If they are agreeable pray for them and soak them in loving prayer. Do not expect or demand immediate miraculous outcomes. Just soak them in prayer and let them slowly come face to face with Jesus who heals them. Repeat as necessary.

7. Encourage them to seek God's Presence in prayer and worship. Do not censure them for seeking God in ways that are outside your personal religious tradition. Many evangelicals are disturbed when a recovering person spends time reading the mystical writers or sets up a chapel at home with a cross and a candle. Remember that the spirit is a world

of symbols and they are trying to reconstruct their symbolic realm. This is a complex task - let them be.

8. Encourage them to express their feelings via art, acting, music, poetry, writing, pottery, crafts, gardening, keeping pets and other non-destructive outlets.

9. Don't argue but do gently correct false perspectives on life. Much of the continuing damage comes from believing untruths about God, self or others. These need to be gently shown to be false and the person shown who they are in Christ and in the loving eyes of God.

10. Give them lots and lots of time to heal and realize that recovery from trauma may happen in bits and pieces over many years. Don't feel it has to be fixed right now. Let God heal them in God's time.

If you are someone that feels that you may have a broken and damaged spirit do not sit alone and try to heal yourself. You need grace and you need special people and places that have a healing effect on the emotionally damaged. Ask the Lord to lead you to the right people and places where you can find the grace you need.

4. Problems Caused By Spiritual Attack

Fourthly, there are those spiritual problems which are the outcome of a *spiritual attack* that has affected the human spirit. For mostly Christians this is just harassment of the believer by an evil spirit external to them. For some people particularly those involved in the occult or grave sexual sin, exorcism may be necessary. For simplicity I will break spiritual attacks into two categories: minor attacks which are generally attacks on our mood, and major attacks that go deep into the spirit and involve a major change in consciousness observable to others.

The classic mood attacks are the sudden swinging moods such as those of King Saul who was afflicted by an evil spirit. These dark and evil moods often accuse the person, others or God and produce hopelessness, despair and discouragement. They can also suddenly give rise to lurid and vivid temptations or can fuel abiding anger and cause an irrational "spirit of ill-will" to develop. These moods have the following characteristics:

- They come over the person without warning.
- They then control their thinking and emotions for a while and take it in a negative direction.

- They leave suddenly when rebuked in the name of Jesus.
- They sometimes can be assuaged by Christian music such as when David played his psalms on the harp for Saul.

Please note carefully the above mood "attacks" are not the same as "demon possession"! In mood attacks the attacking spiritual entity is external to the believer and is engaged in harassment of the believer through their thoughts and emotions.

Other indications of spiritual attack on the human spirit include:
- The sudden desire to give up the ministry or the faith.
- Dislike to the point of hostility regarding the Bible, prayer or communion.
- Sharp painful feelings, doubts from nowhere, accusations of God, self or others. Fiery darts.
- A floating seductive feeling that takes over the consciousness and blots out prayer.
- Altered states of consciousness in which sinful acts are performed.
- The evident presence of an evil spirit, manifestations, voices, etc.
- A preoccupation with strange doctrines or bizarre dietary practices.
- Involvement in the occult, death metal music, pornography, drugs, or Eastern religion.

Major attacks are where the consciousness of the person is greatly altered and it is evident that the person's human spirit has been invaded in some way. A second personality or consciousness may take over the person and speak in a different voice or the person may suddenly enter a trance state (which is often rather sweet and seductive) and which obliterates all moral consciousness. In this trance state the person may perform sinful actions of which they later have reduced or blurry recollection. In such cases exorcism by an experienced practitioner who has the recommendation of sensible and mature Christians may be called for help.

Dealing With Spiritual Attacks:
Here is a general guideline for dealing with minor spiritual attacks on the Christian's emotional life:
- Become aware that it may be an attack of the devil.

- Try and give it a name if you can e.g. "a mood of deep discouragement".
- Resist its effects on you and say a firm "No' to its lies and suggestions.
- If necessary counter its lies with the truth of Scripture or just plain facts. When Elijah was deeply discouraged and said, "I alone am left". God said, "I have 7000 that have not bowed the "knee to Baal" (1 Kings 19).
- Rebuke the harassing spirit sternly in the name of Jesus with the spiritual authority you have as a believer (see Ephesians 1:20, 2:6; Colossians 2:13-15; Matthew 11:11-13).
- It should leave virtually instantly. If it tries another bout later on - then rebuke it again.
- If it returns you may have given ground to it by nurturing resentment or hatred, or actually liking the vivid temptations or believing there might be some truth in the accusations. If this is the case, then remove the ground the devil is using to afflict you by repenting of your wrong attitude and then exercising forgiveness towards others.

When Is Exorcism Necessary?

When there is clear evidence of an indwelling evil spirit exorcism is necessary. These indications include changes in personality such as a male person talking with a female voice or vice versa. They also include various peculiar odors and bizarre manifestations that are quite uncharacteristic of the person; a strong aversion to prayer and spiritual disciplines and especially to communion and an attraction to unclean behavior. Some people are overwhelmed by sinful obsessions and compulsions (unlike in obsessive-compulsive disorder where the obsessions are generally morally neutral acts such as hand-washing or locking up repeatedly) and unusual trance states where sinful acts are performed including a compulsion to suicide and dark obsessions.

Before engaging in exorcism make sure you are aware of your authority in Christ over the demonic realm. See the following verses Luke 10:19; 1 John 5:18,19; Ephesians 1:20, 2:6; Colossians 2:13-15; Matthew 11:11-13; Hebrews 1:14; and 1 Corinthians 6:1-3 and any good and reasonably recent systematic theology. You should also consult some of the books on deliverance ministry recommended in the section below. It is best to learn the art of exorcism from an experienced, wise and balanced practitioner who can show you how to go about it sensibly and effectively. Now let's consider a special kind of spiritual attack - curses.

Curses

Curses are an unusual topic for a book on emotions, but they are real, and are profoundly emotionally disturbing for those who experience them. They are not just angry words or swear words; they are acts of power in the spiritual realm. Curses are mentioned over 200 times in Scripture, and were foundational to the Old Covenant (see Deuteronomy 28-30). God Himself was the first one to pronounce curses – on the earth, on Eve's fertility and upon the serpent. Curses are not just a primitive superstition; they are spiritual pronouncements recorded in Scripture that profoundly affect the very structure of reality in some way.

The world was created by the word of God and is held together by the power of His Word (Genesis 1; Hebrews 1:1-3; Colossians 1:17-20). Thus God's words can change creation and Jesus' curse caused the fig-tree, representing barren Israel, to shrivel up. Blessings and curses are first of all God's words that operate at this fundamental level of creation and "tilt the playing field" of life one way or another. Secondly, curses and blessings can be from evil spirits or flow from the human spirit. Goliath's curses against David were "by his gods" (1 Samuel 17:43) and were ineffective for reasons we shall see later. The David and Goliath encounter was a power encounter of one spiritual system against the other and both contenders came in the name of their respective deities. Shamans and magicians such as Balaam were hired to curse people in Old Testament times and still do this today. Though curses from evil sources are much less powerful than curses from God they still were feared and were able to do much damage. There are twenty two references exhorting believers not to curse others. Curses are finally ended in the new creation (Revelation 22:3).

The origin of blessings and curses is found in the book of Genesis. The first blessing is upon the living creatures, which were told to "be fruitful and multiply" (Genesis 1:22). When God made mankind He also blessed them saying, "be fruitful and multiply" and added a third blessing, "have dominion over" (Genesis 1:28). These three basic blessings of: "be fruitful", "multiply" and "have dominion over" form the basis of all future blessings, such as the Abrahamic blessings, and their reversal forms the basis of all future curses such as those in Genesis 3. Let's look at this further:

Fruitfulness is the ability to joyfully express your inner nature and feel that which you are doing is truly creative, worthwhile and significant. Its opposite is pain in creation, especially barrenness.

Multiplication is exponential increase - increasing as in 2, 4, 8, 16, 32, 64, 128 not additively as in 2 , 4, 6, 8, 10. Multiplication is a huge increase in productivity for a small increase in effort. Its opposite is frustration and futility; putting in a huge effort for little or no reward.

Authority to rule over means dignity, headship, authority, the ability to be ascendant, to be the head not the tail. Its opposite is being humbled, to eat the dirt, to be crushed and humiliated, to be unable to rise.

In Genesis 3 we see the first curses in operation. The woman is made unfruitful, the man is made to work in futility and the serpent is told he will eat the dirt. The three things that make life good are reversed. Life becomes unbearable. Thus when we are cursed we find life very difficult indeed. No matter how hard we try to rise we never quite make it. Time and time we get to the brink of success only to have it snatched away. Curses can affect health, particularly reproductive health. They can affect earning power and they can affect our ability to have authority and command over our lives and people who are cursed may have to endure life-long humiliation.

As a missionary I can say that curses are real and in some cases they are even lethal; Ezekiel talks of magic charms that hunted lives (Ezekiel 13:18-20). Curses are on the rise in Western culture as people dabble more and more in the occult and in organizations where people take secret oaths that invoke curses (such as the Masons). Emotionally curses produce deep confusion and despair and an inability to think straight.

[There is not a lot of good literature on the topic of curses and all such books need to be read critically and subjective material carefully evaluated. Derek Prince's book "Curses and Blessings" is reasonable, Ed Murphy's chapter is good but gives no hint on how to break curses, and Francis Frangipane has some very good books on living in the place of protection from curses and spiritual attack.]

On one hand we do want to acknowledge the reality of curses and to deal with them and to break them. On the other hand we do not want to become overly superstitious and fearful seeing curses everywhere. If your life is affected by sterility, barrenness, constant lack of success and failure to gain any sort of ascendancy no matter how hard you try then a curse may be in operation. If you think this may be the case then do some research on your life and family history and take the matter before the Lord.

The good news is that breaking curses can be surprisingly easy for Christians because we dwell under the protection of the blood of Jesus Christ. Curses have greatest power where the person who has been cursed has committed some great act of wickedness such as involvement in the occult. The reverse is also true. Curses have little or no power over a righteous person and Proverbs says that a curse without cause will not alight on the head of a righteous man.

Scripture reveals a number of ways in which we can break curses and/or be protected from them:

1) Live a righteous life free from major sin and acts of injustice. Abide in the righteousness of Christ where no curse can penetrate (Malachi 4:6; Proverbs 26:2; Romans 8).
2) Put on the full armor of God (Ephesians 6:10-21) which is actually armor against spiritual attack. Ephesus was noted for its magic practices (Acts 19) and its curses and witchcraft. The primary purpose behind Paul writing to the Ephesians was so they could have some understanding of their power, authority and degree of protection in their pagan and occult city. The armor of God is like the Kevlar of the spirit world protecting the Christian against curses, magic and occult practices.
3) God is able to turn a curse into a blessing. He did this when Balak tried to get Baalam to curse Israel (Nehemiah 13:2; Deuteronomy 23:5; Numbers 22 & 23). A brief prayer by Jabez that has received a lot of popularity lately is a case of a person appealing to God to have a curse turned into a blessing and succeeding. In Psalm 109 where David seems to have been the victim of a curse (see verses 17 & 18) he is particularly bold when he says, *Let them curse, but You bless; When they arise, let them be ashamed, But let Your servant rejoice (Psalms 109:28 NKJV).* David did not fear the curse, but instead asked God to bless him and outdo the curse, and then

to turn the curse back on those who uttered it. God can out-bless the most fearsome and disabling curses. It gives us hope that our prayers to God based on the name of Jesus can not only break curses but have them turned into blessings instead.

4) Understand and plead the fact that Christ has taken all the curses due to us when He became a curse on the cross (Galatians 3:10-14). In Christ that ground for curses to succeed against us is removed because on the cross Jesus became a curse for us and took all the cursing that we deserved due to us due to our violation of God's laws.

5) Break associations with the sins of parents and ancestors particularly those involving the occult or idolatry. Exodus 34:6,7 says such sins bring a curse "to the third and fourth generation". We have to break ties with such sins by not participating in occult ceremonies that may be traditional and even confessing such involvement of your parents and ancestors and forsaking them in a prayer of renunciation to God. The essential thing is to make a clear break with the familial sin in your own heart, mind and spirit.

6) Get rid of objects that bring a curse, particularly objects associated with pagan worship, idolatry or the occult. For instance, if you have your Grandmothers pack of tarot cards you need to get rid of them (Deuteronomy 7:25,26). The Ephesian converts were moved by the Holy Spirit to burn their magic scrolls and occult objects. (Acts 19:18-20).

7) Do not engage in secretive or dishonest sins that you think you can get away with unobserved. In Deuteronomy 27: 15-26 certain sins are singled out as bringing a curse, notably the making of idols, incest, bestiality, treating parents with contempt, injustice against migrants, widows, the disabled or the poor, hiring a contract killer, and moving your neighbors landmark or boundary stone. Most of these are crimes that would never be tried in court because of the secret nature of the crimes, the lack of two or three eye witnesses willing to testify or the difficulty of proving the case such as the "my word against yours" case of the boundary stone. The curse was God's way of making sure that such secret crimes did not go unpunished. People knew that if they did these things God would repay. Even in the New Testament God is referred to as the one who punishes those who defile the marriage bed (1

Thessalonians 4:4-6, Hebrews 13:4). If you have done any of the things in the above list then repentance, restoration and an earnest appeal to God for mercy would be a good starting point in breaking the curse over your life.

8) Curses can alight where there is deep abiding injustice against an ethnic group. Saul's bloodthirsty massacre of the Gibeonites, which lay uncorrected for years, later resulted in a curse and a famine in the time of David.

> Now there was a famine in the days of David for three years, year after year; and David inquired of the LORD. And the LORD answered, "It is because of Saul and his bloodthirsty house, because he killed the Gibeonites." (2 Samuel 21:1 NKJV)

David broke this curse by going back to the offended ethnic group, humbly asking how they would like to see justice done and then enacting it. After ten of Saul's sons were hung the famine ended (2 Samuel 21:1-14).

9) Slackness in ministry can result in a curse. The priests in Malachi were under a curse because of their slackness in God's work (Malachi 2:2) and the prophet Jeremiah cries out "cursed be he who is slack in doing the Lord's work" (Jeremiah 48:10). If you are in ministry do the work of the Lord diligently and obey His specific instructions.

10) Put God's interests ahead of your own. In the book of Haggai God puts a curse on the nation (Haggai 1:5-11; 2:16,17) for being self-centered and neglectful of their duty to God. The curse is removed when the people obey the prophets and lay the foundation on the Lord's temple (Haggai 2:18,19) and a blessing is given instead.

There are over 200 verses on curses in Scripture and the above list just touches on some of the main causes and their remedies. Basically a curse can only alight on an area that God has already judged as being worthy of a curse – such as incest, idolatry or murder. Most curses generally last only 3-4 generations though some have lasted since Creation.

Repentance from sin, breaking ties with the occult and taking refuge in Christ who has become a curse for us are the main strategies we can use to break curses. Part of this is putting on the whole armor of God, which is designed to protect us from curses leveled against us in the course of spiritual warfare (Ephesians 6:10-18). When the curse is lifted then the human spirit that has been affected by the curse and been bowed down with pain, confusion and futility will be quickly healed. The person will recover and emotional normality should soon follow.

References On Deliverance Ministry and Spiritual Warfare

There are no perfect books on this difficult topic but there are many good and useful books on deliverance ministry in most Christian bookstores. Among the better ones I recommend Ed Murphy's "Handbook of Spiritual Warfare" and the writings of Francis Frangipane, George Otis Jr. , John Wimber and C. Peter Wagner . Classics on spiritual warfare include "Born For Battle" by R. Arthur Matthews and "Screwtape Letters" by C. S. Lewis . My e-book "Praying To Move Mountains" available from www.aibi.ph/ebooks/ has some short articles on the topic, and it's free. Books to avoid are those written by conspiracy theorists or which sensationalize the topic. Especially be wary of books that "see a demon under every bush" or which place a great deal of credence on the testimony of demons being exorcised or which have extensive lists of behaviors that are supposed to get you demonized (especially if the behaviors are not listed as sinful in Scripture). Such books can bring people into legalism and bondage. God has made us to be aware of spiritual attacks and to have victory over them but not to be preoccupied with them, fearful or overly suspicious.

Concluding This Chapter

Our life perspective may be affected by a wide range of events that damage our human spirit so that it cannot see God or life correctly. This damage tilts our basic perception of reality so that the whole of life, including our emotional life, is dysfunctional. Our human spirit can be deceived or brought into spiritual captivity and bondage by false teaching or damaged through sin, folly, trauma or spiritual attack. Curses can bring immense emotional pain and a feeling of constant struggle and futility. All of the above have Scriptural remedies and can be dealt with and fixed. They are not necessarily permanent.

As they are fixed our human spirit will begin to function as it is meant to function. That is as the place in us that receives God's truth and God's wisdom and which works in co-operation with the Holy Spirit. As our human spirit heals our spiritual sensitivity will increase and we will see ourselves, others and God rightly. When this occurs the process of cooperating with the Holy Spirit to become Christ-like emotionally is made much easier.

Once our perception of life and basic stance on life is relatively healthy we can then go on to create a more functional belief system. This will in turn help us to be stable emotionally since much of our emotional reactivity flows from what we believe is happening to us and our explicit, verbal beliefs that we hear as "self-talk".

Once a person afflicted by a bitter and broken human spirit is healed they will no longer be bitter and broken. They will have a much better outlook on life and see themselves, others and God in a much more gracious light. However, that dark and bitter period of life may have formed certain beliefs in them that have not yet changed. Hence the next chapter deals with constructing a fully Christian and emotionally healthy belief system.

Discussion Questions

1. What is perception 'in and by the Spirit'? How did Jesus demonstrate it?

2. What does Scripture indicate about the ability of non-believers to receive revelation and perceive spiritual things?

3. How much revelation and spiritual perception is given to Christians under the New Covenant?

4. How does accurate spiritual perception help our Christian lives?

5. How does legalism and/or spiritual deception damage our Christian lives?

6. What are the four main areas that cause trouble for the human spirit? What experiences have you had with sin, folly, trauma and spiritual attack?

7. Do you believe in curses? Do you think they can still affect us? How important are fruitfulness, multiplication and authority to success in your life?

8. How much love, joy and peace would fill your heart if you could accurately perceive spiritual things?

The Thoughts and Intents of the Heart
Beliefs, Vows, Desires, Wishes, Games, Life Scripts and Inner Goals

For the word of God is living and powerful, and sharper than any two-edged sword, piercing even to the division of soul and spirit, and of joints and marrow, and is a discerner of the thoughts and intents of the heart. (Hebrews 4:12 NKJV)

The second step in our five-step model is when perspectives give rise to beliefs, which gave rise to emotions. In earlier chapters the term "beliefs" was used very loosely to cover a whole range of internal activity that comes under the biblical term "the thoughts and intents of the heart". In this chapter we will look at that much more closely. In the next chapter we will see how communities form a lot of what we believe and how the group we belong to can affect our EQ.

The "thoughts and intents of the heart" are our internalized beliefs, both formal (such as theological beliefs) and informal and more personal beliefs such as "No one could possibly love me". These beliefs or thoughts of your heart are often reflected in what psychologists call your "self-talk" which is the "chatter" that goes on inside you as you are doing things. An example of negative "self-talk" is, "I wish Susan would call, I bet she won't, no one loves me much".

These beliefs are our idea about what is true or untrue, possible or impossible, plausible or implausible. They contain our conclusions about life and beliefs about God, others, and ourselves. Unlike perspectives, beliefs can generally be compressed into a single sentence such as "I believe that Jesus is God" or "I think I am totally unlovable". The Bible has two categories here; "thoughts" which is fairly much all-embracing and "intents" which deals with the movements of the will as we plan, vow and scheme our way through life. The picture we see in Scripture is that these thoughts and beliefs, desires, vows, and inner goals are generally verbal. When the prophets cry out "I know what you are thinking in your hearts it is such-and-so" it's always a statement, a sentence that encapsulates the heart attitude.

Over time we weave these sentences into a sort of bird's nest structure inside us that we call our world-view. For most people it is a horrific jumble of things they learned at school, life lessons, Grandma's sayings, the latest media opinions and a book they once read. This internal belief structure is more or less functional and gets people by for the seventy or so years they are on this earth. However for some people it can go horribly wrong and cause them a great deal of confusion and emotional pain. It is quite possible to hold conflicting beliefs or inconsistent beliefs or even two entirely different frameworks of belief. Sunday Christians are a prime example. At Church they seem to truly believe the Bible. At work they operate under an entirely different belief system and operate largely without reference to God. Both are real belief systems for them. They choose which one to operate under depending on where they are and who they are with.

In the Old Testament they even had two distinct religions worshipping Baal when it came to farming and fertility and Yahweh when it came to war. Dual value systems such as this have been castigated by the prophets, Jesus, and the apostles from one end of the Bible to the other. From Joshua's "Choose this day who you will serve" (Joshua 24:15) to Elijah's "How long will you falter between two opinions" (1Kings 18:21) to Jesus' "You cannot serve God and mammon" (Matthew 6:21-24) to James and his exhortations against double-mindedness and worldliness. (James 1:5-8; 4:1-7).

 Such people have literally two belief systems - Scripture calls them "double-minded" and says that they are spiritually unstable (James 1:5-8). This instability results from the fact that they are constantly choosing between two or more things they can believe at any one moment. One minute they choose to operate from the biblical belief, the next minute they choose to operate from greed, superstition or expediency. Up and down, tossed here and there like the waves of the sea.

To complicate matters still further Christians do not necessarily believe what they think they believe. Christians are generally still **learning to believe** that which they think they believe. This is the difference between believing something as a notion or as a doctrine and really believing it so that it is operational for you under stress and pressure. A test of this is "How much pressure does it take before you start to doubt that which you are sure you believe? Ask yourself the following two questions:

1. "If I was out in a small boat on the Sea of Galilee and the waves were high and the boat was about to sink would I be calm or would I be afraid?" Would Jesus say to me, "I have not seen such great faith in all Israel" or would He say to me, "Why are you afraid O ye of little faith?"
2. "How low can the bank account go before I start getting anxious and doubting that God will provide? Where is the point at which I choose to panic?".

The difference between the answers we put in the Bible study booklet and the answer we give to the actual pressures of life can be startling. Our notional beliefs and our operational beliefs under pressure are different. This may not be due to double-mindedness but just due to the need to mature, learn and grow. As committed Christians we are continually learning to truly believe that which we think we already believe.

So we can see that the goal is to have a consistent and fully Christian belief system that is the sole one we operate from, and which is operating at the level of the thoughts and intents of our heart and guiding our daily conduct and informing all our emotional responses. This belief system will fill us with joy and give us poise and calm in the middle of life's trials. It will be heart level, practical, biblical, strong and singular. Our lives will ring with faith and authenticity.

Firstly - Why Should We Change Our Beliefs?
Why bother? Why not just put up with the internal bird's nest and believe what we like? What's wrong with believing a mixture of a bit of Hinduism, a bit of Buddhism and handful of Bible verses? Don't I have the freedom to make a mess of my beliefs if I like?

This is true. You have perfect freedom to be as dysfunctional in your private beliefs as you like. You can choose to be unhappy, unstable and unfulfilled. No one will throw you into jail if you chose to believe nonsense. Unfortunately God is not as easy-going as society or the government on this issue. God is extremely interested in what we believe and in the thoughts and intents of our heart. They are not private matters to Him. They are matters of eternal importance that

can decide your eternal destiny and your reward in heaven, as well as your degree of happiness in this life.

Here are six reasons why you should work on your inner, personal beliefs:

1. God cares about your beliefs and weighs them up. He judges the thoughts and intents of your heart (Romans 2:15,16; Jeremiah 11:20; Hebrews 4:12).

2. Jesus expects us to be increasing in our faith and in fact is quite demanding about it! The expectations He had of His disciples included being calm in storms (Matthew 8:26), walking on water (Matthew 14:31), believing in miraculous provision (Matthew 6:30), being able to understand parables (Matthew 16:8), and being able to cast out demons, heal the sick and raise the dead (Matthew 10:8). When they failed to do any of the above they were rebuked (Matthew 17:20). The phrase "O ye of little faith" (see the references in Matthew above) shows that the disciples were expected to learn to believe Jesus with ever-increasing faith. Jesus does not call us to have a static level of faith. Rather we are called to develop a growing "mountain-moving faith" that starts from small "mustard-seed" beginnings (Matthew 17:20).

3. Theology interpenetrates reality. Every belief is theological. Carl Jung used to say that every human problem after the age of 35 was spiritual in nature. In a similar vein even the small voices, the dark mutterings of the human heart and the wretched small-minded beliefs that people have are a form of rebellion against God and a dwelling in darkness. For instance, to believe in your heart that the world stinks is to malign the Creator. To vow that you will always play it safe and that you will never love again is to retreat into darkness and flee the love of God that He puts into people to reach you. Thus all your beliefs have a theological component and need to be brought into the light of the Word of God.

4. How we believe determines what we receive. "According to your faith be it unto you" (Matthew 9:29; 15:28). Conversely having an unstable, worldly or double-minded faith means we will receive nothing from God (James 1:5-8; 4:1-8). Faith can bring healing (Matthew 9:22; James 5:15-18) is a prerequisite for receiving wisdom from God (James 1:5-8), for daily provision and reduction of anxiety (Matthew 6:30-34) and makes all things possible (Mark 9:23).

5. Creedal faith is insufficient. Even the demons have correct theology in the sense that they believe that God is one - and tremble (James 2:19). Thus merely creedal belief is insufficient for salvation. Belief must be authentic, loyal to God, of the heart and worked out in real life (James chapter 2). The great men and women of God all had

extraordinary personal belief systems that set them apart from their generation (Hebrews 11).

6. Letting unbiblical and dysfunctional beliefs linger can cause them to become stronger, more dysfunctional and more painful. Changing them now will take work, but leaving them will make it much worse later on. Keep your heart with all diligence, For out of it spring the issues of life. (Proverbs 4:23 NKJV)

The Difference

Every church has miserable grumpy Christians alongside radiant faith-abounding Christians. Well what's the difference between the two groups? Only the faith-abounding Christians have taken the time and effort to make sure their inner personal beliefs line up with God's Word. Grumpy cynical Christians have decided not to really believe. They would much prefer to complain. Faith-abounding Christians have decided that with God's help they will interpret reality properly and have paid attention to their heart. They have decided that they will "truly believe" and have put effort into their faith. Now they reap joy and have much more successful Christian lives.

An Illustration of Changing Beliefs from The Secular World

Even the secular world has discovered the benefits of working on your belief system. The Dale Carnegie / Zig Ziglar "positive-thinking" movement with its affirmations and personal motivation demonstrated the power of working on personal beliefs. It turned lousy salesmen into better salesmen. It turned unhappy, unenthusiastic people into happy enthusiastic people. It caught a fragment of the truth (taken incidentally from the founders' familiarity with the Bible) and applied it successfully to daily life. Why were salesmen so keen to systematically adopt a new belief system? What motivated them to try? Why wasn't it left in the "too hard basket?"

1. They met other people who seemed successful and who said positive thinking was the key to success.
2. These other people demonstrated an alive and enthusiastic personality they wanted to possess.
3. They compared their personality and results with that of the positive thinkers and decided to change.
4. Positive thinking made intuitive sense and the short sayings had a "ring of truth" to them.
5. The system was skillfully presented.

6. The system was simple and easy to apply.
7. Initial success was swift and this reinforced the effort required to change their beliefs.

If salesmen can diligently work on their belief system in order to sell insurance then surely we can work on our belief system in order to grow in the Kingdom and become mature in Christ? Our target is not just being happy, positive and motivated, though that's not a bad place to start if you are unhappy, negative and apathetic. Our goal is to have a sanctified and transformational set of beliefs that give us the emotions that make us whole Christians and empower service in the Kingdom.

Praxis - A Weird Word For A Great Way Of Changing Yourself
I don't know what your wrong beliefs are so I cannot write a book that says "if you believe X, then you are better off changing and believing Y". That would be long, unwieldy and over-prescriptive. Instead of individual answers I need to give you some sort of a system that you can put into action each day to steadily create more functional beliefs. This method needs to be fairly simple so it can be applied to a wide variety of situations. That method is called praxis (think of practical) and praxis is a cycle of action and reflection. It's like the experimental method applied to real life.

With the disciples we see them having some tough experience such as failing at healing then asking Jesus a question like "why could we not cast it out" and then learning from the combination of action and reflection. Many of us faced the same task as new converts when we first started sharing the gospel. Our first attempt might have been something fairly tactless and naïve like "Dad if you don't believe in Jesus you will wind up in Hell." The resultant reaction may have caused us to consider wiser ways of sharing Jesus with those we love! Then we shared the gospel much better next time around.

Let's look how praxis can help us to change our belief structure and consequent emotions. Here are the seven steps:
1. We enter into a situation where we do not function as well as we would like emotionally.
2. We reflect and ask : "What beliefs are underlying these undesirable emotions?"
3. We probe further and ask: "Are these beliefs true and biblical and in accord with the facts?"

4. We construct new, better, more factual and more biblical beliefs about that situation.
5. We reinforce those beliefs to ourselves.
6. We then re-enter the situation and test our new beliefs to see if they help us function better.
7. We look at the results scientifically and objectively and decide whether to keep the new beliefs, modify the new beliefs or to stick with the old beliefs.

Dysfunctional Situation: You cannot pray aloud in a prayer meeting. You just sit there in silence terrified to speak.

What Beliefs Are Underlying These Undesirable Emotions? : The beliefs might be "I am unworthy to pray" or "I don't have anything important to say" or "They will just think I am stupid."

Are These Beliefs True and Biblical and In Accord With the Facts?: No they are not.

I am unworthy to pray: In Christ you are worthy. You are worthy to stand before God. There is no condemnation before Him. You have open access to the Father. You have just as much right to pray as a pastor or missionary.

I don't have anything important to say: Every prayer is important to God and the prayer points that have been shared are surely important. You can pray for them.

They will just think I am stupid: Who cares? God does not think you are stupid. Besides if the people are men and women of God then your lack of fluency will not bother them one bit.

Construct New, Better, More Factual And More Biblical Beliefs About That Situation: "I am fully worthy to pray, I have important things to say and my lack of fluency in prayer is no issue with God and should be no issue for others either. I will not fear man's opinion. I will be a bold and powerful Christian who can pray for world mission."

Reinforce This New Belief To Yourself: Drill the new constructive belief into yourself. For instance, say it aloud ten times, or write it neatly on a card and place it in your Bible where you can see it each day until the next prayer meeting.

Reenter the Situation and Test Your New Beliefs: Go to the prayer meeting and pray aloud even a short prayer. How does it feel? Did a new confidence emerge? Did you suddenly find new friends? Did someone come up afterwards and say, "Glad to hear you pray." Perhaps there is still some nervousness but you feel you made a major step forward.

Look At the Results Scientifically and Objectively: Rate things out of 10. "OK that was 7.5 out of ten, my new beliefs are much more functional but I am still a bit nervous. I'll keep the card in the Bible another month and give it another try." Perhaps you have noticed that you have also become more confident in meetings at work as well. As we change beliefs in one area it may benefit other areas of our life as well.

This seven step process is very similar to how we unconsciously revise our beliefs from day to day. As life situations confirm or disconfirm our beliefs we continually learn and adjust and retest the beliefs. However, in "real life" we do it unconsciously, partially and are subject to denial and distortion in the process. By making our formation of beliefs conscious, objective, logical, factual and scriptural we are more likely to come up with beliefs that work in healthy and constructive ways. Let's try this process again in another situation - that of finances.

Dysfunctional Situation: Bill feels a call to Bible College but is afraid of the fees and of the loss of income.

What Beliefs Are Underlying These Undesirable Emotions? : The beliefs Bill finds in the "thoughts and intents of his heart" are a whole mixture including:

>"I must always have a good amount of money in the bank."
>"It's foolish to just trust God when you cannot see how to pay the bills."
>"I need to be independent."
>"I would feel ashamed to take money from others and have supporters pay my fees."
>"I'll never get the money back again that I lose in wages and in school fees."

Are These Beliefs True and Biblical And In Accord With the Facts?: Bill reads through the gospels and the Sermon On The Mount in particular and writes down the following conclusions:

"Having a good amount of money in the bank is desirable and good but having the Word of God in my life is even more important. What I will gain from Bible College is worth more than money in the bank."

"It's not foolish to trust God financially; Jesus, Paul, the apostles and many great Christian leaders have done this. I will walk by faith not by sight. God promises to supply my needs if I seek first His Kingdom and His righteousness."

"I might feel I need to be independent but that is just pride talking. The Scripture say I should be dependent on God and inter-dependent with others, giving and receiving in community - particularly with believers."

"It's not shameful to receive from others providing you do not use or manipulate them. If they wish to give, that is God's work in their hearts. Both Jesus and Paul accepted support from others so its OK for me to do so."

"I might never get the money back again but it is like losing earthly treasure to gain heavenly treasure. Besides God is no man's debtor."

Reinforce This New Belief To Yourself: Bill goes to his trusted prayer partner Sam with his thoughts and his responses to them written out. Sam reads them through and talks them over with Bill and says, "You have come to some pretty amazing and biblical conclusions here Bill, I wish I could think like that. You are right, God can provide for your needs." Together they pray that Bill will have the courage to apply to the Bible College and that his financial needs will be met. Bill asks Sam to keep him accountable and to check back with him next week to see that he has actually sent the forms in.

Reenter the Situation and Test Your New Beliefs: Bill goes back home picks up the forms and completes them. He hesitates a few days but eventually posts them off to the college. He feels a sense of relief and gladness that he has had the courage to obey.

Look At the Results Scientifically and Objectively: Pretty good , at least 9 out of 10. Bill no longer feels paralyzed by his beliefs about money. His obedience is no longer limited by his bank account. He has broken through and begun putting into action a new set of beliefs about provision and finances. He still has a bit of hesitancy and nervousness but feels a new world opening up before him. Serving God will be good!

So you see that the praxis method can help you to adjust your real life operational beliefs until they line up with Scripture, logic and the will of God. It may seem a long process at first but once you become conscious of your belief system and aware of your weak areas then you will find correcting one area opens up others, and soon the new good beliefs reinforce one another, and then you feel much stronger inside. This active cooperation with the renewing work of the Holy Spirit can be of great assistance to your practical sanctification.

Faith and Works, Beliefs and Action

Incorrect beliefs can give rise to strong negative emotions such as fear, doubt and hesitancy. These emotions can hinder or even paralyze our ability to obey God. Faith and obedience seem to be connected to some extent via the emotions. Remember what we said earlier – God connects to us through faith, which works through love, which applies specific and focused wisdom and knowledge to do good works. The good works need the motivating power of the master emotion called love. The word emotion comes from the same Latin root as motive or motor. It means to "move toward". Emotions are feelings that move us to action or in some cases block us from action. When the "thoughts and intents of our heart" are not aligned correctly, our emotions will not help us obey God, and may even hinder our service for Him. As we correct these beliefs, then our emotions will tend to follow suit and we will be more able to enact the commands of Scripture and follow the guidance of the Holy Spirit.

This of course has strong theological implications in the faith-works debate. My position is that faith that is of the heart, and continued over time, will result in works consistent with that faith. If a person claims to believe something, but never acts in accordance with that belief it can be assumed that that belief is either held very weakly or is, as James says, "dead" (James 2:20,26).

For instance, someone may say, "I believe in the resurrection of the dead and life everlasting". That is good. Such a person should then do works consistent with a belief in an after-life and a reward in heaven. For instance, they should be able to sacrifice material reward in order to gain spiritual reward or they should do good deeds that no one notices believing they will be rewarded in heaven. But if they live entirely materialistically then they are denying their professed faith. If we were to look at the true "thoughts and intents of the heart" of a materialistic person their real beliefs would probably have very little to do with eternal life. Their belief in the resurrection is simply held for the sake of doctrinal conformity or intellectual conviction and has little power in the person's life. It is in effect a very weak or "dead" belief.

Works are a guide to us as to whether or not our faith is truly alive, saving, living and productive. Our works indicate to the world which beliefs we hold that are strong enough for us to live by and act on. Works are a reliable guide to what we truly believe in our heart. In a sense our works are our true doctrine. Our works are the outworking of those beliefs, which we are prepared to act on, live by and stand for in daily life. Paul is very definite that we are not saved by works of the law. But he is also very definite that faith working through love (Galatians 5:6) should result in good works that God has prepared beforehand for us to do (Ephesians 2:8-10). Faith works, faith is active, faith expends energy to do good.

Jesus' beliefs resulted in action (Acts 10:38) based on compassion (Matthew 9:36-38; 14:14)
On various occasions compassion "moved" Jesus to act in prayer, healing, cleansing and teaching. Thus faith springs into action via love and compassion. Faith that refuses to spring into action through love is lazy, sick or dead.

Moving From Paralysis to Power
The connection between what we believe and how we put it into action is through our inner motive power - our emotions. Our emotions can paralyze our ability to be obedient. When this happens we need to do what Bill did and examine the thoughts and intents of our heart to see if there are some that are contrary to what we are trying to do. As we correct the beliefs in our heart we will find new liberty to obey God and a freedom from anxiety and inner conflicts.

To do this you will have to give up the belief that you are a being of perfect consistency, that all the thoughts and intents of your heart are consistent with each other. As an example of conflicting beliefs take someone who vowed early in life "I will never be poor". Later in life this person feels a strong call to be a faith missionary. It can be predicted that the old vow and the new resolution will be in conflict and that he or she may experience some reluctance, confusion and hesitancy. This attack of hesitancy may be first attributed to a lack of faith or commitment. However, if the early vow is remembered and renounced then the conflict will be resolved. It was not so much a lack of faith as a hindered faith.

How the Mind Works
To understand the power of these conflicting thoughts, intentions vows and desires you have to understand a bit about how the mind handles its data and in particular how it handles time. The mind has no actual awareness of clock time such as hours, days, months and

years. The mind uses event time where actual events are the indicator of when things should happen. For instance, "At two o'clock I will have a sleep" is clock time while "After lunch I will have a sleep" is event time. The event is the "clock". The mind uses event times such as "When I am grown up I will...", "After I am married I shall...", "Until I leave home I will have to", etc.

Events and instructions continue in the mind until the event time is reached for them to terminate. Where there is no termination date included in the instruction it continues indefinitely. Take a student who has often told herself "I've got to study hard all the time" and who has now internalized this instruction. What's wrong? There is no time given for this instruction to switch off. She has not said "I have got to study hard until the exams, then I can relax". Instead she has said "I've got to study hard all the time". Because of the absolute nature of this instruction even on holidays her subconscious will be reminding her that she "has to study". There is no "off" switch, no resolution, and in some cases the study moves from being beneficial to being a compulsion. The overuse of such instructions, without a "switch-off date" can lead to a person feeling very stressed as the programmed subconscious keeps popping up reminders "you must do X now, and Y and Z and P and Q and R..."

The same thing happens if the terminating event does not occur, or is not noted. Sometimes the subconscious mind needs to be told that a particular event has taken place in order for some emotion to be properly resolved. For instance, someone may need to tell himself or herself "you are no longer a small defenseless child, you have grown up now, you can feel safe" or more commonly, "You can relax now, you are not at work any more." Telling yourself to switch off is an important instruction.

Secondly, the mind stores things in "binary states" such as "on" or "off", "resolved " or "unresolved", " accomplished" or "still to be completed", "satisfied" or "unsatisfied", "guilty" or "forgiven". It may also store things as "a cause" or "an effect". (Incidentally, these binary states are elegantly reflected in the time-free verb tenses of the Hebrew language used in the Old Testament.) Memories, thoughts, intentions, vows and inner promises exist in these binary states. The only way to deal with them is to dispute them or resolve them or somehow move them from one state to the other. Thus an old vow using words such as "I will never" or "I must always" can live as an ever-present subconscious reality all through a person's life unless it is resolved.

To illustrate, think of a recurring and embarrassing memory that seems "as vivid as yesterday". When it pops up it has all the intensity of twenty years ago. Time has not healed. Time does not heal. The only way to deal with that memory is to resolve it by switching it off and saying "Hey, that's old history, I've grown beyond that now". One thing some of my clients have found useful is to imagine they are on a boat at sea and dropping their embarrassing memories into the ocean one by one and watching them sink. This resolves them and presses the "off" switch in the subconscious and it moves to the "dealt with" category and it is thus deactivated. Many people have reported that it has brought real release.

Thirdly, the mind works by rather loose associations. Some of these associations (especially with great pleasure or great pain) are very rough and quick while others, processed at higher levels of the neo-cortex, are much more sophisticated. It is not uncommon to experience chains of associations where one thought leads to the next which then leads to something else. This can be quite bizarre in patients with a psychosis. When something "looks like", "feels like", "smells like" or "sounds like" something else then a whole cascade of thoughts, memories and emotional reactions can be produced. The emotion is often transferred from the original to the copy. Someone may react to their boss like their father or to their new spouse like their ex-wife. These associations and the reactions and consequent emotions that follow can produce tragic misunderstandings. "It looks like, therefore it is, therefore I must, because once..."

So inner life plans, vows, self-promises and deep desires retain power in the psyche for as long as they are "active". When, later on in life, we try to do God's will and find that we are "sabotaged" from within it may be that some of these inner motivational factors are at work. Take Pablo the programmer, a fine Christian and a very competent computer technician. He failed first year at University due to heavy drinking just prior to his conversion. He came to me for career guidance and when he did the IQ test his score was so high it was "off the chart". I recommended a medical specialty after doing some other tests but Pablo never even attempted to take the advice. His inner vow, "I must never fail again, I must always be perfect", was totally in control and I failed to get anywhere at all. It has been twenty years now since he failed at University and still Pablo lives a life of inner safety largely wasting his God-given abilities. Old fears, vows, and promises to self can wreak havoc with our potential and so can "games" and "life-scripts".

Games and Life-Scripts

Games and life-scripts were first identified and popularized by Eric Berne who developed Transactional Analysis in his well-known book "Games That People Play". While I do not entirely subscribe to his analysis and the three ego states, his observations are of real and genuine importance. He has observed people very closely indeed. Games and life-scripts are very complex and involve an often sinister "pay-off" for the person playing them. An example is the game "You and Him Fight" where an attractive woman sets up a situation where she brings two men into conflict - the pay-off being the sense of power over men, having people fight over her and her own amusement at their behavior.

Playwrights and novelists are keen observers of these inner games and scripts that people live by and enact almost unconsciously as if it is their fate or doom to do so. Some tragic life-scripts are indeed from God such as that of Judas who was scripted to be the "Son of Perdition" who would betray Christ. On the other hand John the Baptist had a clear life script as a prophet. Such ultimate life-scripts are rare. More often than not we program ourselves and can un-program ourselves as well. Some people create complex scenarios to avoid taking responsibility for their life and actions. For instance, the person who always "tries" but never succeeds, for to become successful would bring responsibility and the fear of blame and failure.

Sufficient to say that the intents of our heart can be very complex like a play or novel and work out over many years with a few central motivations driving the plot forward relentlessly. The person may be completely unaware of the game or life-script. Complex intentions can successfully dwell below the level of awareness - especially if they are somewhat dishonorable!

Thus to move from paralysis to power we need to be able to work with the thoughts and intents of our heart and to bring them into conformity with God's will. Here are some techniques in addition to the seven steps of praxis I outlined earlier in this chapter:

- **Face Up To and Become Aware of the Intentions of Your Heart:** It can be difficult for some people to admit that they are complex and full of conflicting motivations. To admit to sneaky, dishonest, crafty or manipulative intentions is not easy for Christians. Many people are completely blind to this darker side of their character. Pray and ask God to reveal the thoughts and intentions of your heart to you so that you can bring them into the light and deal with them.

- **List the Various Conflicting Intentions:** This is sometimes all that is needed. For instance, a teenager may find that he has two intentions: 1. To be on fire for God and a powerful witness for Jesus. "To still be popular with the cool, tough, non-Christians he knows." Once he realizes that he is trying to do two things at once and that he is asking the impossible then common sense and Christian maturity will help him choose to suffer a little for the Lord. Simply listing the various intentions of our heart then judging them biblically may be enough to resolve the dilemma.

- **Confess Them to God:** Confess your wrong motives and intentions to God and ask His forgiveness and cleansing.

- **Make No Provision for Evil Intentions:** Do not give yourself the means of carrying out your wrong intentions. Deny them what they need to be implemented. If your wrong intention in your heart is murder - don't buy a gun. If the wrong intention in your heart is adultery - don't rent a hotel room. If the wrong intention is stealing from the church offering, make sure someone is with you when you count the money. This principle is what helped Augustine give up his loose living and become a Christian.

> The night is almost gone, and the day is at hand. Let us therefore lay aside the deeds of darkness and put on the armor of light. (13) Let us behave properly as in the day, not in carousing and drunkenness, not in sexual promiscuity and sensuality, not in strife and jealousy. (14) But put on the Lord Jesus Christ, and make no provision for the flesh in regard to its lusts. (Romans 13:12-14 NASB)

- **Put It On Paper:** By externalizing our beliefs and intentions we sometimes can get a handle on them and deal with them. This is often the real benefit of those management exercises such as setting priorities and doing mission statements. On a personal level if you start setting goals and priorities and coming up with a personal mission statement you will often run into awkward, uncomfortable feelings of resistance. When you do get them try and identify them, and write the feelings of resistance beside the goal or priority. Bring the conflict to the surface and into the open. For instance, a student may initially draw up a very demanding study schedule and after an initial burst of enthusiasm look at it and feel "trapped"; perhaps think "this is stupid" and perhaps even desire to quit. He should stop and ask: "Why do I think it's stupid?" and the answer might be "Because I need a life". Once that need is identified blocks of time for socializing can be scheduled in, along with plenty of time for study. Thus the two intentions, "I need to study" and "I need a life", can both be met and conflict avoided. Then progress can be made on the major goal of getting a good degree. So put your thoughts, priorities, goals and intentions on paper, paying attention to internal resistance as you do so. Identify and resolve the conflicts that emerge. This way you can end up with goals that meet your needs and all major conflicts resolved so you can move on in life.

- **Prioritize and Schedule Good Intentions Using Event Time:** Sometimes the paralysis comes from a whole host of good intentions all wanting urgent attention at once; having their "ON" lights flashing so to speak. The resulting overload, confusion and stress can stop us from getting much done at all. Use the event time of the subconscious to prioritize them. First I will do "A", then, after that's done I'll pay attention to "B", then when that's completed move to "C" and "D". Jesus gives nearly all His instructions in event time "after you have", "when they", "wait in Jerusalem until", etc. This is the most peaceful and relaxing way to do things. So when you are clogged up mentally with a whole lot of competing good intentions in your heart write them all down on a sheet of paper and then group them "first these", "then those", "next these", etc. Though the tasks are not done yet the issue of their urgency is resolved in terms your subconscious mind can understand and you will feel more at peace. Try it!

- **Revoke Personal Vows:** Revoke old vows that are now contrary to the will of God. Your promises to yourself are not as important as Christian obedience. Even do something as formal as writing the old vow on a piece of paper and writing "revoked" across it and then burning the piece of paper. Sometimes you may have to revoke a foolish vow you made to God in which case you should tell Him the reason you are revoking it and ask His forgiveness. It is for good reason that oaths and vows are banned in the New Testament (Matthew 5:33-37; James 5:12).

- **Change Absolute Language:** If you say to yourself "I have always got to..." then it's like fixing a mental switch in the "always on" position. You have told your mind that you have always got to do X and it will receive and record that instruction as a permanent injunction, a law of the Medes and Persians. The mind is fairly literal. It will take "always" to mean always and "never" to mean never. Words like "always", "never", "have to", "go to", "perfect" and "100%" jam our mental switches in the "on" position. With enough of them we feel stuck, anxious and stressed as we receive multiple simultaneous urgent instructions that we have programmed into ourselves. It is much better to give yourself an "out" by using language like "generally I should" and reserving the absolute language for situations that are truly absolute.

- **Avoid Psychosomatic Language:** The repeated-emphatic use of the language and metaphors of illness can sometimes make us ill. For instance, men who often tell themselves that their wife is a "pain in the neck" tend to suffer from - you guessed it - a pain in the neck - and people who "can't stand it any more" get knee trouble! This is termed psychosomatic language, somatic metaphors or "conversion" depending on your school of thought and was first noted by Sigmund Freud. Self-talk such as "If that happened... I would die" can become like an internal vow. The promise to die if X happens dwells in the subconscious and is then triggered when the dreaded event occurs. The unleashing of the "I would die" vow can then increase the chances of a major psychosomatic illness. Let me say that it is generally only the repetitive, habitual and emphatic use of such metaphors that makes them a problem. Some self-help books have an alarmist and superstitious understanding and use terms such as "cursing ourselves" and even assign supernatural powers to such language. I am not of that panic-stricken view. The terminology needs to be well embedded in the psyche first, only then does it attain any psycho-physiological power. Even then, research findings show, psychosomatic illness is only at its most damaging where there is some physical weakness in that area already. But still predisposing oneself to it by the inappropriate use of language is to be avoided.

- **Frame Thoughts and Intentions Concretely and Positively:** When you rework your thoughts and intentions it helps if they develop into a concrete picture of a positive desirable future. For instance, a struggling student should frame the goal "I will pass in Mathematics" rather than "I will not fail in Mathematics". When we see the biblical healing commands they are faith-filled, positive and have the desired end state in view. Jesus did not say to the lepers "Leprosy be rebuked", instead He said, "Be clean". Peter and John did not say to the lame man, "Lameness be gone", instead it was "Rise up and walk". We need to be solution-focused not problem-focused. The positive end result is what is to be put before the eyes of our heart. These positive end results in Scripture are also expressed in concrete terms. This seems to work better. "They will beat their swords into ploughshares" has more power in our being than "weapons will be recycled into agricultural implements". I do not know precisely why but when we state our goals and beliefs in concrete, positive, picture terms we seem to lay hold of them much more effectively.

- **Constantly Review Your Plausibility Structures:** We have limits to what we believe is possible and impossible, probable and improbable, plausible and implausible. The anthropologist Peter Berger calls these our "plausibility structures" and says they vary greatly from culture to culture. I was challenged in this area when I was a missionary to Papua New Guinea. A respectable Christian told me that his brother had turned into a python and slithered out the door never to be seen again. While this was a credible normal explanation to him, it was utterly impossible and implausible to me. My plausibility structure was challenged. While I do not advocate Christian gullibility I do advocate reworking our limits so that they line up with scriptural view of what is possible and impossible, plausible and implausible. Jesus says nine times in the gospels "nothing is impossible with God" or "all things are possible with God". His life and miracles reflect His commitment to this belief. The limits we place on our life are often really limits we have placed on God through having plausibility structures inherited from the world rather than from Scripture.

There is so much more that could be written on this but I hope you have grasped the central idea that we need to work on the thoughts and intentions of our heart, becoming aware of what is really going on in there, uprooting the weeds and setting the good plants in proper order. However, this is a large task and it is very hard to do it alone – we need others, and in particular we need a Christian community dedicated to the same ends. That is the subject of the next chapter.

Discussion Questions

1. Does God want you to work on your belief system? How much do you "really believe"?

2. Would you be confident in a small boat in a storm on the Lake of Galilee
3. ? How do you think Jesus managed to totally believe God?

4. Are people always consistent in what they believe? What are the thoughts and intents of the heart? How can they end up in conflict with one another? How can they tangle us up and stop us from doing God's will?

5. At the start of this book I said God links to us through faith, which works through love, which employs specific focused wisdom and knowledge to do good deeds. How does that apply here? How does our beliefs work through love to do good deeds?

6. What is praxis and how can we use it to change our beliefs for the better?

7. How does the mind work? What is event time?

8. Why can vows be emotionally dangerous? Do you think that the intentions of your heart are always "above board"? What can you do to change?

The Learning Organization – Christians In Community Undergoing Radical Transformation of Their Belief Structure

Mystery Quote: *"No one was ever matured in a theatre."*

Let's just pause a moment and think about how the communities we have been part of have shaped our beliefs. Our family formed our first beliefs, our school and social context formed many of our other beliefs and the church community then added yet more. On top of this, networks you have belonged to and groups of friends that you have talked things over with have probably shaped you. Being involved in community shaped an enormous amount of what we believe. Communities have formed both our formal and informal beliefs, our doctrines, our prejudices, our hopes and our paranoias. If beliefs are critical to our emotional health and beliefs are formed in community then fairly logically having the right kind of community will be a big help in emotional transformation. A dysfunctional family is an emotionally destructive community that places wrong beliefs and perceptions in people. The early church was a highly functional community that was emotionally transformational, full of joy and a peace-making, gospel-proclaiming, and miracle-working place to be. It certainly made sure the right beliefs; perceptions and practices were instilled in people. Thus the transforming power of an authentic loving Spirit-filled Christian community that is rightly grounded in the Scripture cannot be underestimated.

We learn, change and grow best in an adventurous, faith-filled Christian community. That seems a simple enough statement but it is one of those important things that are often neglected. Trying to transform ourselves while neglecting the importance of true community is unfortunately rather common. If we forget about community what are the alternatives? I see only two, a) learning alone by suffering, introspection and "bootstrap" self-help books and b) learning in a classroom. Now God does use suffering to teach us and he does use classroom instruction and sermons – however, in my opinion, these are His "fall-back" alternatives to adventurous discipleship in loving community. Let's look at the "fall-back" alternatives first and see why they are less than optimal ways of learning. We tend to do what we have always done and get the results that we have always got.

The Hard Way to Change

"Bootstrap" learning, on our own through suffering, discipline and the use of self-help books, is the hard way to change. Some devotional writers glorify suffering as the true path to spiritual transformation that is intended to show us what we are like and to get us to trust God in all things. Their basis for this has some validity and is more or less as follows:

1. Even theologically correct Christians may have dysfunctional beliefs at the level of the "thoughts and intents of the heart".
2. Generally we are blinded to what we truly believe in our hearts. We like to think we believe X when in fact we believe Y. Our real beliefs shame us so we hide them from ourselves.
3. Generally, only trials and tribulations can expose our true beliefs and allow us to perfect our faith. In trials we find out what makes us anxious and fearful and we can then learn to trust God more fully in these areas.
4. Being perfected in obedience means allowing trials, tribulations and temptations to show us who we are and what we believe. We are then to adjust to a more biblical set of beliefs which we then live by with a single mind.
5. We can do this on our own through Bible study, prayer, discipline, self-control, reflection on our sins, and the use of self-help books.

The problem is that suffering is a very slow teacher. For instance, how many years of financial struggle does a person have to endure before they learn to trust God for provision? Also how do we distinguish suffering that is God's teaching and suffering that is Satan hindering? Though suffering has an honored place in the Christian life it is the hardest and slowest teacher of all. There must be an easier way.

The Slightly Easier but Fairly Powerless Way to Change

A book came out entitled "Why Most People Learn Almost Nothing At Church And What To Do About It". I like the title. It points out an important truth - Church, Bible College and Christian education is not as transformational as we would all like it to be. As a part-time Bible college lecturer I have taken classes in biblical exegesis, theology, church history, and counseling. I see some change, some growth but rarely the transformational change that I hope for. The classroom can give you helpful information once you have realized that you need to change in a particular area and are truly searching for answers. If you are desperate to fix your marriage a Christian marriage seminar may well prove transformational. You were ready to learn. However, most students in most classes are not ready to learn. They are just there to pass the class. Worse yet, because the students are extracted from real life they do not have much opportunity to apply what they have learned in a real life context and thus the learning does not "stick". You see some of them five years later and shake your head at their mistakes. Did they learn a thing? Others, of course, are a source of joy. Books and classes and sermons can only take you so far. Academic, classroom learning is not powerful enough, it cannot blast through the huge blind spots we have. We go to the classroom but we don't really learn much that changes us. So teaching stalls and suffering takes over.

So most Christians end up with classroom teaching where they are teachable and suffering where they are not teachable. Classroom teaching plus years of suffering – are they the only two ways we can be made to change? What about the transformational power of love? What about the challenge of adventure? Can we learn from powerful life-changing experiences? Might these move us along the track a bit faster than teaching and suffering alone? There must be a better way - and there is! It's the method Jesus used to change His disciples and greatly enlarge and transformed their belief structures. It's the process of discipleship and of being a disciplined learner in a learning community. Let's see what led the disciples to be so transformed.

Having Our Beliefs Changed the Jesus Way - How Did The Disciples Learn?

How did the disciples get to increase in faith? How did they learn? How did they go from astonishing incomprehension at the start of His ministry to men of God and founders of the faith at Pentecost? These were the most successful spiritual learners in history, so let's look at how they learned and maybe we can learn the same way.

1. The disciples made themselves teachable apprentices of Jesus. They decided to be learners not know-it-alls. They were prepared to give up significant comfort in order to learn (Matthew 19:27). They broke with their usual patterns of living that reinforced their current belief systems. They left their fishing nets or tax offices and followed Him.
2. They planted Jesus' teaching in their hearts. They probably learned the same lessons over and over again because years later they could reproduce them word for word to their hearers.
3. They had a strong desire to inherit the Kingdom of God. In fact, it

dominated their personal ambitions (Matthew 18:1-5).

4. They expressed a strong desire for specific personal growth e.g. "Lord, teach us to pray".
5. They accepted Jesus' authority over them and simply went where He went, ate what He ate and did whatever He commanded. Even when Jesus rebuked them they did not sulk.
6. They believed that what Jesus said was true, absolutely true and sought to align their beliefs with His (John 6).
7. They watched what Jesus was doing. They saw miracles and had their view of reality enlarged.
8. They asked lots of questions and sought to understand.
9. They discussed among themselves what Jesus said and did. (Matthew 16:7, Mark 10:26)
10. They accepted Jesus' high view of the authority of Scripture. (Matthew 5:17).
11. They took risks in order to learn, such as Peter trying to walk on water or their various attempts at healing.
12. They lived with high levels of ambiguity, confusion and mystery. They seemed to accept mind-stretching confusion as the price of learning anything worthwhile. (Mark 9:32; John 10:6 etc.)
13. They very gradually moved away from being competitive to cooperative. They stopped trying to outdo each other and instead, by the time of the resurrection appearances were trying to encourage and edify each other. They became an encouraging, learning community.
14. They tried to do what Jesus was doing. They started with baptizing people in large numbers (John 4:1,2) and continued to exercise their faith in healing and deliverance ministries and did so with some success (Luke 10:1-24).
15. They increasingly accepted responsibility for ministry. At the beginning they were fairly passive followers. By the end they seem to have roles assigned to them. Eventually Jesus was able to deliver the Great Commission to them without incongruity (Matthew 28:18-20).

The communities in the early church and the traveling bands of apostles and missionaries that spread the gospel in the first century also took adventurous discipleship in community very seriously. The reason we see so little change today is that instead of being adventurous we try to stay in our physical and emotional and intellectual comfort zones. Instead of accepting legitimate spiritual authority and accountability (though it can be abused) we are independent and unteachable. Instead of tolerating ambiguity and confusion we demand simplified, watered-down, paradox-free theology. Instead of letting God set the learning agenda we try to decide what we will learn and how and when. We want to be in control of our learning, our lives and ourselves. We do not want storms as teaching aids. We value the Kingdom a little and the world a lot and consequently we don't take the risks and make the sacrifices to find the "pearls of great price".

Deep and revolutionary change of our belief structures and the emotional authenticity and joy that follows requires a very costly commitment to learning and personal transformation. While the Holy Spirit can work through a course or a book or a set of tapes and produce some personal change this is not the sort of deep change you get with adventurous discipleship over a number of years. I have seen greater change in young people in a one-week Christian camp or a four-week short-term missions trip than in years of good youth group Bible studies. While information has its place and can be transformational if given at the right moment it is not the major means of transforming our beliefs. Revising our beliefs starts with becoming an active learner about life, about God and about people and plunging into experiences and relationships yet always being guided by the Scripture rightly interpreted. To create the right belief structures in our lives we have to try to approximate the conditions the disciples lived under as much as is reasonably possible. The early Franciscans took being like the disciples with total seriousness and turned Europe upside down. It works!

The Importance of a Learning Community
Jesus and the disciples formed a learning organization, a community filled with disciplined learners in which beliefs were transformed and spiritual greatness produced. It is almost impossible to be deeply transformed outside of community or as part of a community that is antithetical to one's new beliefs and growth. Cults take this power to transform beliefs in and through community to a destructive and harmful extreme. It is the growth of the person not the service of the organization that is of critical importance. A true leaning community is the opposite of a cult. It is a place where individual personalities are developed - not squashed into clones of each other. Unlike a cult, a learning community is a place where difference is permitted and where accountability is mutual and constructive not hierarchical and destructive. A true transformational

learning community is a place of great freedom, love, and adventure. I once experienced a Bible study group that was like this and it was an exciting and transformational place to be. I have seen families that were learning communities and mission teams that were on the edge of adventure and both changing the world and the people within the team. Small groups of friends seeking God together such as the Holy Club at Oxford under John Wesley and the Haystack Prayer Meeting have produced mighty revivals. How do we find or create such a learning community?

The Eight Creative Tensions Of A Learning Community

> The elders who are among you I exhort, I who am a fellow elder and a witness of the sufferings of Christ, and also a partaker of the glory that will be revealed: (2) Shepherd the flock of God which is among you, serving as overseers, not by compulsion but willingly, not for dishonest gain but eagerly; (3) nor as being lords over those entrusted to you, but being examples to the flock; (4) and when the Chief Shepherd appears, you will receive the crown of glory that does not fade away. (5) Likewise you younger people, submit yourselves to your elders. Yes, all of you be submissive to one another, and be clothed with humility, for "God resists the proud, But gives grace to the humble." (6) Therefore humble yourselves under the mighty hand of God, that He may exalt you in due time, (7) casting all your care upon Him, for He cares for you. (1 Peter 5:1-7 NKJV)

There are numerous Bible passages describing the ideal kind of Christian community and the atmosphere of a learning organization. One of these is quoted above. It seems to me that learning community revolves around two things – leadership and ethos. I believe good community involves balancing creative tensions. Too much one way and the community becomes dull and bureaucratic and too much the other and it self-destructs in disorganization. Listed below are eight tensions from Scripture that are foundational to good Christian community:

1. Emotional safety - Spiritual adventure.
2. Clear basic doctrines - Room to experiment and discover new things about God.
3. Clear and definite leadership - Being without compulsion, exercising Christian freedom.
4. Sense of history, common purpose and tradition - Open to new methods and new territory; adaptable.

5. Know they are part of the solution – Humbly dependent on God.
6. Homogeneous and united leadership - Great diversity in membership.
7. God has brought this community into being - The drive to add more to the community.
8. Not focused on money - True abundance, care of the poor.

Explanation of the Eight Creative Tensions of a Learning Community:

1. It's impossible to grow very far in God or go on much of an adventure if the atmosphere is emotionally unsafe and you do not know when you will next be criticized or hurt. Christian communities must be safe for learning to occur. On the other hand they also need to stretch people because it is when we are stretched that we learn best. So we also need spiritual adventure. Some churches over-emphasize emotional safety to the point of coziness and become nurseries. Others over-emphasize spiritual adventure and become demanding, strained and critical. Thus emotional safety and spiritual adventure need to both be present in every learning community.

2. Clear, well-established, basic doctrines such as the Trinity and salvation by faith are needed for spiritual stability. Good churches teach solid foundational truths at great depths. Good Christian communities also build on the foundation. They try to find out new things for this generation and discover truth about missions, counseling, etc. This book is one such exploratory attempt to build on the foundations. Good churches explore God's truth so that as Martin Luther said, "More truth may yet break forth from God's Word".

3. Good communities have good leaders. Jesus led the disciples, the apostles led the early church and Paul led his band of missionaries. Leaders impart definite vision and set the clear bounds in which the learning community joyfully operates while treating them with respect. Such leaders lead in freedom and refuse to compel people to follow them. Jesus never forced anyone to follow Him. In fact He seemed to drive many away. (See John 6). Leaders of learning communities are not obsessive, compulsive people who fret over every detail and create an air of dread and compulsion in their wake. They lead in a clear and

definite manner. However it is without any heaviness, without "lording it over" the flock, and without compulsion.

4. Learning communities are well-defined. Somehow tradition helps learning. It is a different kind of education at Cambridge than at a new university – no matter how well-equipped it may be. Some of the most creative and successful missionary societies today such as OMF, CMS, Scripture Union, IVCF and SIM have long histories and a definite sense of tradition that gives them wisdom and the psychological foundations to tackle new ministries and territories. Stability enables learning and innovation. Some small missions have a new "mission statement" every six months which is the path to chaos and an indication of organizational immaturity. We need a solid sense of who we are and what we are about, common purpose, continuity, clarity of vision, and wisdom passed down through the informal teaching and discipling structures of the community. On the other hand such long-lived organizations can become smug and bureaucratic and sometimes have to pass through traumatic periods where the organization must be revamped with new vision. No mission statement can be so authoritative that it can overturn God's will. No tradition or corporate culture can be so "good" that it does not need new ideas from the Holy Spirit. When God reveals a new area of ministry to us we are to go into it boldly, wisely and well. When God speaks about a change in our culture then we are to listen and implement it. The learning organization uses its strong foundations to confidently plunge into new things for God. Balance is needed here. I think we have swung to one extreme – too far away from tradition. Too many organizations are busily doing "this month's new thing" to the point where nothing is built properly and half completed ministries and projects litter the landscape. Folly has become rampant under the guise of the leading of the Holy Spirit or innovation. In fact it is often just an immature "gold-digging" approach to ministry, trying first this for a season and then that until they find "the one" that will take them into the big time. Learning communities are stable and continuous allowing people to learn deep lessons in relative security and to prudently and wisely explore new options for ministry and Christian living.

5. Learning communities know they are part of the solution not part of the problem. They know they have something to offer their members and even to offer the world. They are positive and they are going places. On the other hand they do not think THEY are the solution. They humbly point beyond themselves and say, "Jesus is the answer!.." They combine humble dependence on God with a deep sense of mission and calling and the belief that they can do something for the world – with God's help.

6. To be a bit controversial it seems that homogeneous, united leadership and diverse membership is a Scriptural pattern for effective community. The apostles were all Jewish males mainly from Galilee. They were culturally homogeneous and good friends, some were even related to each other, yet they would lead a church that would soon be comprised of many nations. David's choice of leadership was very homogeneous –people he knew were absolutely loyal to him and had shared his troubles, mainly from his own tribe and clan line. His generals were his cousins! Yet David ruled all twelve tribes. In modern times George Whitfield and the Wesley brothers formed the "Holy Club" at Oxford that ended up becoming the Wesleyan revival. All the early leaders of that movement were educated white males, Anglican clergymen to be precise, yet the Methodist revival touched all levels of society and was very inclusive. The reason for this seemingly unfair principle is probably that if the leadership is not knitted together the whole community will fragment. The leadership needs to be able to deeply understand each other and to get along and have similar objectives and strong loyalties to each other. This requires both cultural and personal affinity. On the other hand no Christian learning community can exclude or demote someone because of gender, race or class. The community is to welcome diversity in membership while it maintains loyalty and unity in leadership. There needs to be a balance even in this – especially in interdenominational works. Nepotism and preferential treatment or the predominance of a particular denomination can destroy a work of God. Homogenous, united leadership is separated from the sin of partiality by a very fine line (James 2).

7. The 1 Peter passage above talks of the "sheep allotted to your charge". God forms the community and it is God who allots the members and builds the Church. To be aware that God has brought you into existence is a good and empowering thing. All

learning communities should believe that they are God's people, called out of darkness and commissioned for His transformational purposes on earth. The early church saw itself as a community formed by divine mandate for divine purposes. This sense of being formed by God and used by God gives a powerful dynamic to the learning organization. However, the learning organization should not be unduly puffed up by this and thus become exclusive or spiritually proud or separate themselves from other believers who do not seem to share their sense of vision and mission. They should not draw boundaries around themselves too tightly. The early church in Jerusalem was a very open, humble and welcoming place. Learning organizations should always be open to new members and believe that there are yet more to be added to the flock, "others not of this fold". They should also maintain open linkages of real integrity with the rest of the body of Christ. To draw the boundaries too tightly is to become a club or even a cult. A learning community sees itself as formed by God and involved in His purposes yet is humble and gracious and open to new people and to fellowship with the rest of the body of Christ.

8. A learning community has a healthy attitude to its financial needs. On one hand it knows what it means to be dependent on God, excited about His provision and free from the love of money. It is thus free to experience His transforming challenges to material comfort. On the other hand the learning organization truly cares about its members and their financial needs. The early church took great care of its poor and in the post-Pentecost Jerusalem church "there was none among them who lacked" (Acts 4:34). Thus it is God's clear desire that His Kingdom should not contain any abject poverty. The twelve fasted from discipline but there is no indication that they starved from want. The New Testament regards God as the Master and money as the servant to be used for Kingdom purposes. Learning organizations need to be free from the love of money, living lightly, simply and adventurously but able to take care of people and their financial needs and use finances to accomplish God's will on earth. Neither crass materialism nor financial disorder is God's will for a learning organization.

The Learning Community, Beliefs and Emotional Health
Let's put this together. First we looked at the disciples as the ideal community members with their high commitment to finding spiritual truth and allowing themselves to be stretched. Lately we have looked at eight tensions that the leadership of a learning organization need to be aware of and bring into balance. In such a community grace, truth and love will meet and people will be transformed in their belief structures and emotional lives. They will learn, they will grow and they will have lots of fun.

How can we do this? How can we create a therapeutic, healing, loving, sanctifying community that really works? I have explored these issues in two e-books that can be downloaded from www.aibi.ph/ebooks/. These e-books are titled Beyond Denominations – The Networked Church, and Temples and Tithes. The first looks at abandoning denominational hierarchical structures in favor of networks of churches in a local area. The second looks at some of the doctrines, particularly misinterpretations of the Old Testament and the Law, that keep Christians in bondage or which confine them in dysfunctional structures. Traditional church structures are not transforming people at the rate they should be. It is imperative for our own personal spiritual and emotional growth to find or create alternatives. Here is my suggested pathway:

- Create a united leadership group that shares the same passion and direction. Pray for 6-8 people (say 3-4 couples) to start things rolling.
- Don't decide on any forms or structures at the start. Just meet in a home and spend some time studying the Gospels and Acts together and looking at early Christian community. Allow the Scripture to speak to you and the Holy Spirit to lead you into the forms the groups should take.
- Act on what God reveals to you.
- Invite others to join you after a while.

On the other hand you may just want to make your current church more transformational. In that case start by throwing out those things that don't work for you and doing more of those things that do work for you. Ask God to show you where to start. Generally, if you spend more and more time doing things that do work for you they will gradually and naturally push out the dysfunctional elements along the way. For instance, if you find that small groups help your people to grow then have more small groups! Get more and more people into small groups and delegate more and more functions to them. Even allow the small group leaders to baptize and administer the Lord's Supper. After a while you will have most of the preaching, teaching, praying, counseling, baptizing and sacraments being done in people's homes in small groups. They will be in small mutually accountable communities and the pastor will be teaching the leaders to lead and dealing with the most complex questions. Maybe everyone will be so involved in their small groups that they won't "come to church" any more. They will just be the church. That will solve the problem of the parking lot.

The above example may shock you but it poses a fundamental question – what is our community for? Is it for the people, for God, or is it for a structure? We need to find a way of being together that makes us most like Jesus Christ. The present way of being together does that a little and is better than nothing. However, there has to be a better way of being church, and thousands, if not millions, of Christians are searching for it.

What has this got to do with Biblical EQ and in particular with our belief structure? Church structure seems a long way from emotional health. To answer that - emotions flow from beliefs and beliefs are formed in community. How far we can go with those beliefs and what they really mean is often reinforced day by day in that community.

An extreme example of dysfunctional communities is the cults. Cults are communities that form wrong beliefs and produce destructive emotional states. Cults are community gone wrong and are a huge danger to emotional health. Just do an Internet search on "cults" or read the biography of someone who has been in one and you will soon see the terrible damage they can inflict. Structure can quietly shape community so that it goes badly wrong. For instance, if there are a small handful of highly coveted church positions in a large church then that will tend to create lobbying and internal politics as people try to get elected. Also if the structure is one of professional performers "on stage" and a large audience in the auditorium then it is natural for people to be spectators rather than actively involved with their faith. I was mulling this over with respect to why mega-churches seemed to be so shallow unless they had good home groups, when God suddenly and almost audibly spoke these words:

"John, no one was ever matured in a theatre." (Hence the mystery quote at the beginning of this chapter).

On the other hand, in the past twenty years or so whole therapy movements have grown up around getting community right – notably family therapy – or they employ community as a tool for healing emotions in T-groups, encounter groups, support groups, Twelve-Step groups and so on. Even in the business world various branches of systems theory and the study of organizational behavior has revealed that structures, beliefs, emotions and behaviors are inextricably linked and that good companies must have good structures if they are to maximize the potential of their staff. The emotional potential of people is released best in a good and rightly structured community. Thus the link between community culture and transformed human emotion is well documented and strong.

When we do get community right it has tremendous healing power. This can even happen on a small scale such as the "Jones family", a loving Christian household that people just keep "dropping in on". There they are welcomed and loved and changed. More counseling is done in the kitchen than in many a pastor's study. Over the years this small functional community of just one family will help hundreds of people towards wholeness as they absorb the atmosphere and feel the love and warmth there. Love is the great transforming force in biblical EQ.

People are matured in families, groups of friends, marriages and stable, healthy groups. They are matured in communities that speak the truth to one another in love. People are not matured in a theatre, even by the best performers. When we turn churches into theatres we rob Christians of the chance to mature. So structures, beliefs, emotions, community, and maturity are all part of one seamless whole.

In the last few chapters we have explored how emotions are formed in the realm of the spirit and the soul and in community. In this next chapter we will look at another place emotions are generated – in our bodies, and turn to the complex topic of the interaction between our physical bodies and our emotions.

Discussion Questions

1. Why is no one ever matured in a theatre? Are you excited about the idea of community?

2. What results do "suffering and classroom teaching" produce? Are they largely ineffective means of making disciples? What percentage of our beliefs come from our communities?

3. What made the disciples the best spiritual learners in history?

4. What are the eight tensions of a learning community? What is your favorite one? How can we prevent communities from becoming cults?

Emotions and Our Physiology

Have mercy on me, O LORD, for I am in trouble; My eye wastes away with grief, Yes, my soul and my body! {10} For my life is spent with grief, And my years with sighing; My strength fails because of my iniquity, And my bones waste away. (Psalm 31:9-10 NKJV)

In Psalm 31 David cries out at how his emotions are affecting every aspect of his physical being. Our body and our emotions are in continual interaction. Yet only recently has Western thought, strongly influenced by Greek mind-body dualism, grasped this rather obvious fact. Anger turns the face red, fear turns it white, a pizza at bedtime can give you nightmares, a pill can make you high, alcohol can relax you and too much coffee can make you anxious (I believe there is even a clinical condition called "caffeine anxiety neurosis"!). I have been an epileptic since childhood and adopted a quite different personality under each change of medication while I was on Phenobarbitole I was "out of it", on Tegretol I was happy, Dilantin made me dizzy and Valproate makes me rather depressed. Our emotions are so heavily modified by our diet, fitness level, medications and other aspects of our physiology that it leads researchers to ask questions such as: Do we really have our own emotions or are all our emotions just a product of our biology? If a change of medication or a bump on the head can modify our emotions completely - were they ours to begin with? Do we have a spirit and soul that is "inside us" and relatively stable and the source of many of our emotions or are we just a bundle of rather well trained biological responses?

The view of this book is that we do have a spirit and a soul and that the emotions generated there are expressed to the world through the body. When we are sad we cry and when we are happy we smile. In a perfect world our body would report the world accurately to us through the senses and express our feelings to the world with poetry, poise and clarity. Unhappily, for now, we live in earthen vessels in a fallen world.

Communication does not happen as well as we would like and we neither understand clearly, nor are as well understood as we wish. Plato saw this dilemma and concluded that the soul was trapped within a material body that was inherently evil. This is not the Christian view. Christian belief has it that the spirit and soul reside in a good body, which has unfortunately been tainted by the Fall. The body now has evil resident within it but it is our present bodies that will be redeemed and transformed at the resurrection of the dead. [It was Jesus human body, the one in the grave, which rose and was resurrected. The grave was empty. Similarly it is our present human body that will be transformed in the twinkling of an eye at the resurrection into a glorious spiritual body. We do not lose our bodies; we have them changed.] Notwithstanding this redemptive hope the body is a problem - perhaps the biggest problem of all.

This interface between the soul and the body is complex and poorly understood yet it is one of the main areas of problems in the Christian life. Is it unspiritual for me to have bouts of depression that are induced by the medication that keeps me alive? Is the terror of a child with high fever and delirium a failure of spiritual nerve? Is post-natal depression a sign of sin in a woman's life? Is the weariness of chronic arthritis or the sudden emotional swings that come to people with spinal damage a sign of unbiblical behavior? I hope you have answered a firm "No" to all these questions. No one with malaria wants bizarre dreams, visions and tropical terrors. No one with a damaged spine wants to suddenly find themselves swinging emotionally. These emotions arise unbidden and unwanted from neurological damage and from chemical imbalances in the body. Yet they affect us deeply and are a large part of our spiritual struggle.

Where emotions have a physiological basis changing the underlying physical condition will often bring emotional relief. When the fever goes the delirium and its terror passes and is simply a memory. If the person manages to give up drinking too much coffee their anxiety levels decline. Thus it makes sense for Christians to visit a physician and to see if there is some underlying physical cause for their emotional condition. There may be a medication with fewer side effects than the one you are using or there may be simple lifestyle changes that can make you feel much better.

The body seems to have an emotional memory of its own as well. A person may find themselves physically repelled by mushrooms after a previous dose of food poisoning despite knowing that the present mushrooms are fine. Many a person has sworn off drinking port after a night on the town. There is a deep physical and emotional reaction to those substances that the body associates with illness and pain and even towards certain odors associated with them.

The difficulty comes when a psychological problem remains after the original physiological issue has subsided. For instance, when a small child becomes afraid of a certain object that may have been the focus of nightmares or delirium. In one childhood measles case the flowers on the floral curtains seemed to turn into huge attacking spiders and this terrified the poor child for days on end. The parents pointing out "there is no need to be afraid of the floral curtains any more" didn't help. The damage from prolonged fear is too deep for common sense. In these cases the body has affected the soul. Counselling and proper therapy are needed. It may even be simpler to buy new curtains!

Repeated physiological stimuli can set off permanent physical changes. These changes include the chemical cravings in alcoholics and drug addicts or some of the neurological changes reported among torture victims and those with post-traumatic stress disorder. Since the problem is now physiological or chemical and seems to be lasting then the response may involve medication, behavioral conditioning or even, in severe cases, neurosurgery. Much research is currently being done on how our neural pathways are affected by our life experiences and the degree to which they can be retrained. It is an extremely interesting but very complex area.

Our emotions have an incredibly complex series of physical correlates that include hormones flooding our system, changes in blood supply, the activation of an emotional region near the stomach, neurones firing and neural pathways, and various associations in the brain. The "fight-or-flight" response [the subject of the next chapter] is a massive activation of the body by the emotion called "fear". According to some recent research our more instinctive fight-or-flight reactions seem to be processed in the limbic system especially in the amygdala. On the other hand our more balanced, less fearful, more refined and thought-out responses come from the pre-frontal cortex. The two areas are connected with the cortical region normally modifying information from the amygdala. When the amygdala or pre-frontal cortex is damaged people lose connection with many of their emotions. These regions of the brain seem to do much of the processing associated with our perceptions of emotional reality.

Damage to these regions can lead to coarse and vulgar expressions of emotion including a distinct lack of impulse control. I once counseled a woman who had tragically been the victim of unethical experimental psycho-surgery and had both her frontal lobes removed as treatment for depression. She was a kind and loving person but her speech was laced with uncontrolled profanities. Her control over finer expression had been totally lost when her frontal lobes had been removed. This unfortunate woman was a born-again Christian but could not attend church because of her constant swearing. Was she really sinful and unspiritual or would we all end up like her given the same neurological damage? I think the latter. Her kind and loving heart was evident. There was not a trace of meanness or hatred in her soul. She was in love and wanted to know whether or not to marry the very patient man who cared for her despite her condition. After a few sessions of counselling I gave them my blessing. The brain was damaged but the person was intact. This leads to the next question – what is the relationship between the mind and the brain?

The Mind-Brain Problem
The philosopher, Descartes, posed the problem of how the physical organ called the brain and the subjective phenomenon of 'mind' interact. Is my mind merely the product of my neural activity - a perfectly predictable thing that obeys the laws of physics so that I have no free will as Thomas Huxley proposed in 1874? Are mind and brain the same phenomenon but viewed from different angles so that the brain is how we view it from outside and the mind is how we view it from inside? Bertrand Russell held this view. The philosopher and mathematician, Leibniz, saw them as parallel universes in perfect harmony but not interacting. Mind and brain were like two matched clocks that kept the same time though they were quite separate and without interaction. The idealists such as Hegel saw the mind as the only reality and the physical brain as simply a creation of the mind. This is regarded by most as an extreme view. Twentieth century philosophers have been taken with the notion that the mind is just a computer program running on the hardware called the brain thus there is no mind-brain duality and no problem. There are almost as many solutions as there are philosophers. Some invoking quantum states and others reverberating neural circuits. It's a fascinating subject and if you have the time just search on the Internet for "mind-brain problem" or "consciousness" and you will find as many articles as you like with as many different theories as you can manage. Well is

there a Christian, biblical and scriptural solution to it? Is our consciousness simply a physical part of us or is there some "entity", a soul or spirit, which is separate from the body and possesses consciousness?

The Bible is quite clear that consciousness persists after death. To put it bluntly the mind continues to exist after worms have eaten the brain. Thus the mind does not depend on the brain for its existence. But does that lead to the idealist position where the mind creates the brain? Not at all! The Bible states that the body was formed before the mind. God made Adam out of clay – Adam's body existed, presumably including his brain, before the spirit of life and consciousness was breathed into him and he became a living soul (Genesis 2:7). Therefore, if the body existed before the mind it is not created by the mind. The idealist position collapses. The separate natures of the mind and brain can be seen as follows: a) We live on after death, therefore, the human mind can exist independently without the physical brain. b) When God created mankind He made the physical body first. Therefore, the physical brain can exist independently without the human mind. This is called the "strong dualist" position. If you think about it it's the only position that can support any sort of free will or morality. If the mind, that is my humanity and reason, is simply a biochemical or computing phenomenon, a somewhat predictable entity like a complicated billiard ball then I am relieved of all responsibility. I am predetermined by a complex set of initial conditions and my reactions are simply nature taking its biochemical course. Hitler and Mother Teresa are just different neurological arrangements and society happens to prefer the latter over the former. For a Christian this is an entirely untenable position despite its appeal to the deconstructed amorality of the modern world.

To me the Christian position seems as follows:
1. Mind and brain are separate entities. Mind is eternal but the brain is temporal.
2. Mind is grounded in consciousness, which arises from the soul that is quickened by the spirit.
3. The brain, as we know it, mainly acts on sense data from the physical world and coordinates the physical functions of our bodies. In maps of the brain complex physical tasks such as the coordination of the thumb take up most of the space. Brain maps show very little space devoted to the existential matters of the mind.

4.   Thus while we are in this physical world we need a physical brain. It's the data link between an immaterial soul and a material universe. The physical brain mediates how our mind communicates with our bodies and receives sense impressions about the external physical world. When the mind expresses itself it does so through our bodies which are coordinated by our brains.

5.   The spirit is designed to handle communication in the spiritual realm directly and intuitively. So when we are not in this material realm, such as when we are with God in heaven, we can have consciousness via the spirit without the presence of a physical brain. A case of this is the souls under the altar, which can speak, feel and communicate with God. (Revelation 6:9,10).

6.   Thus, as we saw in the chapters on perception, we can receive knowledge directly and intuitively from the spirit in Spirit-to-spirit communication. Such communication goes directly into our mind. When it occurs it can be very powerful because it is so direct. When Daniel received prophetic messages it left him emotionally drained (Daniel 10:8).

7.   We can also receive communication directly through our senses into our brain. This input is filtered before it reaches consciousness and does not necessarily get there. For instance, we can come out of a daydream to be suddenly aware that the kettle has been furiously boiling for a few minutes and that our brain knew this at the time but it just was not getting through to our consciousness. Consciousness can ignore sense data. Input to the brain does not necessarily mean input to the mind.

8.   Damage to the brain is mainly damage to our ability to process sensory data and to interact with the physical world.

9.   Brain damage does not affect the mind and our ability to have a soul or a spirit or to experience salvation. Christians working with people with mental disabilities have no doubt about the spirituality of their clients.

10. While this is so, most people have a strong interaction between mind and brain, which produces wisdom, intelligence and creativity. While the mind is ultimately independent of the brain; damage to the brain can reduce

our ability to experience our mind in this life, for instance, in the case of the deep confusion that accompanies Alzheimer's disease.

Thus our emotions flow most fundamentally from our soul and spirit but are then connected to the world and the senses through the body, which includes the brain. This connection is intimate and deep and unless something disturbs it mind and brain appear to be a seamless whole as the body-soul-spirit complex functions as one integrated entity.

In the case of the client with dual frontal lobotomies her ability to interact with and evaluate her vocabulary was missing. She did not know the difference between appropriate and inappropriate words. This was a loss of cognitive processing in the brain not a deficiency of character or spirituality. Also the personality changes that come with medication do not necessarily affect a person's salvation or their spirituality though they do affect how that person experiences his or her spirituality.

Stress
In the following section on stress the published work of Brisbane-based Christian psychiatrist and stress researcher, Dr. William Wilkie, is used and in particular two chapters from his book "Understanding Psychiatry".

Stress is an interesting area in the mind-brain problem because stress is the emotion we experience when our brain cannot cope with all the processing that is required of it. The physical brain is like you desktop computer and if you have too many programs running it can slow down or "hang". There is "just so much" your brain can do at once. Dr. Wilkie theorizes that this is due to the capacity of the reticular formation, an area at the back of the brain that filters incoming data and decides what will get attention and what will be discarded.

For instance, you are driving along a pleasant country road in Australia, listening to the car radio and enjoying the view. Then a six feet tall red kangaroo jumps out in front of your car. Your reticular formation switches the focus of your attention in a split second. Instantly you no longer pay any attention to the radio or the view and every particle of your attention is focused on the kangaroo and how to avoid hitting it. Deciding what is urgent and important and of value for the brain to process is the job of the reticular formation and most of the time it's automatic. You do not consciously think "I'd better stop listening to the radio and looking at the view, I think I'd better concentrate on the kangaroo." That's too slow. Most of the time the change in attention is lightning fast and automatic and not under a great deal of conscious control. Now the problem comes if in addition to the kangaroo you have a truck coming in the opposite direction and there is a ditch on one side of the road and a large tree on the other. In this case you will probably hit the tree. Why? It will likely happen because the reticular formation won't cope with all the situations at once. It will process the huge oncoming truck and the sudden movement of the kangaroo and maybe even the yawning menacing ditch by the side of the road but the tree is just "part of the landscape" and there are lots of trees so you "won't see it" and you will hit it with horrible consequences.

On a much less dramatic scale this happens to busy modern people every day. There is too much to do and "stuff falls off the plate". There are some things that we know we should be paying attention to, that just don't happen. We get that clogged up feeling in our head and we might even say, "If I have to think about one more thing I'll scream" or "Stop the world I want to get off!". That clogged up, "I cannot cope with all this" feeling is what we call stress. We feel stress when we have too many things that are too urgent, too complicated or too important, to be all processed at once. In extreme cases it can lead to burn-out or stress breakdown. Stress breakdown has three stages. Firstly, our system fires warning bells about the overload we are experiencing and we feel stressed, anxious, uptight, and tense. These uncomfortable feelings are trying to tell us that we are doing too much and it would be a good idea if we slowed down. They are saying, "You are driving yourself too fast, back off."

Many people ignore these warning signals, they like "driving fast", living on adrenalin and they have an image of wanting to do more than others. So they suppress the anxiety by an act of will and keep going. They then become in danger of second stage stress breakdown. In stage two the person loses control of emotions and finds themselves getting angry or upset very easily. They can cry one minute and laugh the next. These sudden emotional changes are termed "emotional lability". The person in stage-two stress breakdown also lose their ability to adjust to change and to motivate themselves to get started, though once they have started they can work as hard as anyone else. The system is beginning to crumble at this point and the person becomes subject to psychosomatic disorders as the body tries to slow the person down. These include migraines, headaches, asthma, dermatitis and hay fever. The immune system suffers and resistance bacteria and viruses already present in the person's body may be able to cause disease. These include common infections such as colds and 'flu, herpes virus infections, mouth ulcers, lobar pneumonia, boils and pimples, tonsillitis and urinary tract infections. Most people get the hint at this point and slow down but for some who do not they can go into severe, third stage-stress breakdown commonly called burn-out. This is characterized by three things, and unfortunately they are generally not recognized as being stress related. The three symptoms of third-stage stress breakdown are:

1. Avoidance of sensory stimulation.
2. Development of intolerance.
3. Apparent change in personality.

The brain's circuit breakers have cut in. Everything is being rapidly simplified to reduce the number of issues the person has to deal with.

In order to avoid sensory stimulation the person may retreat to the countryside, separate from their partner, stop having sex, avoid loud music and stop going to shopping centers. Sounds will seem too loud, ice too cold, lights too bright. They will switch off the radio when others turn it on. They will go outside and walk around and just "space out".

Development of intolerance is a mechanism for making life easy to classify so the reticular formation can deal with the backlog. If the shades of grey and complex questions can be eliminated life becomes simple and things can be processed again. If everything can be reduced to the binary states the brain is most comfortable processing, then it can whiz through the decisions. As the decisions are made the clogged up feeling goes and some of the stress can be removed. Racism and intolerance may have their roots in our brains ability to process information and cope with change. Intolerance over things that our intolerance cannot hurt is actually, in a weird way, useful. Say someone was intolerant of Communists in Russia – that simplifies things for them and probably won't hurt the Communists one bit. (I am not justifying racism and intolerance here, its wrong, but it may help to know some of why it arises). The danger is when intolerance is close to home and we apply it to people we know. In third-stage stress breakdown people become totally intolerant of small things such as "If you leave your shaving hairs in the sink I will leave you". I personally know of cases where that has happened. Just a small thing, that was previously tolerated or laughed at, becomes a major drama. Things previously tolerated become unable to be tolerated in third-stage stress breakdown.

Lastly, the person in third-stage stress breakdown may have an apparent change in personality and change their values. They may be unable to resist cult recruiters, they are easily brainwashed, they have sudden changes in beliefs and ideas, and attitudes that required some will or effort to maintain are likely to be abandoned. Some talk of a strange feeling of peace and purity that comes with this process as everything gets radically simplified. There is also a loss of the "law of strength". Normally a slight tap on the knee elicits a slight movement and a large tap on the knee a large movement. The law that a small stimulus generally elicits a small response and a large stimulus a large response is known as "the law of strength" and is a sign of a normal functioning of the nervous system. In third-stage stress breakdown the person ignores the electricity bill and major responsibilities while becoming preoccupied with trivia. When the electricity is cut off nobody in the house can understand why the bill was not paid. All the aspects of the personality change can be attributed to the person avoiding complexity in their life.

The previous section on stress is a summary from the work of Dr. Wilkie. Now let's consider the topic biblical EQ. We have seen that our emotions are linked to our brains ability to do the processing that the mind requires of it. The mind is the key here. It is what is actually telling the brain what it should and should not process. The mind labels the input as important or unimportant, urgent or not urgent. This labeling starts early in life and continues throughout life. Some people develop the anxiety-producing habit of putting "urgent" labels on everything. This is a very stressful habit. Others put the urgent and important labels on things they have no control over. This may be even worse. If the way your mother treats your father is totally important to you, and as a small child you have no control over that, then you will become stressed out, anxious and helpless. Similarly if what the boss thinks of you is important, and you have very little control over that, then work will be stressful for you. If, on the other hand, the quality of your works is important to you, then you can control that. Focusing on your work rather than on people's opinions is less anxiety-producing and stressful and will probably impress the boss as well. Finally, we can put urgent and important labels on totally the wrong things and get into fights over how many angels can fit on the head of a pin. We can totally stress ourselves out with apologetics issues that are of limited importance in real life. It's probably not your job to worry about every one of the 6000 cults on planet Earth and to refute their doctrines one by one. Thus our mind can make it impossible for our brain to work properly. Our mind can give our brain so many tasks to do that it freezes up. The mind can overload the brain. You can ask too much of yourself. In such cases you need to ask yourself the following questions:

1. Am I trying to do too much?
2. Is what I am doing too complicated?
3. Is what I am doing too urgent? Am I trying to do too many things in too short a space of time?
4. Is what I am doing "too important"? Am I telling myself that virtually everything is important?

After honestly answering these questions, I also find it very useful to make a list of all I am trying to do in one column. In a second column I decide whether or not that thing is under my control, God's control or someone else's control. Then in a third column I write down what action I will take on those things where I do have some control. I often find that the thirty or so things that are worrying me can be reduced to about eight concrete steps of action I can take. That eases my mind a great deal.

If the mind can pack the brain too full it can also unpack it. We can learn an emotionally responsible lifestyle where we ignore our egos and the demand to do more, more, more, and settle down to a quiet Christian simplicity that just does what God wants us to do. Paul says, "Make it your ambition, to lead a quiet life" (1 Thessalonians 4:11). That seems a strange use of ambition in the twenty first century. It was probably a strange use of ambition in the first century too. We are to consciously and ambitiously aim at simplicity, quiet living, godliness, and peace. By doing that we will be able to avoid burn-out and establish Christlike and loving emotions.

> That you also aspire to lead a quiet life, to mind your own business, and to work with your own hands, as we commanded you. (1 Thessalonians 4:11 NKJV)

> (Pray) for kings and all who are in authority, that we may lead a quiet and peaceable life in all godliness and reverence. (1 Timothy 2:2 NKJV)

Rather let it be the hidden person of the heart, with the incorruptible beauty of a gentle and quiet spirit, which is very precious in the sight of God. (1 Peter 3:4 NKJV)

Leading a quiet life was Paul's aspiration and prayer and was precious in the sight of God. Rattling around in a stressed out state and living on adrenalin is worldly and foolish and emotionally irresponsible. God can better do the work of the Kingdom with people who live quietly, love deeply and rest in His guidance. Remember Jesus said, "... you will find rest for your souls. For My yoke is easy..." (Matthew 11:29,30). The harried, hurried Christian lifestyle is not spiritual though it may appear so. In 1987 I was on 27 Christian committees and I felt important. And feeling important was about all I achieved! We are important if we do God's will, in God's way, in God's time, at God's pace and live quiet loving lives in all godliness and truth.

Stress can damage us emotionally and spiritually and lead us to make foolish mistakes in ministry. It does not indicate a loss of commitment or a lack of spiritual strength and endurance to adjust your life so that it is quiet and godly. That is God's will for you. My personal test of when I am too busy is when "the fruit of the Spirit start falling off the tree". When patience falls away, when gentleness is not as present as it used to be, when joy is a memory and peace a wished for state, then I know I am too busy.

The thing that finally cured me was when I figured out that nobody really cared how much I produced. But they did care about who I was and how well I treated them. As long as I did something for God that was enough. I didn't have to do much to satisfy them. What they really wanted was to see Christ in me, watch me grow and sense my love and care. You are a fruit tree not a factory and people want to taste the fruit. Fruit trees are quiet and grow best in quiet.

Responsibility for Emotions and Emotional Expression

The September 2001 issue of Readers' Digest chronicles the depression, violence and cruelty that come with the long-term use of "shabu" or methamphetamine. Previously normal people, once addicted, are transformed into cruel monsters that electrocute their wives and kill their children. Drugs and other chemicals can remove inhibitions and make sin much easier to commit. In extreme cases the person becomes pleasure centered and disinhibited and unable to respond to the prodding of natural conscience in any effective way.

At this point they are easily taken over by evil (including demonic influences). Are these people truly responsible for their actions? Can drugs change us so profoundly that we become evil under their influence? When are our emotions "ours"? Can we be held responsible for actions based on our emotions when these emotions are the products of a chemical we have consumed?

This question has obviously got huge legal and spiritual ramifications. Interestingly the Law of Moses had no excuses for drunkenness or other acts of diminished responsibility. It seemed to take the view that you are an adult and are fully aware that alcohol or drugs and can make you become uninhibited and cause you to do foolish things. By choosing to become drunk you are thus choosing to make crime more probable. Therefore, in biblical law, you are responsible for the crime even if you now regret it. Generally, however, most modern law codes make allowances for some forms of diminished responsibility. This is the exercise of legal grace rather than strict justice.

The drug addict is an extreme case of a familiar problem. We all do things "under the influence", things that we do not wish to do. Under the influence of anger we explode, under the influence of lust we commit fornication, under the influence of provocation we start an argument that never subsides. Later we wonder how or why we did such things. All of us are under the influence – of the "flesh". In a similar fashion to the law courts above, God grants us grace as He understands the struggle we have with a fallen body that does not wish to obey His laws (Romans 7).

The Good That I Wish I Do Not Do
Christians are a mixture of Christ-like emotions and evil lusts. While we cannot stop the evil lusts arising within us (because of our fallen nature) we can prevent their controlling us completely. The classic verses on this are Galatians 5:16-18

> I say then: Walk in the Spirit, and you shall not fulfill the lust of the flesh. (17) For the flesh lusts against the Spirit, and the Spirit against the flesh; and these are contrary to one another, so that you do not do the things that you wish. (18) But if you are led by the Spirit, you are not under the law. (Galatians 5:16-18 NKJV)

Christians are capable of victory because of the Holy Spirit within them. They get angry but they do not murder, they may feel strong lust but they walk away from the temptation to commit adultery. The Spirit can bring the flesh under control so that it does not do all that it wants to do. We stop short. God pulls us back from the brink of moral disaster through the work of the Holy Spirit.

This leaves us with two obvious questions that need to be answered. Firstly, what is the nature of the "flesh"? Secondly, "How do non-Christians, without the Holy Spirit, gain any measure of victory over sin?"

The "flesh" is the set of negative impulses that arise from our fallen bodies. Some translations call it the sinful nature but it is not a "nature" as such. It is physical. It is our physical flesh interfering with our quickened spirit and maturing soul. It's what Romans 7 calls "the law of sin in our members".

Some people doubt that our sin nature is physical and is grounded in our mortal bodies. However, it is quite clear that the "flesh nature" will no longer be with us after we die. All sinful impulses will stop when our body dies but while we are in this body we desire to sin. When we leave this body we lose the desire to sin. Therefore the desire to sin is located in the fallen physical body. If you were to kill a born-again Christian and then a few minutes later go to heaven and ask if anything was different about his nature he would say, "All desire to sin is gone, I have left the flesh behind." In heaven we shall neither sin, nor desire to sin.

When sin dwells in the flesh it programs our physical bodies to react wrongly by inappropriately activating physical appetites like food, sex, and comfort and through the corruption of the natural "fight or flight" response. Thus the flesh is sum of the demanding impulses of the body that has been disconnected from reference to God and formed habits and neural pathways inimical to the Spirit. Neural pathways are like tracks through the grass that are worn by much travelling. They connect stimulus with response and sometimes with the wrong response.

I will illustrate with a brief incident in my own life. Prior to my conversion I was quick-tempered and would pick fights. Afterwards I left this behind. Many years later some friends decided to "ambush" me for fun. In a split second I had my fists up before my thinking intervened and then I put them down. The reaction programmed into me by sin was still there in my neural pathways and as activated by my previously well-learned response to "fight-or-flight" situations.

The apostle John says that which is "born of God" cannot sin, nor does it desire to do so (1 John 3:9-11). That part of us that is born of God, that is Christ in us, has no desire to sin. However, that which is, in the words of the gospels, "born of woman" does sin. The flesh, born of human genetics inherits the Fall. The "new man" part of the born-again Christian is born of heaven, born of the will of God, born from above and does not inherit the Fall. The "new man" is born of God, free from sin and even free from the desire to sin. Paul says this new nature is "enslaved to righteousness". Thus Christians are a mixture of the Fallen which is born of human genetics and the Eternal which is born of God.

The Decent But Natural Man

How then can non-Christians lead decent lives as many of then do? Through the law of God written in their consciences by the common and prevenient grace of God and activated by their will. God places some restraint on human evil through various checks and balances including government, the human conscience, the Law, religious teachings and examples, and even though direct communication through dreams and visions, signs and portents, such as Abimelech had when he was warned in a dream not to touch Abraham's wife, Sarah (Genesis 20:3-7). The non-Christian is given much assistance by God to restrain evil but they do not have the ultimate assistance of the indwelling Holy Spirit. The natural man has a conscience from God but is not yet born of God. He can restrain sin to some extent but cannot be truly holy as he lacks Christ in him.

The Mind, the Spirit and the Flesh

How then can a Christian have victory over the evil passions that arise within? This is accomplished by setting the inner nature, the mind, on the Spirit:

> For what the law could not do in that it was weak through the flesh, God did by sending His own Son in the likeness of sinful flesh, on account of sin: He condemned sin in the flesh, (4) that the righteous requirement of the law might be fulfilled in us who do not walk according to the flesh but according to the Spirit. (5) For those who live according to the flesh set their minds on the things of the flesh, but those who live according to the Spirit, the things of the Spirit. (6) For to be carnally minded is death, but to be spiritually minded is life and

peace. (7) Because the carnal mind is enmity against God; for it is not subject to the law of God, nor indeed can be. (8) So then, those who are in the flesh cannot please God. (Romans 8:3-8 NKJV)

After the tussle between flesh and spirit in Romans 7, Paul then presents the secret of life and peace in chapter 8. The mind, which can be renewed (Romans 12:1,2) can be set on the things of the Spirit and bring life and peace. If it is set on the churning and burning desires of the flesh then there is trouble leading to death. We can choose where to set our consciousness, what to meditate on, what to think about. We are not forced to dwell on sin and negativity. Rather we can seek those things which are above (Colossians 3:1-4) and contemplate that which is beautiful, spiritual, noble and true (Philippians 4:8).

This training of our consciousness is vitally important. Napoleon Hill puts this well from a secular perspective when he talks of "Your inalienable right to the full and complete control and direction of your own mind to whatever ends you desire." He goes on to say: "Our mind is the only thing we can control. Either we control it, or we relinquish control to other forces, and our minds and our wills become as chips in a puddle of water, being swept one way then another, and never coming to any satisfactory conclusions, easily falling prey to any negative wind that blows."

For the Christian we need to learn we have control of our minds and to forcibly direct them to the ends we desire, such as eternal life and peace. If we want a victorious Christian life we must take charge of our minds and they must deliberately be directed on the things of the Spirit. The next chapter will look at this in some detail.

Don't Forget the Medical Side and Common Sense

Not all emotional problems based in the body have a "spiritual solution". Exercise, regular rest, a good diet and some basic disciplines can help alter our moods and emotions so we are happier and more easily spiritual. There is nothing terribly noble about praying for victory over emotions that need not arise in us at all with a bit of common sense. If you feel chronically out of sorts get a good "executive physical". Maybe there is something wrong and your body is warning you. If a distressing emotion is being produced by a physical factor we can change, then it is up to us to change it. If your medication is literally "driving you crazy" see if it can be altered. If your air conditioning system makes you grumpy – see what can be done about it or install a fan. If a high level of caffeine is making you tense and anxious, praying for peace may be less effective than changing to decaf or lessening your intake. In short – don't forget to see a doctor and use your common sense and take care of your health to keep you happy in body and soul.

Other Matters In The Mind-Body-Emotions Interaction
There are many very interesting and even speculative areas of study on the area of the issue of the interaction of our mind, body and emotions. For instance:

- **Feats of Strength:** Emotions can not only make you sick – they can also make you strong. Hormones released by emotions can strengthen the body to perform great feats of strength on desperate occasions. This is the positive side of the emotions-body interaction.

- **Dissociation From the Body:** This is when people experience a separation between their consciousness and their physical body generally as a result of severe trauma. Some people report out-of-body experiences where the mind seems to leave the body through dissociation and then return. Paul could say of his trip to heaven "whether in the body or out of the body I do not know" (2 Corinthians 12:2,3). There is also a clinical condition known as Multiple Personality Disorder or Dissociative Disorder where people have multiple consciousnesses in one body, which seem to "take turns". This seems to be the result of the person's consciousness being fragmented by trauma.

- **Amnesia:** This is physical damage that results in a loss of recent memory and in severe cases an inaccurate sense of "self". Severe amnesiacs seem to be locked into the maturity level that they have the last lucid memories of so that a 45 year old amnesiac may remember nothing after he was 17 and still think he is 17 and dress and act culturally much like a 17 year old. The physical structure and memory storage that the mind needs to interact with surrounding culture has been damaged and an inaccurate sense of self results. This shows that our cultural self-consciousness relies on data from the outside world such as time, age, and fashion. When this is disrupted our cultural identity is damaged.

- **Emotions and Cognition:** Emotions release hormones which affect cognition. For instance, in the "fight-or-flight" response blood flow to the brain is reduced and instead it is sent to the hands or the feet. This prepares us well for a good battle but poorly for an exam (where the blood flow needs to be going to the brain). Habitual aggressive or panicky emotions invoke this response which then reduces cognitive ability. Tests on emotionally troubled youth found them under performing on academic tests while better-adjusted and calmer people did much better. This is no surprise to teachers who have observed this for years. Thus emotions affect cognition by affecting the physical structures the brain needs to do its clearest thinking. The mind does not seem able to express itself clearly and efficiently through the body if the emotions have hijacked the resources it needs to do so.

- **Prayer and Meditation:** Goleman reports that "prayer works on all emotions". Numerous studies show the calming effects on the body of prayer and even New Age authors such as Paul Wilson acknowledge that prayer is puzzlingly powerful in achieving states of calm. The physiological effects of a mind focused on God are clear, unequivocal and measurable by modern instrumentation. The mind can bring the body into a calm sate with lowered blood pressure and peaceful emotions.

All these puzzling things contribute to the awe and mystery surrounding how our mind and body interact and how our emotions are produced and coped with.

Conclusion
There is a complex interaction between our bodies and our emotions such that our health can affect our feelings, and our feelings can affect our health. Emotions are produced primarily in the soul and spirit but have very strong interactions with the body. The mind and body are separate but very inter-connected entities. Stress is what happens when our mind overloads our brain and asks too much of us. A quiet and godly lifestyle can prevent stress and assist our sanctification. The body presents the Christian with problems since the Fall. Since the Fall the body has been corrupted by sin and this corrupt physical state is known as "the flesh". The flesh leads to sinful

impulses and negative emotions, is weak, mortal and temporary and we will be rid of it at death. The flesh and the Spirit are at war. Our mind is ours to focus and control and our consciousness is the decisive factor in many spiritual issues and can be focused on the Spirit or on the flesh. Christ-like emotions will flow when the mind is focused on the Spirit. Destructive out-of-control emotions will overpower us if the mind is focused on the flesh. Emotional and spiritual victory depends on having Christ in us, the hope of glory, and in choosing to focus our consciousness on the things of the Spirit. This results in a constructive emotional state known as "life and peace". We should also take care of our health and consult good medical advice. We should also acknowledge that there is much mystery here and much we do not know. The next chapter will focus on how the mind is the secret to personal mastery.

Discussion Questions

1. How does the body influence emotions, and emotions influence the body? How can good medical advice help us with apparently "spiritual" emotional problems?

2. What is "the flesh" and how does it affect the Christian? How does the Spirit control the flesh? What is the role of the mind in all this?

3. What is the difference between your mind and your brain? Are you just a bundle of chemicals?

4. What is stress? What are the three stages of stress breakdown? How can we unload things that stress us? Why is living a quiet and godly lifestyle important?

5. To what degree are you responsible for your actions, even under the influence of drugs or alcohol?

6. How can non-Christians restrain sin and the flesh?

7. What do you think about some of the mysterious areas of the interaction between our emotions, our minds and our bodies?

PART THREE

PRACTICAL APPLICATIONS FOR EMOTIONAL SELF-MASTERY AND EXPRESSION

Finally, we reach the practical section where we look at techniques of how we experience and master emotions and how we act on and react to our emotions. We will learn how to read and understand the emotions of others and ourselves and how to express them appropriately in love. Theologically this section sees Christ in us trying to express His love for the world through us, and in part, through our emotions. Jesus in us, and speaking through us, has His sense of timing, His right phrasing, His poise and presence and His holy and righteous way of being. In the end we should be radiating love, joy and peace because Jesus radiates these things. We should become people with a presence about them who have the deep authority and majestic emotions of the God who indwells us. To do this we need both the theological and the practical. We need to be aware of Christ in us, but we also need to know what to do in any given situation. "Love one another" is not good enough for most people. We also need to know how to love one another and this involves practical information and techniques. We need to know how to switch off our anger, how to help someone who is grieving, how to get a handle on our emotions and how to figure out what someone else is feeling. All of these areas are covered in this section. We also need to know how to let God's love flow through us in spiritual power and that is the subject of the last chapter.

The Masterful Mind

That the righteous requirement of the law might be fulfilled in us who do not walk according to the flesh but according to the Spirit. {5} For those who live according to the flesh set their minds on the things of the flesh, but those who live according to the Spirit, the things of the Spirit. {6} For to be carnally minded is death, but to be spiritually minded is life and peace. (Romans 8:4-6 NKJV)

The decisive factor in Biblical EQ is the mind of the believer. If it is set on the flesh and we are carnally minded the result is death. If it is set on the Spirit and we are spiritually minded the result is life and peace. Chapter after chapter in this book has demonstrated the truth of those two statements in Romans.

The previous chapters have laid the ground-work showing how our emotions flow from our perceptions and our beliefs and how they are affected by our physiological state. This chapter looks at the decisive act of setting our mind on things above, on the things of the Spirit, on mastery of our life and our emotions. Through the mind we gain mastery. This chapter is about experiencing that mastery.

Fight, Flight or Mastery

You may have heard of the "fight-or-flight" response that humans and animals have in response to threat. It does not take high level thinking to engage in the fight-or-flight response. Even the most unthinking of creatures such as an ant can make the decision whether to avoid an intruder or whether to stand their ground and fight. The fight-or-flight response is fast, rough, instinctual, and sometimes quite inaccurate. Mostly it is a useful instinctive response with high survival value, but it is not the stuff of wisdom, ethics, or the Spirit. Under the rush of the adrenalin that the fight-or-flight response releases people can quickly perform great feats of strength; they can also behave absolutely stupidly, because adrenalin signals the body to send blood away from the brain where it is needed for thinking and send it instead to the muscles, where it is needed for running and fighting. When people combine these two aspects of the fight-or-flight response and quickly perform great feats of strength which are stupid, unthinking and ill-informed they have the groundwork for violence and tragedy. When societies give in to their instinctive fight-or-flight responses we see factions, disputes, wars and vendettas breaking out. Survival may seem to depend on the fight-or-flight response but true civilization depends on taming it and mastering it.

Why is the fight-or-flight response so destructive and if so why do we have it? I suppose initially it was not a bad thing. The fight-or-flight response was meant to operate in a human being who was connected to God. This connection would have moderated and altered the response. But now it isn't so well connected and it's become one part of us that has been most affected by the Fall. Cain was the first person in Scripture who was faced with the task of managing murderous rage (Genesis 4:7) and he chose to fight instead. His descendant Lamech boasted of murder (Genesis 4:23,24) and by the time of the Flood his descendants had "filled the earth with violence" (Genesis 6:11). Trusting fallen human beings to choose self-mastery rather than fight-or-flight was a total failure. Eventually Moses came along with the Law, which pointed the way to what was right and wrong and gave very reasonable and agreeable limits for human conduct. The Law also failed. Finally, God sent His Son and the laws of God were written on our hearts through the Holy Spirit (Hebrews 10:16) that we might become spiritual overcomers (Revelation 21:7). This has worked but even so it has been no easy task. Only re-establishing the connection with God has brought any measure of control to the fight-or flight response.

The problem with the fight-or-flight response in fallen humanity is that it eliminates choice and when you eliminate choice you eliminate all sorts of things like freedom, morality, love and decency. When the fight-or-flight response occurs blood flows to the hands and feet and away from the brain. Huge amounts of adrenalin and other hormones take over and the fast action control centers of the brain come into play. Suddenly you are exploding at people, or running, or fighting. In common parlance your "buttons have been pressed" and you are just reacting at an entirely visceral and instinctual level. This is not a bad thing when you are running away from a charging rhinoceros. Speedy reactions may be a very good thing. However, in modern life the provocation that sets off the response may be a cutting remark or a threat to our ego in the office. The feeling of threat is enough to set off the entire chemical cascade that is known as the fight-or-flight response. Road rage involves people reacting to rudeness as if it were the proverbial charging rhinoceros. A minor incident becomes a matter of life and death. The perception of threat and the impact of adrenalin cause us to react without choosing our reactions. Startled people have accidentally shot their family members thinking they were burglars and soldiers have fired on their own troops through the sheer speed and inaccuracy of this response. You cannot be Christlike and filled with rage and gut-level fight-or-flight responses. Neither can you be a timid, always retreating wimp soaring into anxiety attacks like a frightened bird at every alarming news item which is one effect of the "flight" side of the response in modern life. The fight-or-flight response removes our ability to make wise, free and balanced moral choices and is definitely not the stuff on which Christian character is built.

Conversely, it's not wrong to fight under some circumstances if it is a chosen and wise moral act. At other times it's OK to retreat and avoid certain troublesome situations as long as it is thought through, wise and moral to do so. The great biblical warriors like King David fought battles and won victories but they did so out of deep character not out of flash-pan rage. The military heroes of Scripture like Gideon, David and Jehosophat were people of mercy and thought and heart and balance. They were not just big bundles of anger walking around looking for a fight and they were not governed by the fight-or-flight response.

Mastery
The alternative to the "fight-or-flight" response is to achieve mastery of the situation. Jesus always demonstrated mastery and every situation with which He was presented. He neither fought the soldiers who arrested Him nor fled from them but rather throughout His entire trial demonstrated an amazing degree of personal mastery. At no point in His life did Jesus give in to the adrenalin-filled panic of a fight-or-flight response. He could have gathered an army but He did not. Perhaps He could have fled hostile Israel and gone to Greece and been welcomed as a philosopher, but He did not. There were times when He avoided Jerusalem because of the hostility and because His time was not yet come; yet at no point did He react from instinct alone.

His actions were masterful, strong, wise and spiritual. His Spirit-filled mind had total mastery over His flesh and His instincts. This gave Him power, poise, and personal authority that seems to have been the main aspect of His personality that people admired and is frequently commented on in the gospels. The following verses are just some that show how other people saw Jesus as having authority and how

Jesus saw His own authority being used to master situations.
(Matthew 7:29; 8:9; 21:23-27; 28:18-20; Mark 1:27; Luke 4:32; Luke 9:1;
10;19; John 5:27; 7:17; 12:49; 14:10; 16:13; 17:2)

Jesus was not thrown even by encountering the devil in person.
During the temptation in the wilderness Jesus met the devil in a face-
to-face spiritual encounter that must have been of incredible
intensity. The devil was out to destroy Jesus, he was malice incarnate,
and he was beguiling, tempting, and trying to push Jesus into a
wrong response. Jesus neither fled nor fought. Jesus mastered the
situation, resisted the temptations and used His authority to deal with
the problem. Jesus did not flee. He mastered the temptation to avoid
the encounter and thus preserve Himself from possible spiritual harm.
He faced the dangers of the devil at full force. He stood His ground
against pure evil. Jesus did not fight. He did not launch into an
aggressive tirade against Satan. There was no raw and red-necked
stream of spiritual vitriol directed against the devil. Instead Jesus
defeated Satan through the calm use of God's authority based on
God's Word. Jesus mastered the situation.

The biblical example of Jesus in the wilderness shows that even if we
think a situation is utterly evil and threatens our health, identity and
success (as the wilderness temptations did for Jesus) we do not need
to get upset and become reactionary nor do we need to run. We just
need to calmly and authoritatively expose that situation to the truth
of Scripture and the authority of God. We want to end up moving
through life as Jesus moved through Israel, and cope with our
pressures and threats as he coped with His.

Mastery is not sinless perfection. Mastery is more like a combination
of faith, courage, decisiveness and balance. It is having spiritual
authority, poise and power in all situations. It asks questions such as:
How can we master every threat and every frustration with grace,
power and poise? How can we move through a grossly unjust trial
without losing our cool? How can we forgive those that nail us to the
cross? Of course, these reactions are the supreme achievements of a
Perfect Life. They are what made Jesus the spotless Lamb of God.
While we may not always achieve them we can aspire to them and
discipline our minds toward them.

Let's consider my attempts at playing golf. As an under-funded missionary I do not own golf clubs or have a golf membership but once every few years I am dragged out onto a golf course by a friend. When the ball lands in the rough, as it often does, I have three possible responses – fight, flight or mastery. I can become depressed at the difficulty, give up on the shot and pay the penalty – that is the flight response. I can hit wildly with all my might and try and blast it out of there – that is the fight response. I can call up my considerable golf prowess, concentrate carefully, keep my eye on the ball, visualize the wonderful trajectory it will take and get it out of there with just the right touch – this is the mastery response. As you may well guess, it is the most difficult response and the hardest to perfect. I rarely get it right, but it is the one I wish to practice and reinforce. The other two responses just lead to failure. Mastery is the hardest choice but it is the only choice that leads to success.

The Mind

I need to spend a few paragraphs defining what I mean by "mind". By the Mind I do not mean various individual thoughts or mind as intellectual activity or a set of intellectual abstractions. I mean mind as the entire mental framework of the person. We use the word mind this way in the phrases "single-minded" or "open-minded". Mind in this sense is an inner state of consciousness that has certain properties. The mind is controllable and can be focused by the believer. Paul asks us to set our mind on various things such as the Spirit, things above, and the pursuit of maturity; so the mind is something we can focus on God. For those of you who enjoy Greek the phren word family phroneo, phronema and phronesis , phronimos is in view here. Thus the mind is that part of our total consciousness and awareness that we have some control over. In this definition it does not include dreams or the subconscious. The subconscious is part of our mind in a larger sense but not part of it in this narrow sense we are using it here because we have no real control over the subconscious and cannot discipline it or focus it. Neither is mind in this sense the scattered thoughts that drift in and out of a person who is daydreaming or watching TV. Of such people we sometimes say, "their mind was switched off when they watched the movie". Their inner consciousness was inactive. Thus the mind is what thinks when you do some real thinking. The mind is where you receive and mull over wisdom and where you make real choices about your actions. That's your mind. It is that part of your consciousness that you can control and exert and which bears a close relationship to the "real you".

Throughout this book I will continue to emphasize that the mind is the only part of our consciousness that we can control, and therefore it is of vital importance. I do not mean to imply that we are all mind by doing this or that the mind is superior, it is part of an integrated whole which it directs. The mind is like the wheel on a ship's bridge that controls the rudder. The navigator plots the course and then the wheel is turned to a definite bearing and the ship holds that course. The course of the entire ship is determined by where the captain sets the wheel. The wheel is the only part of the ship that can be focused on a direction or course of action. The engine will drive the ship anywhere, the cargo hold does its job, the air-conditioning makes it bearable but the wheel, connected to the rudder sets the entire direction and destiny and decides which port the ship will go to or even if it will be shipwrecked through carelessness. The mind is that part of us with which we steer and plot our course. It's the only part of us that can do that job. Therefore it is decisive.

We need to love God with our whole being; mind, spirit, soul, and strength. All these parts of us are vital and important but it is the mind that directs the spirit, soul, or energy and strength onto God and His purposes. The mind is the critical point where the decisions are made and the course committed to.

The mind in the sense of the *phren* word family generally means the wisdom and understanding especially of the righteous (Luke 1:17, Ephesians 1:8). This mind can be set on various things. When Jesus rebuked Peter he said he was "not mindful of the things of God, but the things of men" (Matthew 16:23; Mark 8:33). The legalistic Romans nit-picking about food and drink were literally "rules-minded" in the Greek (Romans 14:6). The mind can be set on the flesh or the Spirit (Romans 8:5,6) and things above (Colossians 3:2) or on earthly things (Philippians 2:19), which caused Paul to weep. Due to the renewing and infilling of the Holy Spirit we can even have "the mind of Christ" (1 Corinthians 2:14-16) and when we are humble servants we have a mind like Christ's (Philippians 2:5). On the other hand we can have a childish mind (1 Corinthians 13:11; 14:20) Unity of mind is important and Christians are to be one-minded and like-minded (Romans 12:16; 15:5; 2 Corinthians 13:11). This word family can also mean the careful, prudent mind, that which thinks of others, the mindful and thoughtful person (Philippians 1:7; 4:10) though the word "mind" is rarely used in English translations of this aspect.

Thus it is clear from the New Testament that the sort of mind we end up with is entirely our choice. We can focus our mind on God's interests or man's interests, the Spirit or the flesh, the things above or earthly things. We can choose to be humble, like-minded, unified and thoughtful of others or we can choose to be puffed up, childish, contentious, worldly and carnal.

Mastery and the Mind

Mastery is a product of the focused and disciplined mind bringing the whole person into submission to an over-riding ethic or ethos. Throughout history everyone from Zen monks to Spartan warriors and corporate traders have discovered this. People have become masterful human beings by disciplining themselves in all sorts of pursuits from archery to fencing to philosophy. That is why competitive sports, while trivial in themselves, have shaped many a person for the better. The somersaults of a champion gymnast are in themselves quite pointless. They don't feed the hungry or make any great philosophical point. It's not doing somersaults that makes the gymnast great but their discipline. The sport builds mastery and mental strength into the gymnast so that when the days of gymnastics are over the character remains. Another point, the focus must be external to self. The gymnast does not find self-mastery by focusing on self-mastery. He or she finds self-mastery by focusing on somersaults.

The mind is the only part of our consciousness that we can focus and direct therefore it is the only part of us that can give us mastery. A million dollars will not give you personal mastery. People who win the lottery often end up poor because of their lack of personal mastery. The money has not made them masterful. A strong body will not give you mastery except of certain physical skills. Athletes can be enslaved to alcohol or drugs. Education will not give you personal mastery; there are many well educated people who are small-minded and weak-willed. Willpower won't give you mastery as the will can simply become stubborn and inflexible, unable to adapt to changing situations and thus lead to inevitable defeat. Even religion won't give you mastery. Many people are enslaved by cults, caught up in bondage to religious guilt or overtaken by idolatry and superstition. Only the adaptable, flexible, trained, focused and disciplined mind can bring mastery.

Please be clear about this, I am not advocating mentalist philosophies, mind science, Christian Science, or think and grow rich kinds of mental mastery. They are half-truths. The mind is not a terribly significant force in itself. The mind does not have the ability to create heaven or hell as Blake thought. God creates heaven and hell. Reality is His creation, not ours. The mind does not create the world but it does enable us to move through it with poise and power. The mind is not God. The mind works best when it is set on God. In biblical terms personal and emotional mastery is a product of the mind set on God and imbued with His Word and authority. The unaided mind operating by itself cannot produce mastery of the kind we see in the life of Jesus Christ. For that kind of mastery we need more than positive thinking. We need a direct connection to God and the mind must be resolutely set on God, on the Spirit, on things above, on the Kingdom, and the righteousness thereof.

Directing the Christian Mind

So we see that we are faced with three universal truths: Firstly, that personal mastery is the only wise option. Secondly, that such mastery is solely a product of the mind. Thirdly, that the mind becomes masterful as it is disciplined and focused on something outside itself. This book maintains that the highest degree of mastery can only be attained when the "something outside itself" is God. You can achieve a sense of mastery by focusing your mind on fencing or gymnastics or horse-riding but you won't end up like Jesus just by focusing on those things. The mind must be directed onto Christ. That is its proper place.

This directing of the mind is a forceful and decisive activity. It is hard to put into words. It is not concentrating on Christ, neither is it speculating about Christ or studying or daydreaming about Christ. It is not even thinking about Jesus as such. It is not an internal, reflective or meditative process. It's similar to standing outside yourself and directing yourself onto Christ. It's like standing at the top of a high-dive tower and looking down and plunging in with total commitment. It's choosing where your life energies will be focused and your mental processes directed. It's like going outside yourself but towards Christ at the same time. I suppose you could call it faith, or at least faith is very much involved in it. I am stuck for an analogy. It's a little like those missiles that lock onto their target or a cat focused on a mouse. The whole of the mind is fixed on Christ and directs the total life energies of the believer in that direction. As this focus is attained everything else is entrained; the emotions, the will and the responses.

Just as someone absorbed in a video game entrains all their concentration, emotions and will into the game so a Christian absorbed in Christ, with their mind set on the Spirit, inevitably brings their whole life into conformity with Jesus.

It may not be immediately obvious but when we direct our mind to a purpose it means that we commit ourselves to the rules and techniques that the particular purpose requires. For instance, in writing this book I must follow the rules of the English language. I am hardly conscious of that because I have internalized many of the rules. Now and then the spell check or grammar check on this computer alerts me to where I am going wrong, then I correct it. That is part of writing, part of the project, and part of being focused on writing a book. Following the rules of English grammar is not bad or awful. It's not a restriction on my freedom or a legalism or a lack of grace. It's just required. Mastery of anything means sticking to the rules. Similarly, following Jesus has rules. Submission to the commandments of Jesus Christ is not optional if we are to stay focused on Christ and know life and peace. Obeying these commandments is not the whole of the Christian life but they are part of the discipline of the Christian life. They make it flow and if you are to have mastery in the Christian life you must decide to obey the rules. You cannot just make up the spiritual life as you go along any more than you can decide to reinvent English grammar every time you write.

Deciding to totally set your mind on Christ and achieve total life mastery is the very hardest thing you will ever do. But what are the alternatives? To potter along lamely is not much of a life. To refuse it totally is to go into eternal darkness. But the effort seems tremendous, the focus too narrow and the rules too hard. The focus must be kept or we are unruly. We are prone to distraction. We are far too easy on ourselves. We don't want to get up and practice. We want heaven from our armchairs. So we make a commitment to Christ, then that fades, then another one, then a spiritual breakthrough, and then a slack patch. We are all over the place. Our minds are set on ourselves, or on our finances, or on the opinions of the Christian community or on the success of our ministry. We find easier goals and substitute foci. We become anxious, stressed, harried and spiritually weak. We need to come to a point of final decision where we look at the mess, pull ourselves together and decide with all that is within us to focus ourselves totally on Christ alone and pursue single-minded, focused, disciplined mastery.

People are drifting around in ministry without a real and solid connection to God because the cost of staking everything on Him is too high. You must come to that decision. The Christian life is unlivable without it. You cannot dabble in the eternal. You must commit totally to it and direct your mind to it.

Prerequisites for Self-Mastery
The absolute prerequisites of spiritual progress are that you are born-again with a new nature from God, that you have the filling of the Holy Spirit and that you are single-mindedly devoted to God in obedience to His word. Without these three things you do not stand a chance.

Unless you are born-again you do not have a new nature. Without the new nature it's an impossible job. If you are not Spirit-filled and led by the Spirit in your daily life then you will not have power over the flesh (see Galatians 5:16-18) and you will struggle continually and lose continually. If you are not single-minded you will be double-minded and double-minded people receive nothing from the Lord (James 1:5-8). You will be left wallowing in your doubt and indecision. These three things are the basics. Before you can successfully apply the techniques in self-mastery you must have these three things in your life.

Practical Techniques for Emotional Self-Mastery
It's fine to talk about the need for a personal relationship with God and having one's mind set on things above but how will that keep someone from exploding the next time someone cuts them off on the highway? What are the practical tips for mastering our "fight-or-flight" response and for mastering life?

There are thus two levels to emotional self-mastery. Firstly, we must set up the foundations of the new self and the God-focused mind. That renews our connection with God and sets up some spiritual lines of control over the fight-or-flight response. Then we must learn the practical details of responding to life intelligently and wisely.

- Pay attention to your physical state. If you realize that your fists are clenched and your neck is rigid and you are physically tensed up and alerted for danger then try to undo those physical states. Unclench your fists, rub your neck, relax your posture. The fight-or-flight response is partly a physical response and as we undo its physical correlates it will lose much of its power. Perhaps try to relax or use deep breathing if you are tense, guarded or explosive.

- Be aware of the magnitude of your emotional responses and the quick "zoom" to anger or anxiety that the fight-or-flight response produces. Learn to recognize when you are zooming to disaster and practice keeping a lid on it.
- Take time to think. Use your God-given right to choose your response. Do not just respond on auto-pilot. Once you stop and think you are far more likely to choose a good and much more optimal solution.
- Disengage. If you have started to move into attack mode pull back the troops! Go for a walk, cool down. Pray about it.
- If you are going into a situation that you know aggravates you (such as dealing with an annoying person) try to make a conscious decision about how you are going to respond in that situation. Then rehearse your balanced and biblical reaction over and over in your mind. Perhaps seven times or seventy times seven? (see Matthew 18) Train yourself mentally to respond rightly just like professional golfers 'see the ball going in the hole' even before they make the shot. Use mental rehearsal to disarm potential conflict situations.
- In the converse of this – don't mentally rehearse the wrong response. Don't see in your mind's eye a picture of yourself strangling the boss of the phone company. It may be very satisfying but it is not helpful. It is educating yourself in the wrong direction.
- Use the "what would Jesus do?" question as a quick reference.
- Question your perceptions of threat. Is this really a life or death issue? Am I getting tensed up over nothing? What does it say about me if I am so easily riled? On the flight response: Is it really that bad? Is the world going to end over this? Is this fear, anxiety and emotional reactivity helping me? Has running away from things helped or hindered my life?
- Learn to find your emotional center and to live from it and to know when it is in balance and out of balance. This is quite difficult for many people.
- Some people will push you wanting you to explode so they

can take advantage of your immature reaction. Be alert to this and deliberately respond the opposite way they are pushing you (1 Corinthians 4:12). For instance, when they revile you, greet them with a blessing. Christ who, when He was reviled, did not revile in return; when He suffered, He did not threaten, but committed Himself to Him who judges righteously (1 Peter 2:23).

- Remember that when you react rightly to unjust treatment that "great is your reward in heaven". So rejoice and give yourself a pat on the back when you keep your cool. Positive reinforcement for good behavior. (Matthew 5:11)
- Do not return evil for evil (Romans 12:17). Leave retaliation to the Lord (Romans 12:19). If we return a blessing instead we will inherit blessing (1 Peter 3:9).
- If people rip you off and insult you don't escalate it into a life or death struggle over honor and pride. This is what Jesus means when He says "do not resist him who is evil". (He does not mean that the police should not arrest robbers!) Rather it means "don't let the evil person push you into a full-scale, adrenalin-packed, fight-or-flight response". Deny the natural man's urge to strike back. If he slaps you, turn the other cheek, if he takes your cloak, let him, if he makes you walk a mile, go two. If he says "give me money" let him have some (Matthew 5:38-42). Deny your reactivity and show you are made of different stuff.
- Don't let unkind, ungrateful, stingy, mean, or small-minded people get to you. God is merciful to the unkind and ungrateful and we have a great reward in heaven when we do likewise (Luke 6:35). Brush their meanness to one side without taking it too personally and treat them as well as you can with reasonable safety (because some are quite toxic).
- Do not get your ego hooked into the game of "Christian comparisons" such as my church is bigger than your church. This only leads to fuming and fighting.
- Do not let theology push you into the fight-or-flight mode. For instance, "I won't study the Second Coming it's too contentious" (flight response) or "You are a heretic and I will torch you verbally since the law won't allow me to burn you at the stake" (fight response). The mastery response is to learn about the Second Coming and other aspects of theology and

grow in God and only debate under circumstances that are harmless to the hearers (such as with good friends in the ministry) unless, of course, there is an urgent apologetic reason. Even then your speech should be seasoned with salt.

- Learn correct responses by modeling mature Christians and by studying the heroes of the faith.
- Make a personal commitment to grow in this area.
- Have some friends keep you accountable for your reactions and encourage you to maturity.
- Enjoy the feeling of grace rather than the feeling of explosive emotional power.

Overcoming Paralyzing Fears

The flight part of the fight-or-flight response has not received a lot of attention so far. It's not as dramatic and many people simply dismiss it as weakness or nerves. When it blossoms into full-fledge agoraphobia people disconnect from life for fear of having a panic attack in public. Fear can create a state of life that is almost unbearable. The person becomes over-reactive, nervous, withdrawn and anxious and may be filled with phobias and obsessions. Dr. Claire Weekes has done some wonderful and compassionate work on this and every pastor should read her books which are listed under "agoraphoba" in the reference section at the back. Below I will briefly summarize my understanding of the central points of her work.

Life circumstances cause the person to reach, at some point in their life, a point of nervous exhaustion in which fear that already exists cannot be suppressed or controlled by the will and during which new fears can be easily implanted. (See the section on stress in the previous chapter)

Strange frightening thoughts then appear in a tired mind. The person worries about these thoughts. This further activates the fight-or-flight response and exhausts the person and so they have even less energy to control their fears. More fears then surface, the person then worries, and so on in a vicious circle. The strange thoughts in the tired mind eventually reach such an intensity that they lead the person to the threshold of panic. A small incident then triggers a full-scale panic attack which may become the first of many if this spiral continues.

Mastering such fear means moving away from the fight-or-flight response. Instead of trying to fight the fears or run away from them they are just accepted. This position of not fighting and not running away disengages the fight-or-flight response, lowers the adrenalin levels and helps the person think. They are encouraged to go slowly because the need to "hurry" or take action activates the fight-or flight-response. They are encouraged to rest, eat properly and recover strength and get over their prior depletion. This enables them to get some perspective on their fears. They are told that the only way to deal with fear is going through it and her famous phrase "even jelly legs will get you there" has helped many agoraphobics. Of great importance is floating through experiences. The problem with fearful people is they engage life too tightly. When you grab life too tightly it bounces you around and you end up either struggling with it or fleeing from it. A bit of detachment can lead to peace of mind and Claire Weekes teaches "floating through" normally traumatic experiences such as shopping in a large mall. The person floats through the shop door, floats around the store, floats up to the counter, floats out the money and pays for the goods and floats out again. The person is slightly detached but not dissociated from reality and is able to do the task that was impossible before. Dr. Weekes has reduced a whole lot of complex medicine to four short phrases that are of great help to those who have panic attacks - and to the rest of us as well!

1. Face; do not run away.
2. Accept; do not fight.
3. Float; do not tense.
4. Let time pass; do not be impatient with time.

Hints on working these out in your life are contained in her excellent books which are listed in the reference section of this book. Mastery of fear means setting the mind in the right stable position. We set it into the situation but without fighting it. We are calm. We are like Tiger Woods looking at a golf ball in the rough. It's no big deal, small problem, he can handle it. Neither are we tense. Some people believe that being tense is being responsible; being tense means you are putting the effort in. That is a mistake; being tense ruins the golf shot and also ruins life. Jesus was not a tense person and Jesus was the most responsible and committed person who ever lived. And mastery means letting time pass. Jesus never seemed to care about time. Abraham and Moses took years, seemingly wasted years. By letting time pass we actually use it best. The people who look the most hurried and who have the most time-consciousness with their organizers are generally the junior executives. The members of the board seem unhurried–thoughtful, careful, responsible and wise, but unhurried. There is a lot of spiritual wisdom for anxious people in the four phrases above. As an exercise, think of Jesus in the Garden of Gethsemane and during His trial using the four concepts above – facing, accepting, floating and letting time pass. Before I leave the topic of fear I want to deal with a peculiarly Christian form of fear – reacting to new and powerful spiritual experiences.

Reacting to New and Powerful Spiritual Experiences
New and powerful spiritual experiences often activate the fight-or-flight response. The result is over-reaction, division, fear and anxiety. I hope you can see that there is no place for angry, reactionary responses or panic stricken flight from strong emotions or unusual spiritual experiences. Flapping around wildly is not the correct response. Rather we need to analyze that emotion or experience in the light of Scripture, holding to what is good and rebuking that which is evil. Discernment is a mastery response not a fight-or-flight response.

Because we are creatures and not the Creator we have a certain inbuilt dread and fear of the numinous. The old writers talk of "the dread of God". The powerful and the spiritual evoke emotional reactions within us and those reactions are often immature. We become reactive and fearful unable to cope with emotions and experiences that are unfamiliar to us. Instead, when evaluating a new teaching or experience we should say, "I'm a mature person with a good brain and I know the Scripture fairly well, I'll just sit back and watch, I'll hold to the good bits I find here and reject the junk, I don't have to fear what's going on. I'll pray for protection and discernment, stay within my boundaries and work it out as I go along."

We need to accept that we are complex creatures with complex emotions in a complex world created by a God far beyond our comprehension and that sometimes we will encounter things that rattle and disturb us. We need to accept the experience "as is" then evaluate it in the light of Scripture, holding to the good and discarding what is of evil.

Avoiding a black and white stance where it's got to be "all of God" or "all of the devil" is important. People who take black and white stances lump people into one category or the other; thus they have very blunted discernment. This leads often to damaging evaluations and serious mistakes in judgment. Jesus never named an opponent or launched a personal attack against an individual. Rather in every debate He found the good (*do what the Pharisees tell you*) and dismissed the evil (*but do not do as they do*). See Matthew 23:2,3.

Let's apply this. Suppose you hear a sermon that is in major error. What should you do? Leave the church and never return (flight) or talk to everyone indignantly and start a church split (fight) or seek a peaceful but powerful solution (mastery)? The person with a good biblical EQ would work out carefully what was incorrect and then talk it over with their pastor. If he or she did not respond he would take then the matter to other responsible leaders in the church in a peaceful and caring fashion.

To give a further teaching example, how should we react to a controversial theologian like Bishop John Spong? A wise approach is to write against the controversial doctrine without attacking the person. We can defend the truth of the resurrection and expose the error of wrong, theology and logic without engaging in personal attacks or feeling overwhelmed by heresy. Our stance should be emotionally mature, clear, authoritative, biblical and balanced. The emotionally competent Christian should never fight (do not resist him who is evil); nor should we flee (when you have done all, stand), rather we should demonstrate courage, self-mastery, integrity, power and competence when these various challenging doctrinal situations arise.

The Problem or the Solution
Fear looks for the problem but faith looks for the solution. Fear generates the fight-or-flight response but faith generates intelligent thinking and personal mastery. In this section I want to talk about being "solution-focused" as an alternative to being "problem-focused" and as a way out of the fight-or-flight spiral and as a huge step towards personal mastery.

I first came across this concept in the work of William Hudson O'Hanlon and Michele Weiner-Davis in their book, "In Search of Solutions", which looks at a new approach to brief family therapy. It's a brilliant book and I highly recommend it. It has revolutionized my clinical practice. However, I have as usual sought to go a 'bit deeper" and seek its application to the Christian life. It is my conclusions, based on reflecting on their work, that I will present here.

Their concept is that instead of trying to analyze the problem down to its last detail, we should instead search for the solution. A youth in trouble with the police was brought to one of them for counseling. So instead of asking "why do you break the law" they asked "when don't you get into trouble?". The youth replied, "When I play football". "How often can you possibly play football" the counselor questioned? Soon the youth was playing football and other sports in his every spare moment. He was not getting into trouble any more because the time that has been given to doing bad things was now given to doing harmless things. They found a solution. In just two sessions of counseling his delinquent behavior was reversed. But if the therapists had taken the "find the problem" route they would still be analyzing his childhood and he would still be in trouble with the police.

Imagine two motorists in identical situations with their tires punctured by nails. Problem-Focused Pete bends down and finds the nail in the tire and says, "Why is that nail in my tire?" He then searches around for sources of nails. Finding none he walks around looking for where the nail may have come from in the life history of the road. Finally he sends the nail off to the government analytical laboratory hoping to get to the source of the problem. Meanwhile his wife and kids are furious but Problem-Focused Pete leaves them in the now hot car because he must get to the source of the problem. A few days later the answer comes back from the government laboratory and Problem-Focused Pete is still there, by the side of the road, searching for where the nail came from. Solution-Focused Sam gets a puncture, says "how can I fix this?", gets out the jack and the spare, fixes the tire and is on his way in fifteen minutes. It's a lot less intellectually satisfying but his family is eating pizza soon after, while Problem-Focused Pete frets by the side of the highway.

Sometimes in counseling we end up so focused on the problem that we miss really obvious solutions. Instead of getting our clients on the road as soon as possible we end up analyzing the nail to bits. Being solution-focused means looking for the solution, not focusing on the problem; finding the way forward for people and situations, not getting stuck in the "blame game"; doing what works and succeeds and stop doing what does not work and just frustrates.

Some of the basic concepts as I understand them are:

- Just find a solution. Don't ask why the stream is flooding or sit around analyzing the water quality – just find the bridge and walk across.
- Avoid the paralysis of analysis. If you puncture the tire on your car with a nail don't analyze the nail, change the tire.
- Don't see problems everywhere. Learn to see solutions everywhere.
- Big problems sometimes have really simple solutions. Scurvy was a huge problem among sailors for centuries and the British Admiralty refused to believe that fresh fruit was the solution saying "such a large problem cannot have such a simple solution". It took the death of one third of the British navy from scurvy in one year and the urging of Captain James Cook to get the Admiralty to see that big problems sometimes have simple solutions.
- If you do what you have always done you will get what you have always got.
- Ask what is working and do more of it. Discover the positive and reinforce it.
- If it's not working stop doing it.
- Don't fix the blame – fix the problem.
- Forget about reacting to the problem and just start searching for the solution.

The person who is chronically poor and unable to pay their bills does not need to ask: "Why am I poor and unable to pay my bills". That will just lead to them blaming themselves, their wife, their parents, the government, their employer and God. They do need to find a solution and ask the questions: "How can I best bring my finances under control? How can I make myself wealthier? How can I solve this financial mess?" The solution-focused approach will work better and faster than all problem-focused analysis of their poverty.

When we become problem-focused we start finding people to blame and enemies to accuse or we get wound up over the size of the problem. Basically, we soon end up in fight-or-flight mode. When we start searching for solutions we start thinking, we start using our mind, we start praying, we start digging into the Scripture, we ask for wisdom, we tally our resources and we move forward step by step in faith believing that God has a solution. In other words we start marshalling our resources towards mastery.

Jesus had an amazingly solution-focused approach to life. There was always a solution. There were no "problems" for God. In the gospels Jesus says "nothing is impossible with God" or "all things are possible with God" a total of nine times. Jesus finds solutions for blind people, lepers, demon-possessed Legion, Lazarus in the grave, five thousand hungry listeners and a boat full of disciples on a stormy sea. Whatever the problem there was always a solution and the solution always gave glory to God. The faith of Jesus searched for, found and activated solutions.

Jesus never gave a long-winded analysis of things when the disciples asked "Why". In John chapter nine when they asked "why was this man born blind, who sinned, him or his parents" He cut them short. The analysis was not needed and not helpful. What was needed was a solution that would give glory to God. So Jesus healed the blind man. Jesus did not teach His disciples to analyze problems and write treatise on them. He taught them how to provide solutions by healing the sick, raising the dead, cleansing the lepers and preaching the Kingdom of God. (See Luke chapters 9 and 10).

Obviously a fairly basic level of analysis is needed. You do need to identify if the person is blind or lame or demon-possessed so you can know what to do. But you don't stop right there with the analysis. You move from the analysis, by faith, to the solution. This is where mastery comes in. To move through life with mastery is to be able to see the solutions in every situation and to implement them to the glory of God. This requires a changed mindset. Instead of a fearful, helpless, analyzing, quarreling and useless mind we need one that is bold, confident, faith-filled and solution-seeking and this can only come through the power of the Holy Spirit as the mind is fixed on God.

Conclusion

We are to move away from the visceral and self-defeating reactions of the fight-or-flight response to the noble, practical, solution-focused and faith-filled responses of the sanctified believer. The instrument for doing this is the mind. The mind is the only part of our consciousness that we can focus and deploy. We can use it to stop automatic responses and to master our emotions. We can focus it on God and things above and be connected to His eternal power. We can use it to give us poise and power when we face our fears and to search for positive faith-filled solutions to pressing needs so as to give glory to God. The disciplined, focused mind is the only instrument we have to bring us out of our negative emotions and into life and peace. Mastery is the only wise alternative and mastery comes from the mind and the mind set on the Spirit is life and peace. The next section will deal with getting a handle on our emotions; first identifying them, then choosing those we will express and those we will deny.

Discussion Questions

1. Explain the differences between fight, flight and mastery?

2. What is "the mind"? What are some things it can be set on? How do we focus and control the mind?

3. Dramatize and enter into Jesus temptation in the wilderness. Imagine that your body is absolutely starving, you have been utterly alone for forty days and now you are being assailed and tempted by concentrated pure evil. How do you cope? What would you naturally be tempted to do? How do you achieve mastery over such a situation?

4. Why do we need to set our mind on God to achieve mastery? Why cannot we achieve mastery in our own strength just by practice?

5. What does it mean to be "solution-focused"? How is it different from being "problem-focused"? What sort of difference does it make to the way people tackle life?

6. How should we react when we come across theological error or strange and powerful and new spiritual experiences?

7. What are the four concepts that can help us tackle paralyzing levels of fear? How are they very similar to many biblical concepts?

Getting a Handle on Our Emotions

(John 11:35 NKJV) **Jesus wept.**

Like it or not God has made us to be emotional beings. He wants us to have emotions – His emotions. He wants us to weep over the lost, be moved with compassion for the oppressed, be outraged by injustice, provoked by idolatry and angry at the hard of heart. He wants us to love the sheep in our charge, be caught up in the agony of intercession and have hearts full of hope. The Christian life, properly lived, is awash in emotion. However, it is not merely sentimental, trite or unstable. Truly Christian emotions have a majesty about them. They ring of the Kingdom and participate in and agree with the Truth.

People and their emotions are like bells. Some people are like alarm bells going off anxiously and loudly. Some are chipped and cracked and when they "ring" the sound seems painful or like the bells on old-fashioned trams noisy, clanging, rattling. Yet others are like shop bells being rung by everyone that enters their life. Some are like a carillon, gentle, and beautiful and silvery. Finally, there are those that are deep and resonant and summon the countryside to worship. The aim of this book is to produce people who ring true and ring deeply with the emotions of God; people whose very emotional presence is a declaration of the Kingdom of God. To do this we must get a handle on our emotions, we must be able to name them and we must start to choose which emotions we will express and which emotions we should deny.

Identifying Our Emotions

Many people cannot clearly identify their emotions. They simply use general words and phrases such as "good", "bad", "up" and "OK", instead of more specific and useful words like "disconsolate", "elated" and "perplexed". For others feelings are just a confused blur. Yet others are so hurt that pain overwhelms all other finer feelings and for those people the emotional choice is constant pain or oblivion. Many chose oblivion via drugs, alcohol, or promiscuity and increasingly they escape into the total oblivion of death through suicide. Such people need help. They need to untangle their emotions and work through to peace. So being able to "feel their feelings" and being able to identify and name their emotions is a crucial first step.

Another reason why good emotional identification is important is that mistaken emotional identification can lead to spiritual disaster. For example, take the common confusion between love and lust. A young person who confuses these two can end up in a disastrous relationship. Love and lust are opposite 1 Corinthians 13 soon reveals that: "Love is patient (but lust is impatient), love is kind (but lust is cruel), love does not envy (but lust envies all things), love does not parade itself (but lust struts its stuff)… and so on. If we think we are feeling one thing but are in fact feeling its opposite all sorts of havoc can be unleashed. Regret and repentance can seem similar. However, regretting being found out is far different from repenting from sin. Unless we can correctly identify emotions in ourselves and others we can make serious mistakes in judgment.

For information about emotions and the fine differences between them the Psalms, classic poetry, novels and good literature are excellent sources. The great writers and poets have put their emotions into words with such fine skill that others through the years have found them to be important and accurate descriptions of emotions. Whole poems can focus on a single emotion such as Keats' "On Dejection". The portrayal of emotions by great authors helps us to get in touch with our feelings and to discriminate between them. When a poem particularly resonates with us then it is probably evoking an unexplored feeling that needs to surface.

Of course writing our own poetry, keeping a diary, painting, joining a drama group or attending a twelve step group or workshop can also be ways to get in touch with buried feelings and gradually sort out the emotional knots within. As we do so it is initially important to simply accept the emotions that surface rather than leaping to spiritual judgments before the process is complete.

Making spiritual judgments about the emotions we experience is often counter-productive and causes us to express some emotions and repress others to conform to a spiritual standard or model that we have been taught in church. This can confuse us emotionally and spiritually and is the subject of the next section.

Emotional Modeling – Choosing the Emotions We Express and Repress

Most Christians have a strong belief about what the perfect Christian is like. Some may think the perfect Christian is an extroverted evangelist. Others may think the perfect Christian is a quiet and ascetic mystic, while yet others may think that the perfect Christian is a blessed and joyful believer living a happy and contented life. This model of the perfect humanity shapes our emotionality. For instance, people who think the "blessed believer" is the ideal Christian tend to emphasize the importance of joy as an emotion. They also tend to deny painful emotions such as grief or disappointment, which do not fit with their model of the joyful contented Christian. This process of valuing some emotions and denying others based on our idea of the "model Christian" is very common. Let's look at how your mental model of perfect humanity may be affecting which emotions you repress and which emotions you express. The following table lists sixteen different models of ideal humanity along with their central premise, the consequences for the expression or repression of emotion and the key weaknesses of the model. Each of them is in some way a human cultural creation; each falls somewhat short of Christ who should be our model.

Model Of The Ideal Person	Expressed Areas	Areas Repressed	Weaknesses and Limitations
The Blessed Believer: The ideal Christian is a person of great faith who prays fervently and receives great blessing from God and lives in abundance and happiness free from anxiety and turmoil. Salvation is easily and joyously and often instantly received. Abraham, Isaac, David and Solomon are seen as models, can easily focus on material blessings as a sign of God's approval.	Praise, gratitude, thankfulness, joy and contentment. "Rejoice in the Lord always". Salvation is from misery to happiness. Happiness is a sign that Jesus is in your heart.	Sorrow, depression, grief, anxiety, genuine doubt, feelings of weakness and inadequacy, disappointment, any sense that life has treated them in an unfair manner. Negative emotions are construed as indicating a "lack of faith and victory".	Model fails when life appears to be far less than blessed such as when life appears to be unjust or unfair or when pain is overwhelming or during grief and sorrow. Job is the classic example of a blessed believer being challenged by life.

The Penitent Pilgrim: The pilgrim is escaping judgment and heading away from the World which is doomed. The Christian life involves separation from sin and worldliness and the serious pursuit of salvation which only relatively few attain and which is a perilous journey. Pilgrim's Progress. Lot escaping Sodom. James	Sorrow for sin, seriousness, self-examination, correction of faults, penitence, intense prayer, travail, joy over forgiveness, righteous anger, woe, and pessimism over the world.	Frivolity, laughter, flippancy, playfulness, sensuality, attraction to worldly things, sexuality, pride over achievement, romance. Positive emotions are treated with suspicion.	Can become legalistic and joyless. Fails to give proper place to the goodness of Creation and creates rebellion in people brought up in this system who learn life is not as grim as portrayed.
The Independent Achiever: Emphasizes being in ministry and achieving things for God. A Christian is measured by the size of his or her ministry and how they achieved it alone as their personal vision. Strategic thinking, business skills and personal success are highly prized. Models include Nehemiah and the apostle Paul.	Faith, hope, vision, optimism, joy, and the emotions of the will and the mind.	Tend not to be artistic and may lack compassion at times. They avoid necessary introspection and reflection. Doubt and fear are repressed rather than faced.	Can lead to burn-out. Works for some people but can destroy others. Their spouses often suffer.
The Sacrificial Servant: It's what you give up for God that counts. The Christian "has no rights" and is there to "spend themselves for God" and "burn out for Jesus". Spiritual indicators include remoteness of where one serves and the poverty of conditions. David Brainerd is a model example.	Enthusiasm and passion for God and devotion to the cause.	Most emotions are repressed or sublimated including most natural affections.	At times is the stuff of cults. Tends to love God alone and sacrifices self, family and neighbor to the cause.

The Serene Saint: Like Yoda in Star Wars these are the unruffled and wise contemplatives full of peace and deep emotions. Their goal is tranquility of soul and union with God and self-mastery.	Tranquility and peace, gentle emotions, prayerful devotion, saintly emotions, mercy.	Anger and most intense emotions including sexuality are repressed.	Can be weak at critical moments and fail to tackle issues of justice and practical issues of life. Can become very selfish and inward.
The Radical Revolutionary: Enjoys turning over the tables in the Temple. Seeking after justice they identify with the Old Testament prophets. The ideal Christian is a counter-culture revolutionary who brings transformation to society and justice to the poor.	Righteous anger, passion for justice, indignation, wrath. Vision, hope and even optimism may also be present.	Tend to be overly serious and lose natural playfulness and joy. Gentleness and meekness may also be lacking.	In some contexts this is very much needed in others it is totally inappropriate. Not a whole of life perspective for most people.
The Evangelist: The ideal Christian sees many people saved. They are master communicators who are always witnessing. They have strong personalities are enthusiastic and clear sighted.	Black and white emotions. Enthusiasm, passion for the lost, Joy, exuberance.	Reflective quiet emotions are often seen as impractical.	Lacks any understanding of ambiguities and complexity, a very confined and narrow model.
The Aggressive Apologist: Defends the faith from error at every turn and exposes heresy, cults, witchcraft and deception as well as contending with other belief systems. The ideal Christian is knowledgeable, theologically correct, logical and able to debate others so that they convert to Christianity or correct their ways.	Reason, logic, righteous indignation, anger, forcefulness, suspicion, evaluates and discriminates.	Playfulness, gentleness, creativity, sympathy, mercy, emotions of the heart.	Tends to distrust emotional expression and be overly logical and dry. Can make a person very rigid in their later years.

The Ecstatic Enthusiast: Led by the Spirit they are "on the move for God" and express strong enthusiasm for spiritual things. Spiritual ecstasy is a sign of God's presence. The day of Pentecost is the ideal Christian moment to be recreated at every opportunity.	Trance states, ecstasy, passion, enthusiasm, joy, exuberance, praise, thanksgiving.	Critical faculties, analysis, contemplation, thinking, reflection and negative emotions such as pain, grief and disappointment.	Tends to spiritual burn-out and can be very unstable and insufficiently critical. Tends to fall for fads and is too simplistic for many of life's deeper practical issues.
The Reasonable Man: Wisdom and Reason are the voices of the Spirit who leads Christians into a balanced and moderate life that reflects proper priorities and which is well adjusted to the social context the believer lives in. Extremes are interpreted as a sign of a dysfunctional personality. Solomon is a model.	Reason, analysis, ethical reflection, conventions and social mores, well-tempered emotions, kindness, gentleness, reasonableness. "Moderation in all things".	Strong emotion of all kinds is disapproved of as well as any major breach of social standards.	Unless the Bible is taught clearly and strongly this rapidly tends to an insipid worldliness and spiritual skepticism.
The Perfect Man: Like Confucius' concept the perfect man is without inappropriate emotion or any visible faults. Emotion is carefully guarded and kept under control. The perfect man is upright, ethical, has perfect manners and social perception, and is extremely humble and meek.	Proper behavior, loyalty, humility, meekness, convention, submission, restraint, ethics, duty. "Being without fault in one's conduct in life".	Anger, pain, any socially disabling emotion, anything that may cause loss of face.	Because how others perceive the Christian is of ultimate importance it can produce harshness and hypocrisy. Very individualistic and tends to ignore larger social issues.

The Good Samaritan: Love of neighbor expressed as social action and deeds of mercy mark the true Christian. Kindness, gentleness, mercy and helpfulness are the premier virtues.	Mercy, gentleness, kindness, hospitality, inclusion, practical deeds of love and compassion.	Exclusion, rejection, unkindness of any sort, tries to develop a very inclusive and non-theological faith.	Has much merit but can become just social work without a true saving gospel being proclaimed.
The Principled Idealist: Characterized by seeking the high and noble life lived by principles and virtue and self-renunciation for the Ideal Good. People are valued by their principles, intentions and ideals without reference to actions. There is a pursuit of absolute excellence at the personal level and of a Christian Utopia at the corporate level.	High ideals and aspirations, concepts, ideas, justice, philosophies, ambition, personal striving for high goals, vision, personal principles, ethics, mission statements, nobility, virtue, the Absolute Good, Utopia.	The mundane, earthy, concrete details of daily life are scorned. Attention to detail and diligence are often lacking. Earthiness and pragmatism are perceived to be unspiritual. Tends not to allow feedback from results.	Frequently disorganized. Also godly ambition and personal ambition can easily be mixed. Often so focused on the external goals that they lose personal insight and can become dishonest and treacherous.

The Perceptive Pragmatist: Able to sum up life quickly and fix problems on the spot. A Christian is measured by their capacity to be useful and by their skills in judgment, analysis and implementation.	Analysis, evaluation, enthusiasm, practical knowledge, authority, wisdom, toughness, shrewdness, energy.	Empathy, kindness, compassion, mercy. Most emotions are not felt deeply and they tend to be deemed as irrelevant.	Tend to come unstuck in mid-life and feel a deep sense of meaninglessness. May neglect relationships. May see virtue as impractical.
The Intelligent Instructor: A learned Christian who teaches well and can exegete the difficult verses of Scripture. The goal is knowledge of God. Wisdom and knowledge are equated with progress in the Christian life. Academic prowess is prized and church is often made into a classroom. Ezra is a model.	Thoughtfulness, balance, evaluation, discipline, kindness, gentleness, logic, intelligence, knowledge, reasoning, debating, humor, moderate emotions suitable for the classroom.	Strong passions are suspect and practicality may be lacking. The subjective and non-cognitive areas of the Christian life tend to be deeply distrusted. Lack of celebration and praise.	Can become dry, dull and overly rational. Praise and worship tend to be seen as only teaching tools. The central idea that knowledge of theology is progress in God is deeply flawed.
The Child of Nature: Still living in the Garden of Eden and feels free to express all kinds of emotion. Spontaneity, freedom, expressiveness, artistic skill and creativity are high on the agenda.	Nearly all emotions are freely expressed. Creativity, joy, freedom. The inner child is given freedom to play.	Discernment, wisdom, truth and responsibility. Can be undisciplined and immature emotionally.	Can become overly sensual and fall into moral disorder. There is a tendency to anarchy and irresponsibility. Lacks power and authority.

So we see that the Christian's mental model greatly influences which aspects of life they pay attention to and which emotions they express or repress. In fact we probably choose our own model partly because we are naturally more comfortable expressing one set of emotions than another. This may be due to, among other factors, our culture, our denomination, or to our natural temperament.

I find God paying a lot of attention to those areas outside my model. He challenges my preconceptions and stretches my view of what I should be like. The gap between my natural comfortable model of the

Christian life and the life of Jesus is a gap He wants closed. He wants me to model myself after His Son and does not allow me to invent my own destiny or a "better idea" of how I should be sanctified. For instance, I am naturally rational and cognitively oriented and uncomfortable with high levels of emotion, so God in His desire to make me like Jesus, has made emotions a real area of challenge and of study for me.

God will not be satisfied with you being less than Christlike. He will work on the difference between the model of faith you have adopted and that displayed in the Scripture. Your mental model of the ideal Christian undoubtedly has many Scripture that support it – but here and there it can be improved and, in fact, needs to be improved if you are to be fully like Jesus. In my Christian life I have had to do a major revision of my faith about every seven years or so. I move from a certain model to a more Christlike one, then that in turn is challenged and revised and so the process goes on.

Changing Our Mental Model

How then do we correct our mental model of the Christian faith – particularly one we are quite committed to? For a start, read one of the gospels and note the difference between how you act and react to how Jesus acts and reacts. Would you be happy being a friend of publicans and sinners? Would you let a prostitute touch your feet? Would you say, "You cannot serve God and mammon" with conviction? At those points where your model and the gospel model disagree you must decide to change and become like Jesus. Other clues are inner discontent with where you are (maybe it's your model of Christianity that's wrong), or a desire for something more. Go with your questions seeking their answers in the Scripture and "brick by brick" you will build up a more mature idea of what it means to be a Christlike person.

The central questions of changing mental models are "Can I be more like Jesus than I am now?" and "What is my actual working notion of the Christian life? Is it what Jesus meant by the Christian life?" To doubt our mental model of the faith is not the same as doubting God. I do not doubt the authority of the Scripture but I do periodically question how I have interpreted them and the mental pictures I have generated. Thus changing mental models means being honest to God and the Scripture. It also means being tough on one's personal comfort zone, church culture and traditions. It is honest biblical reflection on where we are spiritually, in the light of Scripture.

You may need to make a calculated decision to move beyond your culture and upbringing, accepting that which is good and rejecting that which is evil and moving to maturity in Christ. The Jewish Christians in the book of Acts had a most difficult time doing this because they were so sure of then superiority of Jewish culture and practices and of the need to be circumcised. Their model of Jesus was that He was "a good Jewish boy who kept the Law" – and He did! However He also accepted Gentiles! Chapters ten to fifteen of the book of Acts detail the terrible tension Peter and the Jewish Christians faced when the Gentiles accepted the gospel. A church-wide conference had to be called to resolve the issue. Changing models of faith was not easy then and it's not easy now.

It requires the power of the Holy Spirit if radical change is to occur and if we are to have the courage to be more Christlike emotionally than our community believes is desirable. For instance, people who bring prostitutes and drug addicts to church may not be welcomed with enthusiasm. Departing from our comfortable model of Christianity to a genuine Spirit-filled and Christlike existence will have a huge cost and be understood only by other seekers on the same journey. [Remember that this is your quest and that you may not be able to take your church with you. You may see the need to change while they are content with where they are. You do what you must do to be like Jesus. That's your responsibility. They will have their time and path to Christlikenessness.]

To sum up – we need to get a handle on our emotions by first of all identifying them and secondly making a conscious decision about which emotions to express and which to deny. Our mental model of the Christian faith will greatly affect how we express or repress emotions. Our mental model serves as a sort of Christian master plan that guides our destiny, thoughts, emotions and behavior. It is shaped by culture, conditioning and our community of faith with its traditions, as well as, our own conclusions about God and Jesus. It needs to be revised now and then when it has outlived its current usefulness. We need to move to ever more Christlike mental models and these in turn will pattern our thoughts, behavior and biblical EQ. As we become Christlike we will express and repress the right emotions, in the right way, and at the right times for the glory of God and the extension of His Kingdom. This leads us to a problem – what about the emotions I have today, right now, before I have changed a bit. How do I handle them? How should I evaluate them? How should I react to them? That is the subject of the following chapters.

Discussion Questions

1. Name as many emotions as you can. If you have difficulty, use Roget's Thesaurus. What are the differences between the emotions? Why do we have so many words? How do they have different facial expressions? See if you can imitate the emotions of dejection, surprise, happiness, fear, anticipation, puzzlement, and exuberant confidence. How does it feel when you do this?

2. What are some ways that you can keep track of your own emotions? Are there some emotions that you just do not want to feel?

3. What do you think of the idea of people being like bells? What sort of bell are you? How do people "sound" emotionally to you?

4. What emotions should we repress as Christians? Which emotions should we express?

5. Which of the mental models listed above is closest to your own? Where do you need to change to be more like Jesus? Which is closest to that of your church? Where does it need to change in order to be a bit more like Jesus?

6. How do you feel about such a major change? What is the difference between a "nice church culture" and a "Christlike church culture"?

Acting on and Reacting to Our Strong Emotions

Therefore my spirit is overwhelmed within me; My heart within me is distressed. (Psalms 143:4 NKJV)

Handling strong emotion is not easy – and life in the Spirit is frequently full of strong emotions. Love, righteous anger, compassion, ecstasy and joy in worship can be transcendent and powerful emotions that sweep the believer along. In the face of such powerful emotions what should we do? How should we act on our emotions? How should we react to them as they well up inside us? That is the subject of this chapter.

Self-Control, Repression, Grieving and Quenching
There are two main spiritual errors when it comes to the expression of emotion in the Christian life. The first is giving expression to carnal emotions such as wrath, bitterness and clamor. This is called "grieving the Spirit" and is mentioned in Ephesians 4:30,31. The second error is the repressing of holy emotions that arise within us because of the work of the Spirit. This is called "quenching" the Spirit and is mentioned in 1 Thessalonians 5:19. Holy emotions frequently have an intensity about them that makes many people fear their presence and they repress on them. *Self-control means managing our emotions so that fleshly and carnal emotions such as wrath and bitterness are kept out of the Christian life and holy emotions such as compassion are given full expression in the best manner possible.* Thus, as we saw in the last chapter, self-control does mean repressing some emotions – but not all. The Christian life is about holy emotion – not a dead and passionless existence. However, before we can control our emotions and manage them appropriately we must become aware of their existence.

Repression is the opposite of self-control because it denies the existence of the emotion and does not enable us to control it in any way at all. That is why people who use repression of emotion as a main device in their Christian life are often subject to outbursts of rage. They, in fact, have no real control of their emotions and no insight into their emotional state. Before I go any further I want you to stop and think about the concept of "permission to feel emotion". This is denied to many people. They are told from a young age to keep emotions, particularly negative emotions, completely under wraps. Once this is successfully internalized such people may have to give themselves "permission to feel" those emotions that they have denied themselves over the years. Such emotions may include sensual emotions, pleasure, anger, disappointment and grief. Gradually coming to feel long lost emotions can take some time. There is frequently a deep fear that control will be lost. It needs to be remembered by such people that they have successfully controlled that emotion for perhaps thirty or more years. They know how to put the lid on the box when they have to. It is most unlikely they will truly lose control but the experience will feel new and a bit scary at first. Eventually the recovered emotions will lead to the deeper resonances of life and a fuller and more meaningful existence.

The aim of biblical EQ is that we move from repression and denial of emotion to proper self-control of emotion. Thus the Holy Spirit will not be "quenched" by good emotions being stifled or "grieved" by inappropriate emotions, such as wrath or bitterness being expressed. This makes the person of the Holy Spirit absolutely central to the Christian's true experience of emotion. It is as He is released in His fullness that we move into the emotional life of our Saviour. It is as we are led by the Spirit that we experience His moving within our souls, His passion for the lost, His hatred of sin, His love of holy things, His rejoicing in the truth. Self-control is an aspect of the fruit of the Holy Spirit and operates under the leading of the Holy Spirit so that we enter into holy emotions and forsake fleshly passions and ungodly wrath and dissension. Through the leading of the Holy Spirit and His infilling we become a joyous, loving, holy and zealous people filled with holy emotions and the fruit of the Spirit (Ephesians 5:18-21; Colossians 3:16-17; Galatians 5:16-23).

True Holy Spirit led self-control is neither apathetic and stoical on one hand nor irresponsible and indulgent on the other. The Holy Spirit leads us to express emotion wisely and truthfully but also joyously and with depth and intensity. Shallow sentimentality is not found in the Scripture. People of faith are deep, resonant and have a grounded-ness about them. The people of the Living God are most fully alive. That is what makes Christianity attractive. Many people say of the time they first met Christians, "they had something about them, a joy that I really wanted."
The Holy Spirit filled believer is emotionally alive and emotionally substantial.

Self-Control and Other Control

If we are not self-controlled we are other-controlled. In other words if we do not take charge of our emotions then they will be up and down with every change in the weather, every different circumstance, every tiny provocation. If we do not take positive and definite control of our emotions we will simply be flotsam and jetsam on the sea of life. Basically, the choices are self-control or other-control; mastery or madness in its various forms.

There is a common myth that other people can "press our buttons" and make us explode with anger or burst into tears or react emotionally. "He made me so mad", "She seduced me; she made me have sex with her" and so on. Most of the time this is just plain untrue. Generally, you were able to master your emotions in that situation but you chose not to.

Say you are in a heated domestic argument, with much shouting and red-faced anger and the telephone rings. So you pick it up and suddenly your voice is calm and rational, you say hello nicely and take the message. In doing so you just took control of your strongest and angriest emotions. You mastered yourself, in a second of time; just in order to answer the phone. You knew how to calm down and you did. You knew how to stop shouting, and you did so. You demonstrated instantaneous movement from powerful emotions to complete rationality; switching off your fight-or-flight response as you did so. It was impressive. The phone incident demonstrated that you do possess the power to instantaneously master strong emotions. You can do so easily and routinely in order to avoid embarrassment. Why then do you not more often use the power you had when you answered the phone? That is the power we call self-control and you do have it.

The phone incident shows we have an "off button" for the fight-or-flight response. We can switch it off suddenly and completely. The off button is like the red emergency button they have on trains where I come from in Brisbane, Australia. The red button is behind Plexiglas which must be broken by effort but once that button is pressed the whole train with its hundreds of tons of locomotives and carriages comes quickly to a grinding halt. Your fight-or-flight response may seem like a runaway train but you have the red button and with a bit of effort you can stop it completely.

Hitting the red button is as easy as saying "Stop" to yourself in a firm and commanding tone of voice (either audibly or inaudibly). The red button can be pressed *as soon as you decide to take charge* of yourself and your emotions. This involves coming to the realization that you should take command of you emotions, then doing so by switching off the fight-or-flight response and returning to a rational way of being. Let's break down the phone incident and see how that happens:

1. You are caught up in the argument. Your face is red, the anger is surging, you are floating on the adrenalin and in a strange way the rage feels good. You are letting it fly. You are half-aware that the rage is controlling you but you don't care. You are going with the flow of the fight-or-flight response.
2. The phone rings, you pick it up.
3. You realize the call is important.
4. You realize your present responses are inappropriate.
5. You decide to take control of your emotions.
6. You switch off the fight-or-flight response by pressing the "red button".
7. You return to a rational and intelligent way of being as you take the call.

The critical point is when you decide to take control of your emotions. Realizing your emotions are inappropriate is not quite enough. You must make a definite inner decision. Some people realize their emotions are inappropriate but think "what the blazes" and let emotions fly over the telephone as well! That inner decision, that choice between "what the blazes" and "I'd better cool down" is critical. That's the equivalent of breaking the Plexiglas. It's the bit of effort that's required to stop the whole shuddering train. After that decision is made pressing the button is easy. When you put yourself in control of yourself you achieve mastery. When you decide to put your mind in charge and not your adrenalin you win. You must make the firm and definite decision that even when emotions are powerful you are going to be in charge of them. This is not repression, it is self-control. It's the sane, rational, functional part of you being in control of your emotions. It's deciding to appoint your Spirit-filled mind as the CEO of Myself Inc.

This is very powerful. No one can make you react emotionally unless they use so much force, such as torture, that they actually break you. If you definitely decide not to laugh, say at a dirty joke, no one can make you laugh. If you definitely decide not to cry, say in order to stay together in an emergency, then no one can make you cry. Your emotions are yours to express or repress. You are in control of them. You can stop them and you can let them go. Your mind can decide how you will or will not react as long as you make the decision to put it clearly and absolutely in charge of your life.

Some people fear people of strong minds and say they are repressed and even that they have "deep inner rage" which in a few cases is true. Repression and rage live together in some people. However, we are aiming at a Spirit-filled Christian use of the mind. We want the mind to be strong and strongly in control but we also want it to be holy, renewed and spiritual. We want the mind to permit holy and appropriate emotions and to stop fleshly and inappropriate emotions. We do not want to quench the Spirit. Thus we need discernment about when to press the button. We do not want either total emotional repression or a runaway fight-or flight response. We need a balanced middle ground. We need to discern our strong emotions. Thus we do not need to run away from strong emotion whether it be positive emotion, negative emotion or even deep spiritual emotion. The presence of strong emotion should not panic us into a fight-or-flight response or shut us down into repression. We should evaluate the emotion rather than react to the emotion, we should master the emotion and not just flee from it or try to beat it to death. The mastery stance requires discernment and discernment requires understanding of emotions, their sources, their place in our life and their relative values. The following few sections deal with how we can respond with poise, power and wisdom to the strongest emotions such as temptations and powerful spiritual experiences.

Emotions and Discerning the Truth

Before we decide to let an emotion control or direct our behavior we need to know whether or not it is leading us in the right direction. Can we safely follow our hearts? Are emotions a good guide to truth and to right behavior? If the Holy Spirit produces good emotions are all good emotions a sign of God's Presence? Can we tell the truth of a doctrine or the authenticity of a movement by how it makes us feel? Not at all! "It feels so good it must be right" is a downright lie!

While the Holy Spirit produces joy and peace, the presence of joy and peace does not necessarily indicate the presence of the Holy Spirit. People can feel at peace after a bottle or two of wine! People experience joy and peace when they convert to Buddhism, a New Age group or even to Islam. People join cults because they feel better there than at church. Cults can feel warm, loving, tranquil and enlightened. Cults often meet the emotional needs that were not met in the local church and someone has said "Cults are the unpaid bills of the Church." Thus good feelings are no guide to good theology. The opposite may also be true, bad feelings are no guide to bad theology. We may experience negative emotions when we are being confronted with the truth. The prophets – who spoke the truth – found many people reacting negatively to them. The truth was not producing good feelings in those who heard. Negative emotions are no indication of error and positive emotions are no indication of truth. Thus good emotions are not a guide to good theology neither are negative emotions an indication of wrong theology.

If this is the case is it "too risky" to cultivate a Christian subjectivity? Not if we place emotions in their right place as a response to truth and a guide to action. Emotions are a valid response to truth but not a valid guide to truth. Jesus reacted emotionally as He perceived the truth but Jesus did not arrive at the truth via His emotions. He arrived at the truth via Scripture. Jesus wept when He saw His friends grieving at Lazarus' grave. He was moved by compassion when He saw people sick, harassed and lost. His emotions were a response to His perceptions in a framework filled with God's truth. However, Jesus never said, "I feel X, therefore I will believe Y". His emotions moved Him to act and His actions were based on truth revealed from the Father. His emotions did not show Him what was true or false – they just moved Him to act on what He already knew from Scripture to be true or false. We do not follow our emotions, rather we need to follow truth – and express emotion as we do so.

Bob was a 50-year-old executive having a mid-life crisis. Somewhere along the road he was told, "just follow your heart". He followed his feelings into an "emotionally fulfilling relationship" with a younger woman and a painful divorce that he now deeply regrets. The adultery felt great. However, it was not of the truth. The good feelings were not an indication of a right course of action. These good feelings can be intense, global and very convincing. There is such a thing as very strong temptation. There are emotions that can lead us into adultery, drugs and alcohol addiction, gambling, and acts of self-destruction. These emotions feel true, authentic and valid at the time. They may even feel "cosmic" and like a form of self-awareness, self-discovery or enlightenment. Affairs can seem totally "right" in their initial phase; the first drink for an alcoholic "feels terrific", and the guru makes people feel "at one with the Universe". Unless there is a solid examination of the truth and awareness of the consequences these powerful emotions can lead people to shipwreck their lives.

Following our heart can be truly catastrophic. However, repression is not the answer. [In fact repression can be the indirect cause of the catastrophe as temptation comes strongest to our repressed unmet needs.] Rather than repressing our emotions and unmet needs we need to be aware of our heart and discipline it according to the truth. During a mid-life crisis the best advice is "acknowledge your feelings but follow the truth." It is perfectly OK to acknowledge to yourself, "I am strongly tempted to have an affair" as long as you stare that fact in the face and decide to refuse the temptation because you love God. It can also help to look at the consequences and say, "I will not do so because that is wrong and destructive and would make shipwreck of my life." By acknowledging the temptation and refusing it you can grow in emotional and spiritual maturity.

There is however an aspect of emotion that can guide us and is meant to guide us. Emotions can act as a "preliminary analysis" of a complex situation prompting us to give it more thought. For instance, our emotions can also make us uneasy about someone and after we look harder we find out they have a reputation for being dishonest, predatory or cruel. Our emotions can give us the hunch that there might be real potential in a certain situation. Once our emotions have alerted us we can then examine the situation objectively and see if our emotions have informed us correctly.

There is a place for hunches, gut feelings, emotional signals and awareness of emotional atmosphere. Emotions are able to reduce a very complex situation down to a certain feeling or impulse and they do this very quickly and efficiently. A young man sees a lady and feels "Wow, she is the one." This judgment may be made in a second or two. That judgment, however, will need a lot of further examination before it can validly lead to marriage. Emotions are thus meant to be initial assessments of complex situations – but only initial assessments.

This is useful in that our emotions select the situations that our reason will go to work on and analyze. A young man cannot analyze the suitability of every young lady he meets – that would be impractical. Rather he thinks about those he is attracted to. Thus his emotions select first and his thorough evaluation follows later. Emotions can make us attracted, suspicious, repelled, guarded, curious or astonished at a given situation. Sometimes this initial impression is validated by further thought at other times it is proved totally wrong.

In our own culture and on familiar territory our impressions can be quite accurate. However, the further we are from home base the worse our emotional judgment becomes and the more we must rely solely on objective evidence. Inner impressions have a place in our discernment of situations and we should listen to them. God has placed them within us. However, we need to be careful in relying on them and not mistakenly think that we are always right. If there are significant consequences from following those impressions we should be very careful and check the facts carefully before proceeding. These impressions cannot replace reasoning, rather they alert us that reasoning should commence on a particular issue or line of thought. They are a stimulus to think not an alternative to it.

When emotions are damaged the ability to form accurate impressions of situations also suffers. Emotionally damaged people tend to be prone to mistakes in judgment. They rush into love, they hold back from friendship, they gamble on foolish ventures, and they run from shadows. The ability to sense what is happening in a situation, then to sit back and analyze it adequately, is out of kilter. People who have been emotionally damaged should not enter into a significant relationship or project until they have healed to the point where they have functional and accurate discernment. They should look at their decision-making and be careful – seeking the advice of friends and family and striving to be as objective as possible. Even if their ability to assess situations was good before it will not be as good now. This loss of judgment can be alarming but it is temporary and will pass in time as emotional healing takes place.

Spiritual Experiences

Many of our most powerful emotional experiences are spiritual experiences. The spiritual life and the emotional life are thus very closely connected and our meaningful spiritual experiences are nearly always highly charged with emotion. Truth for the believer is real and living and meaningful and the discovery of truth – those great "Aha!" moments – is frequently deeply emotional. When Ezra read the Law the Jews wept (Nehemiah 8:1-9). Truth and emotion went hand in hand. The scientific age with its view of truth as clinical and unemotional is rooted in Greek Platonism not in biblical (and especially Hebrew) reality. In the West it has led to false dichotomy between theology and emotionality that is even reflected at the level of denominational differences. Part of the appeal of the New Age is having teaching that is expected to be emotionally and existentially meaningful.

Thus it is the testimony of men and women of God down through the ages that deep spiritual experiences were also often powerful emotional events. Many biographies after biography give accounts of nights in anguished prayer, times of breakthrough and joy, deep sorrow over sin, and being astounded by the presence and power of God. Revival in particular is seen as full of emotion. However, this has led to the common error that only deeply emotional experiences are truly genuine spiritual experiences. The true convert is expected to weep or be joyous or have certain feelings. The emotion, which often accompanies spiritual change, has in some cases become required. That is simply not a biblical stance. The biblical sign of true conversion is a life lived so that repentance is demonstrated and the "fruits of repentance" are shown. The life, not the emotions, is the true indicator of piety.

Variance in Emotionality
Thus a highly emotional person is not more or less spiritual than a relatively unemotional person. The emotional volume level is not terribly important. What is important is that we have the right sorts of emotions. We should feel some sort of contrition when we do wrong. We should feel compassion for the hungry. We should feel indignation when blasphemy occurs. These are proper and holy emotions. Improper and unholy emotions might include rage over a trivial insult or jealousy over a person's success. The question is not whether the emotion is loud or muted but whether it is holy or fleshly.

Ecstasy, Trance, Dreams and Vision
A vision does not make a saint. Powerful spiritual phenomena are recorded both for genuine prophets, seers and mystics and for false prophets, cult leaders and mischief-makers. Most Christians seem to

have a significant dream or vision at some point in their life. A few have them often. However, most dreams, visions and experiences of trance seem to be of fairly limited value. I am a missionary and while writing this book I took ill with a tropical fever and spent a few days in delirium. During the delirium amazing and disturbing visions came to me every time I closed my eyes. These visions were a sign of a high temperature (not of great holiness) and antibiotics "exorcised" them from my mind. The experience, though interesting, was of little spiritual value and I did not gain anything from it. It was just interesting spiritual stuff and that's about all. Even when a dream or vision has a distinctly numinous and awesome quality about it there is no guarantee that it is genuine and useful – until Scripture tests it.

At no point are Christians exhorted to enter into altered states of consciousness. Rather they are at times warned about excesses in this area and placing too much emphasis on dreams and visions (see Colossians 2). To balance this I have, during my missionary career, seen the great value of dreams to pre-literate tribes-people in Papua New Guinea and among Muslims. People frequently come to Christ or make a definite change for the better in their Christian life because of a dream in which Jesus or an angel appeared to them. The fruits of the dream show its validity and such valid dreams fit within the biblical pattern. However, they occur naturally without any special inducement or the use of drugs.

Thus we need to take our dreams and visions seriously and evaluate them wisely and in a balanced and biblical fashion. Writing then down is helpful and then leave them in the notebook while you pray and consult the Scripture and perhaps a wise Christian or three. Here are a few guidelines for doing the evaluation:
- Chronological date setting is not found in Scripture, so I doubt any dream that uses actual times and dates (e.g. 18th September 2003) to forecast the future. The Scripture use event time, (e.g. seven years after the appearance of the man of lawlessness) not clock time, when setting the prophetic calendar.
- If after your dream or vision you find yourself convinced of your own spiritual importance then pause, stop, think. Spiritual pride is not what God wants. The dream or vision is not Scripture and is very probably not a new chapter in the book of Revelation. Calm down, evaluate it very carefully and then share it with a few other mature Christians. Humility will help you sort out the truth.
- Dreams and visions and spiritual experiences can come from

God, from your own imagination, or from the devil. Those from God are scriptural and edifying and point to the complete sovereignty of God and glorify His Son Jesus Christ. Those from self tend to be filled with daily events or political events and are often self-centered, those from the devil are tempting or terrifying or accusing.

- I do not think it is presumptuous to say, "Lord, if that dream was of you please give it to me three nights running and substantiate it with Scripture and other signs." God allows us to test the spiritual realm (1 John 4:1-3). This is especially so if the dream points to a major change in life direction.
- No dream that contradicts Scripture, invites you to sin, fills you with pride or terrifies you out of your mind is from God.
- The power of the emotion in the dream does not tell you how important or spiritually valuable the dream is. You can have powerfully emotional dreams following too much pizza but they are of no spiritual value. The spiritual value is determined by carefully weighing the dream against Scripture.
- Many dreams do not carry direct symbols that are easily interpreted (like the fig tree for Israel). Most of the language of dreams and visions comes from within your own subconscious and the metaphors you use to yourself. They are like the cartoons in the paper. So if in your dream your wife has a knife in her neck it may not mean she is going to die. Instead it probably means that you are finding her to be a "pain in the neck" and that the argument over the dishes has made its way into your dreams. After you have written down your dream look for the metaphors you commonly use and see if any have popped into it. This is a good starting point for interpretation.
- Doctrine flows from Scripture in context not dreams and visions. A dream may serve as an illustration of a doctrine (I once had a wonderful dream of Jesus as the Shepherd) but they are not the source of doctrine. A dream or vision can be your subconscious making truth real to you in pictorial form but it does not invent new truth. Nebuchadnezzar's dream of the tree in Daniel 4 merely told him he needed to become humble – it illustrated an already existing doctrine and carried God's warning of the consequences of sin (as many dreams do, see Genesis 20:3-7).

- Some people experience vivid dreams in response to political events in the news. Hundreds of such dreams and visions have been sent to me over the Internet and at least ninety-seven percent of them have been substantially wrong. They generally predict invasions of America or Australia, gigantic tidal waves, and huge earthquakes. My theory is that such dreams represent a way of dealing with anxiety over the instability and wickedness we see around us. They carry a spirit of fear and anxiety within their structure and seem to lack substance.

- Demonic dreams tend to fall into four categories – inflating, accusing, terrifying or seductive. Inflating dreams convince the person of their own importance and generate spiritual pride. Accusing dreams "reveal" the supposedly secret sins of another person or convince the dreamer of their own inevitable damnation and judgment. Terrifying dreams use fear as their main weapon and often involve demons and masks and sometimes leave the person struggling to breathe. Seductive dreams involve very realistic and vivid dreams of sexual acts and are powerfully alluring, playing on the deep sensuality in the person to make them wake up with a strong desire to sin.

- Dreams can result in distraction from ministry. Quite a few of my colleagues in the ministry have moved out of flourishing but difficult ministries and gone to a place they saw in a dream to start a "new and exciting ministry". In every case I think they have ended up disillusioned. My theory is that sometimes the pressures of ministry make us want out and our subconscious manufactures a way out for us in the form of a spiritually acceptable dream or vision. Such callings should be tested over time.

Powerful spiritual experiences and dreams and visions are not to be feared nor fled. Neither are they to be over-rated. Rather they are to be carefully tested and the truth extracted from them.

The Point of Balance

Archimedes once said, "Give me a lever long enough and a place to stand and I could move the earth." But where can we stand to get a grip on our strong emotions? Tis' a fine notion to think that we can stand outside our strong emotions, evaluate them scripturally and then bring them into submission to the Holy Spirit. But this fine notion seems very impractical to many people caught up in the roller coaster ride of their own powerful emotions. Here are some hints that may help you find a "place to stand" so you can take charge of your own emotional life.

- Make a definite and clear decision to place Jesus in charge of your life with your Spirit-filled mind as His CEO. Your mind, set on the Spirit, has delegated authority from God to bring the rest of you under control and into line with His purposes.
- Realize that you are the boss. You are the master of your emotions. They are not the master of you. You have a right to tell them what to do. They are your emotions after all, your property so to speak.
- Realize that you have the control panel inside you. You can press the "red button" and take control of the fight-or flight response. You can modulate the volumes of emotions and control them.
- Don't disown your emotions. You have to own them before you can boss them!
- Realize that the apparent authority of strong emotions is largely illusory. They are just part of you, they are not. They may feel compelling but they have no right to compel you at all.
- Think. Use logic. Stop and think hard about where your emotions are taking you. Check the consequences of the actions. Choose to be rational and sensible.
- Evaluate the truth of the propositions the strong emotions are putting to you such as "It would be a good idea to punch X" or "You should follow your heart and have an affair". Even if these things feel true, right, authentic, satisfying and fulfilling they may be wrong (See Genesis 3!). Choose to stand on God's Word.
- Apply the principles in the chapter on mastery.
- Be constantly filled with the Holy Spirit. Just pray, "Lord, fill me with the Holy Spirit and grant me wisdom and self-control and fix my mind on You." That is the sort of prayer He delights to answer. I recommend the Campus Crusade booklet, "How To Be Filled With The Holy Spirit". I believe you will find it helpful, and very practical and easy to use.
- Be aware of your weaknesses. Know that "under such and such circumstances I tend to react in X manner". Check yourself. Watch yourself carefully. Have friends keep you

accountable and have them pray with you and help you find your point of wisdom and balance.

- Get it very clear that the Holy Spirit is wise and intelligent and His leadings are wise and intelligent. Don't destabilize yourself by following many crazy ideas thinking they are leadings from the Holy Spirit. Stand in wisdom and do not move from it.

By practicing the above techniques on a daily basis you will gradually learn how to generate dignity, power and poise. Day by day you will become a stronger person not tossed here and there by every emotion that comes your way. You will hop off the roller coaster of your own emotions and start to take charge of yourself and your destiny. Best of all you will learn to be a Spirit-filled Christian and be able to consistently demonstrate the fruit of the Spirit.

Once we have started mastering ourselves we can more fully engage in profitable relationships with others. To do this, and to minister grace, we need to be able to recognize and understand their emotions, which is the subject of the next chapter.

Discussion Questions

1. Are strong emotions a problem for you at times? How are they a problem?

2. What is the difference between self-control and repression?

3. How are grieving the Spirit and quenching the Spirit opposite kinds of spiritual errors?

4. What is the "red button"? How can we switch off the fight-or-flight response?

5. What is the place of emotions in forming our doctrines and telling us what is right and what is wrong? Why do we need discernment? Do good emotions mean we have found the truth?

6. Do you think that Jesus had powerful spiritual experiences? Did He rely on emotions or experiences or Scripture when it came to forming doctrine and understanding truth?

7. Many powerful spiritual experiences are recorded in Scripture and some still happen today. How should we assess and handle them?

8. Jesus seemed to be always poised and in charge. He had obviously found a "place to stand" in order to manage His emotions and manage life. What are some things that can make people lose their poise? How can you find such a "place to stand"?

Recognizing and Understanding Emotions in Others

But Jesus, knowing their thoughts, said, "Why do you think evil in your hearts? (Matthew 9:4 NKJV)

As I write this chapter the news is filled with the horror of the terrorist attacks on the World Trade Center. Emotions such as grief, sympathy, sorrow, anger, anxiety and perplexity are openly being expressed. The world teeters on the brink of war and there is anxiety about the stock market's ability to open on Monday. The air seems charged with highly contagious emotion. Now how can I recognize all this from a television screen? What gives us the capacity to read another person's emotional state and to respond to it? What happens when we fail to do so?

There are approximately thirty common emotions that are reasonably easily recognized. These include, fear, surprise, apprehension, sadness, elation, doubt, anxiety, guilt, contentment, sexual interest, curiosity, anger, frustration, annoyance, and laughter amongst others. A sensitive, discerning person may be able to recognize hundreds of different types of emotions while an abusive person may recognize as few as nine or ten. Criminals frequently have trouble recognizing or identifying with the emotions of their victims. Sociopaths are almost completely unable to recognize emotions in others in any meaningful way.

It seems sophisticated neural processing is needed for the recognition of emotions and that it is based in an almond shaped part of the brain called the amygdala. (Damasio et al. found that bilateral damage to the amygdala impaired the recognition of emotion from facial expressions.) To give you an idea of how complex this task is, "affective computing" or teaching computers to recognize emotions in humans struggles, even on fast computers, to obtain a 50% success rate on just eight basic emotions. The complexity of the task of accurate emotional recognition means that it is a task we are learning all life long.

But isn't emotional recognition simply a "natural attribute" with some people being naturally sensitive to others while others are brutish and insensitive? There is plenty of evidence in the EQ literature that emotional recognition is partly genetic wiring and starts very early in life. However, there are two schools of thought. One school says EQ is truly innate, that we can be damaged but not improved, that EQ is set very early in life and is mainly genetic, and that like IQ it can be reduced (say by a blow to the head or emotional abuse) but not improved. Thus this view maintains that a sensitive person can be hurt and become emotionally clumsy but that a person born with a brutish disposition cannot become sensitive.

The other view is that EQ, while having a genetic component is a teachable skill. My experience from teaching EQ seminars is that about 85% of people are teachable to varying degrees but 15% have not even the faintest desire to improve emotionally. I think that on the whole EQ is more learned than genetic.

Emotional Recognition and Christian Ministry
Sensitive and caring ministry to others depends on being able to accurately recognize and understand the source of emotion in others. Without this skill pastoral care will be clumsy at best and damaging at worst. Tasks such as counselling and prayer ministry require a fine feeling for personal emotions. If God has called us to ministry He has called us to minister grace to a hurting and damaged world and called us to be able to understand people – including being able to "discern" or "recognize" their emotions.

This is becoming increasingly difficult as in our multi-cultural societies ministry means recognizing emotions of people from different backgrounds, genders, and ethnicities than our own. Any pastor of a church of any size in the modern world will have to be able to discern the feelings of people of half a dozen races and a wide variety of professional and economic backgrounds. We cannot run away from this challenge but must embrace the learning required to be emotionally competent ministers in a complex world.

Interestingly some research done with the Penn Emotional Recognition Test suggests that introverts have better skills at recognizing emotions than extraverts. Given that extraverts are more socially active this seems surprising. Perhaps introverts have greater sensitivity which makes them withdraw from numerous interactions through overload. It also gives some truth to the stereotype of the loud, insensitive extravert! Thus quiet sensitive counsellors and spiritual directors may indeed be the ones to look for when you want your emotions deeply understood.

In recognizing another person's heart the thoughts, intents and feelings need to be surfaced. Jesus, our model, was deeply emotionally aware and "knew what was in the hearts of men". He did not just recognize the surface emotional issues but the deeper undercurrents of the heart. There are some gender differences in what people conceal and what they are willing to reveal though these are far from absolute. In general, I find men are willing to talk about their plans and intentions and tend to conceal their feelings while women tend to conceal their plans and intentions and are more revealing of their feelings. While it is relatively easy to recognize the six basic emotions of happiness, sadness, fear, anger, surprise and disgust it is very hard to recognize thoughts and intentions and the more subtle emotions such as apprehension and tentativeness. Reading people deeply takes time and practice and wisdom. Here are a few clues I have found helpful:

1. Start from a neutral position as free as possible from your own baggage. The more emotion you are carrying – and thereby projecting onto others, the more inaccurate you are. A study by Walz showed that aggressive men saw more anger in other people than was really there. The aggressive men were projecting their own anger onto others. This mislabeling led to behavior problems in life as they reacted in hostile ways to this perceived but non-existent aggression.

2. If you do have a great deal of pain, do not try counselling others until you have dealt with it. This is why I recommend that Christian counsellors and ministers who have been recently divorced take two years out from the ministry until their emotions have been worked through. There is generally too much baggage there to be accurate in reading emotions and to be therapeutic in counselling.

3. Do not take the latest bit of psychology you have read and dump its conclusions and observations on everyone. I have a lot of time for the MBTI personality test and similar instruments but personality typology can become an obstacle to judgment when taken too literally. In general, look at the

objective facts about the person first then much later employ your theories.

4. There is no prize for the hastiest judgment. Suspend religious judgments until all the facts are in. Hasty labeling of clients and leaping to spiritual conclusions is unwise and potentially damaging. There is plenty of time to come to conclusions, so use it wisely and well.

5. Listen to understand and not to judge. There is indeed a place for confronting sin – after we have fully understood the situation. If we seek to understand first and listen intently and with intelligence and wisdom our words of admonition will be far fewer, much more on target, and more easily accepted by the parishioner.

6. Expand your own emotional vocabulary. For instance, use words like exhilarated instead of "up" and "satisfied" instead of "good". By becoming aware of a wide range of emotional terms as they apply to yourself you will be soon able to pick up these finer emotional tones in others as well. Roget's Thesaurus is a good starting point.

7. Use the "mirror principle" to work out what the other person is thinking. By the mirror principle I mean the observation that what "A" thinks of "B" is generally the mirror opposite of what "B" thinks of "A". For instance, if you think someone is very tall then you probably look short to him or her. If you think someone is not too intelligent you probably look like a complicated intellectual to him or her. If you think that certain people are quiet and polite they probably think you are loud and rude. And if you think young people are loud, over the top and energetic they probably think you are staid, quiet and a bit on the slow side. People are often seeing you in an exact mirror image of how you see them.

8. If you can get hold of a "chart of emotions" do so. These charts have dozens of different facial expressions with the emotions labeled underneath. A counsellor should be able to help you get hold of one.

9. Don't just read one aspect e.g. facial expressions, voice, body language or verbal statements. Survey the whole person and watch for patterns as a whole. Just reading body language alone can lead you astray. For instance, a person with their arms crossed may be just cold from the air-conditioning – not rejecting

what you are saying at all. You need to look at all the other factors as well.

10. Try and figure out what they are not saying as well as what they are saying. For instance, if a client talks freely about everyone in their family with the exception of their father – about whom they are totally silent, then there may be something worth exploring.

11. Study crowds and pick up on social distance, actions and reactions – the location of the person in the room, who they are talking to, how many people they move amongst and the degree of animation they are showing. For instance, a person who is feeling timid may be in the corner of the room, the person who is feeling lonely may be on their own, the socially insecure may be glued to just one person and the tragically disconnected person may be near the bar and drinking a bit too much.

12. Assume that even the most seemingly irrational behavior seems intelligent to the person doing it. Then try and work out what that reason is. What thought is behind it? What need are they trying to meet? What emotion is driving it?

False Positives and False Negatives

Most of us have an area that we "get wrong" consistently when reading others. A "false positive" is when you think someone is happy and they are not. It is mistakenly thinking the situation is better than it is. Most men think their marriages are good when their wives think otherwise. Thus the men have a "false positive" when it comes to reading their wives' emotional state. A "false negative" is when a person thinks a situation is bad when it is in fact good or OK. For instance, a person from a rejecting family may see anger or rejection around them in normal friendly social situations. They have a "false negative" when it comes to reading others emotions. They "fill in the blanks" with rejection and find it difficult to believe they are accepted. These false attributions can have enormous social consequences; the young man who thinks a girl loves him when she does not and goes away heartbroken, the husband who thinks his wife is flirting with other men when it is not the case and becomes enraged "over nothing", or the feeling in many offices that "the boss does not care about us" when that is often far from the truth. Learning to read other people's emotions accurately can thus save us much pain.

False reading of other people's emotions leads to mistaken action and reaction on our behalf. People react to "shadows" instead of realities and defend themselves from perceived emotional threats that simply do not exist. For instance, if we believe that the boss hates us and is about to fire us we may start a rumor campaign or even resign our job to avoid the rejection. What a surprise if we get promoted instead! We do not just react to circumstances we react to our interpretation of those circumstances, particularly the emotional perception – whether we are liked or disliked, accepted or rejected, valued or despised. Most people will stay at even a lower paying job if they perceive they are liked, accepted and valued. Therefore people who habitually see the world as disliking them, rejecting them and despising them are going to find life tough going. They, like Cain, will be a wanderer on the earth. This is indeed tragic if their fears are unjustified and their rejection only in their own minds.

To continue this thought for a while we need to look at how "false negatives" can affect us socially and politically. When people constantly misread others intentions towards them and this spreads to an entire group then entire churches, denominations, cities and even nations can become embroiled in it. This group aspect of emotional misunderstanding is often indicated by phrases such as "they hate me" or "they are up to something" where "they" is rather loosely defined. Eventually false negatives can come to include whole classes of people e.g. "all men are lustful rapists" or "all Americans hate Muslims" which, of course rapidly leads to prejudice. If this kind of thinking goes far enough, the false negative can involve an all-embracing projection of fear and suspicion upon the total environment. This fear and defensiveness produces a harsh defining of boundaries between those who are "in" and those who are "out", those who are with us and those who are against us, or even between those who are of God and those who are of Satan. Fear, paranoia, prejudice and hatred can all flow from allowing false negative attributions of others to grow and become believed.

How do these false perceptions come about? They mainly come about through three basic errors in observation and logic:
 The first error is **not gathering all the facts**, or using a biased source of facts. Take the prejudice "all Muslims are terrorists". If we base our sampling on action movies where all the Muslims are terrorists we may arrive at this conclusion. However, if we gather all the facts we will find that there are over 1 billion Muslims and that there are maybe 10,000

muslim terrorists. So if we do our sums we see that only one in one hundred thousand Muslims are terrorists. Thus the complete facts do not bear out the prejudice that all Muslims are terrorists. If truth be told, the facts paint the opposite picture.

The second error is choosing to **unjustifiably filter the facts** so that some aspects are emphasized and some heavily discounted. For instance, take the radical feminist rhetoric "all men are rapists". This is easily disproved statistically. However, someone being shown the statistics on rape might say, "OK, not all men have been caught as rapists and maybe not all men have raped someone – but they would if they could" and thus the false negative is maintained by using a "filter" which keeps the prejudice intact.

Thirdly, we can **have no facts at all**. The whole thing can be imaginary. We can be so completely inaccurate in our reading of people that we get it completely wrong to begin with. This is often due to our family background training us to see things a certain way e.g. training us to see rejection where there is none or being unduly suspicious of others motives.

Another source of error that I find is becoming common in Christian circles is "mystical attributions" such as "I sense in my spirit that so and so has a Jezebel spirit". This often lacks an objective basis in fact. Where I have seen it in operation it has been a power play that makes the speaker look spiritual and perceptive and labels their enemy with a stigma that is difficult to contest or remove. Unless there is substantial good evidence for such a judgment these mystical observations that are plucked out of the ether should be treated as insubstantial and perhaps even as dangerous. At best they come from being misled about the nature of the gift of discernment. Genuine discernment is both spiritual and intelligent with the Holy Spirit operating through a renewed and quickened intellect not just through impressions.

People who operate through inner impressions alone are liable to serious error. Those who have a genuine gift of discernment are generally characterized by a sharp mind, a habit of continual observation, a deep and quiet graciousness, a listening spirit and the ability to keep their conclusions to themselves. While the spiritual man does indeed judge all things he does not do so irrationally and hastily or solely on the basis of an inner intuition. True spiritual judgment is solid and substantiated. When Jesus said the Pharisees were "whitewashed tombs" He was able to clearly point out why in factual terms such as the devouring of widow's houses. He did not say, "In my spirit I just know you are whitewashed tombs, don't ask me why!". The spiritual perception is a new framework that encompasses all known and substantiated facts. Jesus said it is like reading the weather and knowing that a certain wind means rain and another means heat. First there is observation and fact, then there is interpretation of all the observed facts in the light of Scripture and the guidance of the Holy Spirit.

At this point take a minute and ask yourself the following questions about the way you form judgments:
Do others say that you are overly critical or defensive?
How often do you properly gather the data?
How often do you sit down and calculate things out and check the facts?
Do you thoroughly search the Scripture using a concordance or computer Bible or do you just pluck verses from here and there?
Do you "look on the negative side of things"?
Do you filter out positives?
Do you over-emphasize negatives?
Do you anticipate rejection when there is none?
Are you often suspicious of people and then find out that your suspicions were unjustified?
Do you draw sharp boundaries between groups of people, lumping them together as "in" or "out", good or bad, with you or against you?
Do you fix on the negative and ignore the positive?
Does one bad part make the whole thing wrong for you?
Do you go on inner intuitions and dark emotions separate from objective evidence?
Do you feel that you must play judge, jury and executioner?
Do you imagine terrible things about people and imagine them doing evil deeds? (e.g. "I am sure our neighbours are bank robbers.")

If this partly describes you then you need to be aware of these tendencies and strive to counteract them. If you have a constant sense of rejection you may need to tell yourself: "I am probably just imagining this, I always see more rejection than there is." If you are overly suspicious stop and ask, "Is this the real picture, are my suspicions based on solid evidence, not just wild fancies"? If you are constantly defensive and see criticism in every remark, then try to re-interpret those remarks: "Maybe they were just making a constructive suggestion, maybe it wasn't a personal criticism at all."

This involves standing outside your own mental processes and evaluating them. It's called "meta-cognition" or thinking about thinking. You think about the way in which you think and as you do this you correct that which is unhelpful, illogical, irrational or untrue. In the realm of emotions we do this by realizing that our thinking about our emotional environment and other people may be wrong. We then think about our thinking and challenge our negative perceptions with the simple question, "Is this really so?" Is it really so that my wife is having an affair? Is it really so that my neighbor is a bank robber? It is really so that everyone is out to get me?

Good emotional recognition means picking up the emotions that truly are present in the situation such as love and acceptance and not projecting into it emotions that may not be truly present in the situation such as criticism and rejection.

False positives are generally not as dangerous as false negatives but can be just as difficult to recognize and deal with. The pastor may build a castle from a compliment and may start to believe that everyone likes him and become oblivious to his weaknesses. The naïve and sheltered may honestly believe that all people are beautiful and have good intentions – and only find out otherwise in one of life's hard lessons. The missionary may think that the village accepts him because it is polite to him while underneath they are seething with anger at his cultural blunders.

The indication of false positives is constant disappointment. The girl does not love you. The wonderful business opportunity sends you broke. The church does not renew your call. The village eventually tells you what it thinks. There is a balance here. On one hand it's good to be positive, optimistic, hopeful and full of faith. It's OK to strive high and fall flat now and then – that's part of the journey; an honest mistake. On the other hand, it's lousy to be constantly and continually disappointed, ripped off and hurt. Let's be blunt, it's stupid, it's folly, it's not listening to your warning bells. There is often a fine line between faith and folly and pain is a warning of folly. Blows are made for the backs of fools. If you are constantly disappointed in relationships then perhaps you are just too optimistic about how much people love you. If you are in a constant state of shock and your plans come down with a thud at regular intervals perhaps a reality check is in order.

There are two main sources of false positives which are a.) being conned by others and b.) being conned by ourselves. Sometimes the two works together so that people who want something from us play on our vanity and then we go home and strut and preen and daydream about how wonderful we are. As we do this we edge closer and closer to catastrophe and disappointment.

Let's get a tough but fair biblical perspective on this. All people are sinners, and for the vast majority of people self is on the throne. What does this mean? It means that most ordinary people are primarily acting in their own self-interest and are not particularly concerned about your interests except as they may intersect with their own interests. They aren't terrorists or bank robbers but they are not saints either. They are just plain selfish with a few bursts of altruism at Christmas time and during a crisis. After these seasons of good-will it's back to looking after number one. Neither are most people interested in the fine points of being terribly good, honest and ethical, as this conflicts with their more selfish interests. Sure they are not as dishonest as a con artist, but they are not at all interested in becoming like Mother Teresa.

This means that selfishness rules and that real love and appreciation is relatively rare. The Bible does not paint the picture of a world filled with good, nice people who we can trust and who really love us. Neither does it paint a picture of a world full of terrorists. It paints the picture of a selfish world that has disconnected itself from God. This should be our picture also. If we see everyone as "nice" we probably have a wrong picture, or a very low standard of what being nice is. If we walk into a new group of people and believe we have been instantly accepted and that everyone loves us and is only thinking about our welfare – then perhaps you should double check. Maybe behind their acceptance they have a selfish motive. They may want your money, your membership or even your soul. Normal people are only that nice when it is in their self-interest to be that nice. Always ask, "Who benefits?"

It does not hurt to ask the question, "Is it really so?" in positive circumstances, especially if they are unusually positive, and most especially if things seem "too good to be true". I have no intention of plunging you into doubt and cynicism, that's why I dealt with false negatives first. I do not want you to be ripped off by nice salesmen of shoddy goods, used cars, cheap real estate and fake watches; or in the spiritual realm by cults and some televangelists. My experience is that perhaps a dozen people, tops, really love us, and act in our interest and care about us. That's good and it makes life worthwhile. The rest of the six billion people on the planet are only being nice in order to get something. Now that's OK if it's a fair trade, but sometimes it's not a fair trade and we are being conned or used, in which case we get disappointed. You cannot trust the six billion like you trust the twelve. You need to be careful and cautious and wise.

By nature I am a positive, faith-filled optimist who loves seeing people achieve and being involved in big projects and grand schemes. Unfortunately, I am nearly always way too optimistic and trusting and I need help with the details. I value the input of people who can help me see reality. It is so easy for me to delude myself and see success where there can be no success. I have a bias towards "nothing is impossible with God" and that is a good bias and a godly bias. However, I have needed to adopt the solution-focused thinking mentioned earlier in the book and to meticulously look at the data and ask tough realistic questions if I am to make the impossible possible in the real world. There is a balance between say, believing in everyone/selecting the best possible staff; or between seeing all things as possible/choosing projects that are wise, sane and profitable that will not bankrupt Frontier Servants.

The questions I find most helpful in digging out reality are:
- Who profits?
- What is their track record?
- What is this leading to?
- Why do they want me in particular?
- If I look at their actions alone, separate from their words and stated policies, what picture do I get?
- What are the statistics on this? (business opportunity etc.) Are they showing the stats to me? Are the stats they are showing me reliable and verifiable?
- How much extrapolation is going on here? Am I taking a little acceptance to mean total acceptance or a little profit as an indicator of great riches to come? Am I just daydreaming?

- What percentage of people who do this are truly successful? Are the trainers and speakers rich and everyone else poor? Does the business itself generate money or does talking about it generate the money and the business itself is a scam?
- What are the obvious, logical interests of this person/group of people?
- What about the big four areas of self-interest which are money, sex, power and status; are they involved in this, if so, how?
- What do they want from me? Can I deliver those expectations? Should I deliver those expectations?
- Will I get a fair deal at the end of the day?

The above questions may seem at first to have little to do with our emotions. But they do have a lot to do with avoiding disappointment on one hand and not becoming overly cynical on the other. They are questions that will bring you to the truth of the matter and help you get in contact with reality, which is ALWAYS good for us emotionally. These questions do not have to give negative answers. You may indeed find out that you will profit, that it is a fair deal, they do really like you and they are reliable, honest people with a good track record. If so, good! Go for it! The above questions will help you sort out the wheat from the chaff and the rogues from the rest. They will enable you to lead a less ripped off life and guide you to worthwhile and profitable areas to spend your time, money and life energy. In fact, I regularly watch the investment channel, CNBC, which is a bit weird for a missionary who has no investments of any sort. I do this because I want to find out how realistic and successful people think. The interviews on leadership, and the tough questions people ask and the emphasis on facts and data are healthy for me as I am someone who needs to come down to earth regularly and not get lost in my nice, comfortable, but thoroughly impractical, theological speculations.

Other than being conned by others we can be conned by ourselves. We can mistake mere politeness for genuine love or being given a position on a committee for genuine acceptance. We project our own faith and hopefulness into the situation. We extrapolate and we build castles in the air. We build expectations of love and warmth and hope and success that go way beyond the facts, and that this world may not deliver on. Pride and vanity alter our ability to objectively look at ourselves and our plans and others. Pride and vanity puff us up so that it becomes painful to be honest with ourselves and hard to look reality in the face. We need to come to a "sober estimate", not a wildly projected estimate, of ourselves and of reality. When we have a fair idea of who we are and who others are we can see past flattery and politeness simply accepting them as normal social nonsense. We can then instead listen to the real heart values and concerns of those around us. We can hear what they are really saying. We can learn to cope with the truth; which well may be that "we are mainly selfish and only love you a little bit". If we are to perceive the emotions of other people truly to understand and communicate with them well, and attain to a high biblical EQ, then we must be humble and meek to hear what is really there.

But what will this do to our self-esteem? If we cannot con ourselves how do we stay happy? If we have to face the truth, such as "we are mainly selfish and only love you a little bit" - is that worth believing? Why not stay with the illusion? Living in touch with reality is far more emotionally functional and will eventually cause your self-esteem to grow and cause you to become more successful. How? I'll give you a common example from Christian culture.

Christian workers ask people to pray for them and support them and they get a lot of positive vibes. With even a little bit of extrapolation they may think "All these people love me and hundreds of people will pray for me and support me, they really care for me". Buoyed up by all this they become euphoric and surge into ministry on cloud nine. They perceive the emotions of others as being altruistic, positive, caring and full of love. Everyone is nice and they are happy. But six months later there is a huge crash. People forgot to pray, and people didn't support, and people were just being nice. It wasn't real. Your brochures went in the bin. So bitterness overtakes the Christian worker. Anger and resentment rise to the surface. All those broken promises hurt and they hurt badly. If the Christian worker is fortunate they wake up and say: "That's life, I should not have expected a fallen world to be that nice. I'll divide my supporters into three groups. Those I know well and who I know want all the details about what I am doing, then those who I think will support regularly but are not terribly interested in the details of the ministry, then the flaky ones who will support me once or twice then give up. I'll divide my effort proportionately and expect my prayer support and human understanding from the first group, my economic support from the second group and a bit extra now and then from the third group but I will not rely on them". Thus the Christian worker adjusts to reality, takes a sober and realistic view of people, and works out how to move forward in a solution-focused way. They succeed. Life stabilizes, ministry happens, and self-esteem grows. Reality is good for you.

What's Going On Here?

One of the big barriers to correctly reading the emotions of another person is that we cannot understand how on earth they could possibly react that way. We make light of reality of the other person's emotions. People may react in immature ways but we still need to try and understand the source of their immaturity. Writing someone off as "just unspiritual" without understanding why they are unspiritual does not contribute to the solution. It only contributes to the problem. Let's take the teenage "you don't love me" explosion as a classic case. The teenager stomps to their room, slams the door and accuses their parents of not loving them. Why? Is it a means of gaining emotional distance so they can feel free to grow up? Are they hurting and disappointed over a personal matter and were not listened to at home? Writing off the reaction as unspiritual or trying to cast out the demon of rebellion will only make things worse and rob the parents of insight, understanding and valuable relationship building opportunities. Humoring the reaction then searching for understanding is far more profitable.

- Firstly, acknowledge the emotion as real. It may seem bizarre but it is nevertheless being expressed.
- Next, search for the concept that the person is acting on or reacting to. With the teenager the concept they are reacting to may be "you don't listen and you don't understand".
- Try to put that concept in a single phrase or sentence. Once you have boiled down what they are reacting to in one sentence you have probably got the gist of the matter.
- Then ask, "Why have they come to that conclusion, is it a mistaken conclusion or a correct conclusion, and what can I do to help the matter?"

With those four simple steps you can go a long way to sorting through emotions. In addition bear in mind the three levels of a difficult conversation I mentioned earlier in this book – Facts, Feelings and Identity:

What are the facts of the situation?

How are they interpreting those facts and generating certain feelings?
What are they sensing about their identity – is their core being under threat in some way?

To sum up this chapter – as Christians we need to be sensitive to the emotions of others so we can minister grace to a fragile and hurting world. This means we need to be able to accurately read other people's emotions. If our judgments are inaccurate it is often because of false positives or false negatives. We need to review our thinking patterns so they are both faith-filled and positive but also realistic and humble. Much can be gained by distilling the thought behind a person's emotion into a single sentence. This sentence provides the key thought that they are acting on or reacting to. It can also help to ask about the facts, feelings and identity issues involved.

Once we have identified another person's emotions we need to know how to respond appropriately. That is the subject of the next chapter.

Discussion Questions

1. How important is it for people in ministry to be accurately able to read the emotions of other people?

2. What are some of the main ways in which we make errors in judging other people's emotions?

3. Jesus "knew what was in the hearts of men"; what do you think this must have been like for Him?

4. What is a "false negative"? How does it come about? How can we overcome our tendencies to think people do not like us?

5. What is a "false positive"? What are some of the dangers from false positives? How can being realistic in our expectations improve our Christian life?

6. Jesus and the prophets often distilled a person's attitude into a single sentence beginning with a phrase something like "In your hearts you think…". Pick four well-known people such as movie stars and try to put in one sentence what they might be thinking in their hearts.

The Appropriate Expression of Emotions

A time to tear, And a time to sew; A time to keep silence, And a time to speak; (8) A time to love, And a time to hate; A time of war, And a time of peace. (Ecclesiastes 3:7-8 NKJV)

Once we are in touch with our own emotions and the emotions of others we need to put those feelings into words so that they touch minds and hearts and minister the grace of Jesus Christ to the world. With Jesus as our model and some guidance from the Wisdom literature of Scripture we will look at how to speak and act with emotional understanding and appropriate expression.

Issues of Timing -There Is a Time

We are not free to just "let fly" with our emotions. According to Scripture there is an appropriate time for each and every form of emotional expression. This is not chronological time such as "at 3 p.m. you may weep" but event time linked to life events and happenings, "at a funeral it is a good time to express sympathy". An emotion "out of time" is jarring and unedifying and may even be cruel. Laughter at a pastor's joke is appropriate; laughter at a person's misfortune is not. Each expression of emotion has its time and place. Each is "beautiful in its time" (Ecclesiastes 3:11). Emotions in their time are truly of the Spirit and a blessing to others.

Generally, our emotions should be matched to those around us so we "Rejoice with those who rejoice, and weep with those who weep" (Romans 12:15). Emotions should be congruent in both type and intensity. For instance, if people are rejoicing loudly it is appropriate to rejoice loudly with them, if they are weeping quietly it is appropriate to weep quietly in sympathy. When Mary and Martha wept over Lazarus – Jesus also wept. In times of deep suffering and anguish silence can be the best counsel (Job 2:13). Culture, circumstances and social dynamics normally tell us what emotional expression is appropriate in any given situation but this can be modified by the Holy Spirit from time to time.

People who get the social timing of emotional expression wrong can quickly become social outcasts. The classic comic figure is someone who always makes a mess of things in social situations. At the other extreme are people who always blend in perfectly. Such people may lack authenticity and become false and hypocritical, weakened morally by over-compliance with the norm. The "time to speak" is dictated ultimately by the Holy Spirit not social convention (though such conventions are useful and we should know them). Jesus and the prophets often seemed to be "speaking out of turn" in setting forth God's message to their time and place. Others such as Ezra and Daniel seemed to fit much more closely into the warp and woof of their social situations.

However, God calls us to speak we should remember that it is His interests we are serving with our every word and every expression of emotion. Our communication is to flow from the Spirit and be for the edification of others. It is not our own interests we serve or our own need for expressing ourselves. Ultimately love of God and love of neighbor should govern the expression and timing of our emotions. Let's look at a few scriptural guidelines on how we can do this.

Issues of Intensity - Being Strong With the Strong and Weak With the Weak

We need to match our emotional expression with the strength of the person and the depth of the spiritual needs of those around us. When Jesus spoke to people who were strong, hard and stubborn he was strong and harsh and direct (Matthew 23:1-10). On the other hand, with the broken and hurting He was so gentle that it could be said of Him "a bruised reed He will not break" (Isaiah 42:3). Paul makes the puzzling statement "with the weak I became weak" (1 Corinthians 9:22). This means that Paul did not overwhelm weak souls with his powerful personality. Instead Paul measured the strength of his reactions to what the person needed and could take. Paul also tells us to "uphold the weak and be patient with all" (1 Thessalonians 5:14) and that no one was weak without him becoming weak (2 Corinthians 11:29). On the other hand, when Peter was in error this same Paul "withstood him to his face" (Galatians 2:11). The revivalist, Charles Finney, used to classify sinners into "hardened", "awakened" and "penitent" each requiring a different approach from the evangelist.

We see a good example of this principle early on in the book of 1 Samuel when Hannah is weeping before the Lord (1 Samuel 1:9-18). Eli the high priest at first sternly rebuked Hannah thinking she was drunk. It was a "strong" response – and in this case it was inappropriate. On realizing that Hannah was pouring out her soul before the Lord Eli changed from a "strong" to a "weak" or gentle response. He became conciliatory and replied "may the Lord grant your petition". In doing this Eli adjusted his emotional expression to suit the spiritual needs of the situation. Eli was big enough to admit his mistake and adjust his response.

We are to be both priest and prophet. Is the person strong and hard and do they need to be brought to repentance? Then be strong and speak like a prophet. Are they troubled in soul like Hannah? Then minister grace like a priest.

Issues of Place - Private and Public Emotion
In 1 Corinthians 14 Paul writes about the use of the gift of tongues saying that private tongues were for private moments and not for the general worship service. This established the principle that only things that are edifying to the church as a whole should be brought into the public domain. Private spiritual and emotional experiences may be very helpful to the person in private – but they are not for general public consumption.

In church life we have different levels of sharing; that which we share with God alone, and that which we share with our family and close friends, that which we share with a cell group and that which will share with the general public. As a rule of thumb the higher the level of emotion the more private the sharing should be. Emotional sharing is restricted to where it can safely edify the people who hear. Even between Jesus and the disciples at the Last Supper Jesus said, *"I still have many things to say to you, but you cannot bear them now"* (John 16:12). He limited His most intimate sharing to what the disciples could cope with and be edified by.

The principle of "for the edification of all" needs to be carefully weighed when there is sharing of intimate personal testimonies, or the use of the prophetic and the visionary and even during times of passionate intercessory prayer in a known language. I know a woman who is a powerful and prophetic intercessor who groans and travails before God. Unfortunately, her private travail, pain, anger, and righteous indignation are voiced with such deep intensity in the evening service that people are not edified but only embarrassed. This has caused many to leave that service or even find another church. It is the right emotion in the wrong place. While it is deeply sincere and not sinful as such, it is simply not edifying or helpful to the church body. Her emotional outpouring that has its place before the throne of God in private is out of place in a general worship service. Powerful private emotions, even when they are holy emotions, are not for general public consumption. Let's see how even Jesus and the apostles observed this rule.

Much to the frustration of Bible scholars and students of prayer, Jesus never revealed publicly the nature of His private prayer times with the Father. Neither did He reveal to His disciples much about His dreams and visions or describe in any detail His experience of the spiritual world. Also Paul was very reticent in describing what was probably his most powerful spiritual experience in 2 Corinthians 12. Scholars still debate whether this was Paul's experience or that of someone he knew. If Jesus and Paul and the apostles were highly reticent to speak about their private spiritual experiences and if countless great men and women of God since have shared with reticence, perhaps we should be very careful about expressing these sorts of things in public. I am especially careful about the expression of private dreams and visions or the numerous accounts of trips to Heaven or Hell. In Colossians Paul sternly warns Christians about people who take their stand on visions they have seen and depart from the Head, which is Christ (Colossians 2:18,19).

The exception to this is in small groups where intimacy has developed over time and permission for deep sharing is an understood part of the group dynamics. Those who followed David in the wilderness, the twelve disciples of Jesus and the various missionary companions of Paul are Scriptural examples of small groups that seemed to have lived and shared at a very deep level. Cell groups, Bible studies and twelve Step groups are all places where sharing and emotional expression can go deeper for Christians. We all need outlets for our deep emotions and while friends and family should provide this, often they do not do it very well so some alternative structures need to be created. If our private world fails us we cannot just take our overwhelming emotions public. They need to be shared in private with a counsellor, a therapy group or a small group that will willingly accept emotions at that level and keep them in confidence. It is simply not safe to share yourself in public with a fallen world which is not committed to respecting you and your privacy.

How can we know what is appropriate expression of emotions and spiritual experiences? Firstly, we need to ask these questions: Does it match the emotional tone and volume of the group? Is the sharing much more intense than what other people are sharing? Is it much "deeper" than the group normally copes with? Is it in a tone of voice that is much louder and strident than the other sharing? Is it about matters that other people cannot cope with or have no personal experience of? Are people looking awkward and embarrassed? Are you expecting people who hardly know you to act as family or close friends, or even to be therapeutic for you?

Secondly, we need to ask if God meant us to share it in the first place. With some visions God told people to "seal up the scroll", and yet others were to be announced. When the seven thunders spoke the apostle John was not allowed to write down what they said (Revelation 10:3,4) but to Ezekiel God said, "Son of man, eat what you find; eat this scroll, and go, speak to the house of Israel" (Ezekiel 3:1). We need permission from God to share our dreams and visions and without that permission the general rule should be to keep quiet and wait on God for His timing for that revelation.

Thirdly, we need to spiritually evaluate that which we think the Lord has told us to share, especially if it has a high emotional content. Often the best thing to do is to carefully write down exactly what you think God wants you to say – just as the prophets wrote down their revelations. Then wait on it in prayer for at least forty-eight hours. Then finally share it with two or three others that you trust and who can help you if you have accidentally said something that is not quite in line with Scripture. Many churches have the policy that all prophecy should be passed by the elders before being aired in public and this seems to prevent much abuse of the prophetic.

Fourthly, we need to be careful about the presence of young people and those with more sensitive and impressionable dispositions. Some horrifying sermon illustrations (especially one about a father letting his son be killed in a swing bridge to save a passing train) are so emotional that they can only be described as manipulative. These can scare young people in the congregation leaving them with distorted views of God and church. Sermons need to be G-rated when children are present.

Fifthly, ministers need to be extremely careful about sharing intimate or sensational information from the pulpit, especially that of a sexual nature. There are certain lines we need to draw when dealing with social evils and Paul refuses to comment about certain gross perversions that "should not even be mentioned among the saints" (1 Corinthians 5:1: Ephesians 5:3). Sensational and vivid material is seldom edifying unless it is masterfully handled. It tends to spark unhealthy associations, start rumors, and lead to idle curiosity or inform people about things they are better off being ignorant about. Confessions in particular should only be made to God alone or to highly trusted and confidential others. If some details have to go public because of the public nature of the offence they should be kept to an edifying minimum.

Finally, deep emotions should only be shared when there is genuine trust already present – not to elicit trust or as an act of manipulation. Some clever people use emotional sharing to build trust – which they later violate. Proper emotional sharing is built on pre-existing trust and is not a tool to manipulate others.

Once we have the timing of our emotional expression right and decided on how private or public it is to be we then need to make sure that we deliver a clear, unambiguous and balanced message.

Issues of Balance – Ensuring You Get Both Parts of Your Message Across
Emotions are often mixed and in order to express them clearly we need to give a picture of all the emotions involved in a particular situation and their relative strengths. For instance, consider a Christian father watching his daughter go out on her first date with a godly young man from the church youth group. He may say something like: "Jill, Steven is a good choice and I am pleased that you have chosen to go out with him and not some other guy. He is a guy of real character and I am sure he will treat you well. However, that skirt you have chosen is a bit too daring. I know it is your first date and you want to be attractive but I want you to change it right now. I also want you back here by 10:00 pm and no later. That will make sure that your Mom and I can feel that you have a responsible attitude to dating and we can trust you in the future. Have a good night and have fun and don't forget to pray. I hope you enjoy the

movie, it sure sounds good."

Here the father is expressing a wide range of concerns each in balance with the others giving a coherent message. The anxiety is not out of balance with the love and the clear rules are set in a general context of approval, care and concern. This is what I call the "light and shadow" technique. It involves expressing all aspects of an issue, its boundaries, the light and the dark and the various contrasts so it cannot fail to be understood.

Often I use the phrases "I am saying" and "I am not saying..." e.g. "I am saying you need to redo that work, but I am not saying that you are a bad employee. I continue to value your services." By giving the contrasts, by clearly stating what you are saying and what you are not saying, the message is made completely clear and misunderstanding is removed. The concerned father in the illustration above may have just said, "You are not going out in that skirt" without any further explanation. If he had done so the daughter may have leaped to a range of rather dramatic and negative conclusions. By including the reassurances, and placing things in context, potential misunderstanding and conflict was avoided. Paul often uses this technique in his epistles where he reassures the church of his prayers, love and concern and then firmly corrects a wide range of issues.

This use of the "light and shadow" technique takes a while to master. First of all you have to know the main fears of the other person and then you have to possess the courage to address them directly. For instance, in getting someone to do some very sub-standard work again you might say, "This work is well below your best George and I'm disappointed that you produced it. You are in no danger of being fired but I very much want you to do your best and do this over again. I value your work and I think highly of the contributions you have made in the past but this is just not good enough. I am sure you will do a better job this time around." The obvious fears of dismissal and of being thought incompetent are addressed and reassurance given. At the same time the message that it is not good enough is clearly and firmly conveyed.

This raises one of the trickiest questions in human communication – how much emotional truth can we tell in a given situation? We may have the timing right, the choice of audience (private or public) correct, a balanced and tactful statement but how much do we tell people about the emotional truth of the situation?

Issues of Emotional Truth – Why Not Fake It Till You Make It?

Is not some pretence a normal and even an essential part of life? What about people who are in constrained social roles such as an archbishop or mayor where a high degree of emotional control is required? Do you really want an emotionally honest policeman during a crisis? Aren't we supposed to be joyful? What's so wrong about faking a bit of enthusiasm?

Christians do not express emotions for mere impression management, or for personal catharsis under the guise of authenticity. Emotions are expressed for the glory of God, for the edification of His people and for the love of one's neighbor. Thus a police officer in a crisis will not vent his feelings but maintain good emotional control and a professional demeanor as that is the right, loving and most edifying course of action in a crisis. Contrary to some pop psychology books, this is not repression. It is, in fact, responsible Christian emotional management. It is not pretence; it is self-control.

Pretence is when you pretend to be experiencing an emotion that you do not really have within you. Self-control is when you bring a real and existing emotion into line with God's will. "Faking it till you make it" tends only to produce good actors and skilful hypocrites. False emotion ends up deluding people and eroding our morality. We cannot lie about our emotional state without lying about ourselves and the danger is coming to believe the lie and losing touch with ourselves forever. On the other hand should we not be so in love with "total sincerity" that we answer the question "how are you?" with a list of woes and complaints!

Our emotions should be true and not false but they should also be appropriate and edifying. We are to express true emotions that are modulated by the circumstances, timing and needs of the situation. We think before we emote. We aim to edify, to be appropriate, to inject those feelings into the situation that encourage, uplift or console. We balance truth with grace, bringing both to bear on the situation. Jesus did not retreat from expressing emotion. His emotions were real and authentic and spiritual. There was a solid and appropriate truth about them. Yet they conveyed grace and fitted the moment perfectly.

Thus we should never fake an emotion except if you are actually an actor. Christian emotion is to be real, but it is also to be self-controlled. The emotion revealed should fit the circumstances and it should edify others. If I am boiling mad nothing is gained by "being honest". I am far better off maintaining self-control. But neither should I fake happiness in order to disguise my anger. That ends up being self-distorting and untruthful. God is self-revealing but He is also self-concealing! He reveals the truth about Himself, a bit at a time, as we can manage and cope with it. He does not reveal all of Himself at once. Similarly, we need to reveal the truth about ourselves, so we cannot pretend emotionally, but we need to fit that truth to what others can bear.

Conclusion

In this chapter we have seen that there is a proper time for each and every form of emotional expression and that this is an "event time" not a clock time. We also saw that emotions have a proper intensity that depends on the person – being strong with the strong and weak with the weak. Emotions have their proper audiences. Public expression of emotions should edify the general public and private emotions belong in private settings. We have also seen a little on how to balance emotions in our speech and how to express them wisely and truthfully for the glory of God and the edification of others. Much more about appropriate emotional expression can be learned by observing people of integrity in your own culture and surroundings. Watch how they handle situations and how the delicate balances are achieved, what is said and what is left out, how they encourage and how they rebuke, and how they carry the image of Jesus in their behavior. The final chapter will be about love. After all, is not love our aim as we express our emotions?

Discussion Questions

1. Read Ecclesiastes 3:1-11, what does it tell you about the timing of emotional expression?

2. How forceful should we be with people? What does it mean to be strong with the strong and weak with the weak? Have you ever been in a situation like Eli where you have realized that you have needed to change your approach?

3. How openly can we share our emotions? Which emotions are best kept private?

4. "Let everything be done for the edification of others." How does this principle affect the way we communicate personally? How does the principle affect how we should communicate in church?

5. List some ways in which misunderstandings can cause big problems. How can using the "light and shadow" technique help avoid this? Use the light and shadow technique as you tackle the following problem: "Some good natured but rather active teenagers sit down at the back of the church, nudge each other and are a bit playful during service, though not in a bad way. Some of the crusty members of the church are affronted by this and have come demanding that something be done. You need to say something to both groups here. What do you say and how do you say it?

6. Should you fake it till you make it? Why not?

Love Is a Many Splendored Thing

To know the love of Christ which passes knowledge; that you may be filled with all the fullness of God. (Ephesians 3:19 NKJV)

Ephesians 3:19, quoted above, is my favorite Bible verse. It never fails to make me gasp in awe and wonder, especially the last phrase "that you may be filled with all the fullness of God". According to St. Paul, you and I can be filled with all the fullness of God. That is absolutely mind-boggling. If this verse was not there in Scripture I would have called it heresy and never dared to invent it. It's too much, and I cannot absorb it fully. God means us to become like Jesus who was the fullness of Deity in bodily form (Colossians 2:9). We partake of that sort of fullness and are to grow up in all aspects and be like Him.

I am saying that we can partake of the fullness of God and be filled with it. I am certainly not saying that we become God. We will not be "Him who sitteth on the throne". We will be the ones waving palm branches and having white robes and singing Alleluia in Heaven. Whatever being filled with all the fullness of God means, it does not turn us into an object of worship, or make us the creator and sustainer of the Universe. Being filled with the fullness of God is sharing a nature, and is what theologians call "participating in the communicable attributes of God". The incommunicable attributes such as the "*omni*'s" belong to God alone.

This promise that through love we can be filled with the fullness of God is a marvelous promise in the midst of a wonderful prayer. Let's look at the whole of Paul's prayer and put it in its proper context.

> For this reason I bow my knees to the Father of our Lord Jesus Christ, (15) from whom the whole family in heaven and earth is named, (16) that He would grant you, according to the riches of His glory, to be strengthened with might through His Spirit in the inner self, (17) that Christ may dwell in your hearts through faith; that you, being rooted and grounded in love, (18) may be able to comprehend with all the saints what is the width and length and depth and height; (19) to know the love of Christ which passes knowledge; that you may be filled with all the fullness of God. (20) Now to Him who is able to do exceedingly abundantly above all that we ask or think, according to the power that works in us, (21) to Him be glory in the church by Christ Jesus to all generations, forever and ever. Amen. (Ephesians 3:14-21 NKJV)

There is a succession of ideas and "spiritual stages" here, each of which leads to the next and forms the foundation for the one to come:

1) We are strengthened with might through His Spirit in the inner self.
2) This leads to Christ dwelling in our hearts by faith.
3) We then become rooted and grounded in love
4) We comprehend with all the saints the greatness of the love of Christ.
5) That we may be filled with all the fullness of God.

The other chapters of this book have dealt with stage one - being strengthened in our inner self and achieving personal mastery. They have also dealt with stage two – being focused firmly on Christ so He dwells in our heart by faith and we experience life and peace. Then in the last few chapters we have started exploring stage three – being grounded in a loving lifestyle where we express ourselves in edifying ways.

In this last chapter we will further explore stage three – becoming rooted and grounded in love. Next we will study the last two stages – comprehending the greatness of the love of Christ and being filled with all the fullness of God. All three final stages involve the mystery called love. The practice and the experience of love leads us to the fullness of God. The high reaches of the spiritual life are about perfecting our ability to love God and love one another. Love is the ultimate in biblical EQ. The ultimate use of our emotions is love of God expressed in worship and that is the use they will be put to in Heaven. The ultimate state of our emotions is pure love. The ultimate height of our emotions is when we can love our enemies.

> "You have heard that it was said, 'You shall love your neighbor and hate your enemy.' (44) "But I say to you, love your enemies, bless those who curse you, do good to those who hate you, and pray for those who spitefully use you and persecute you, (45) "that you may be sons of your Father in heaven; for He makes His sun rise on the evil and on the good, and sends rain on the just and on the unjust. (46) "For if you love those who love you, what reward have you? Do not even the tax collectors do the same? (47) "And if you greet your brethren only, what do you do more than others? Do not even the tax collectors do so? (48) "Therefore you shall be perfect, just as your Father in heaven is perfect. (Matthew 5:43-48 NKJV)

If we love our enemies we attain spiritual perfection. Loving our enemies and blessing those who curse us leads us to become sons of our Father in heaven (Matthew 5:43-45). In verse 48 Jesus' apparently absurd command is "you shall be perfect, just as your Father in heaven is perfect". This seems as 'ridiculous' as saying we can be filled with all the fullness of God. The two apparently absurd statements are, of course, connected. Love leads us to be in the fullness of God, and loving our enemies makes us perfect like our Father in heaven. Both perfections are attained through strenuous love. God desires us to dwell in perfect love where we can love friend and foe alike. The path to spiritual perfection is the path of loving our enemies, overcoming our fight-or-flight response, exercising our biblical EQ skills and dwelling in a perfect benevolence towards all, free from animosity, hatred, revenge and the spiteful impulses of the flesh. That is high ground indeed.

Love is, of course, the fulfillment of the law, the perfection of biblical EQ and the one great attribute of the Christlike nature. It's part of what Americans call "motherhood and apple pie"; a global sentimental statement that makes us all feel warm and with which no one dare disagree but which is apparently of little real consequence or practical value. In most Bible studies everyone present can tell you such things as love is a good thing, it fulfills the law and we should be doing more of it. The Good Samaritan was very nice and a wonderful example. We should all love God and our neighbors and that means everyone. Amen. So I'm going to skip all of that. You already know it. Instead, I'm going to ask a few tough questions, e.g., "Why don't we love very well at all? Why are we still mainly selfish and only love a little?" Paul talks of the love of God being poured out in our hearts and in this love transforming us from glory to glory and even making us perfect and filling us with the fullness of God. Was he just joking? Is that just theological waffle or is it for real? If it's for real how can we get hold of it?" These are some of the real, "where the rubber hits the road", questions of Christian living and this book is all about those sort of questions, especially where they intersect with our emotional life. But first a definition of love:

> **Love is a lawful and practical way of life which we live out from Christ within us in a common benevolent connection with God and with others.**

Love is lawful
It rejoices in the truth and takes no pleasure in evil

(1 Corinthians 13:6). The true follower of God in the Old Testament was someone who "loves Me and keeps My commandments" (Exodus 20:6; Deuteronomy 5:10). In the New Testament love is demonstrated in keeping the commandments of Jesus Christ (John 14:15, 21; 15:10; 1 John 5:3). In 2 John love is even defined by obedience: "This is love, that we walk according to His commandments" (2 John 1:6). Thus love is not some kind of maverick sentimentality that can ride roughshod over laws and do what it likes in pursuit of the grand passion. Love is God's nature at work and God is lawful and holy so love is lawful also.

Love is practical

As we saw in the chapters on beliefs our emotions are meant to move us to Christian action. Faith working through love should move us to do the good deeds that God has prepared beforehand for us to do (Ephesians 2:8-10; Galatians 5:6). The parable of the Good Samaritan (Luke 10:29-37) shows that loving your neighbor often involves practical action. This is backed up in innumerable passages in Scripture most notably James chapters 2 and 3 and in 1 John, particularly 1 John 3:16-18.

> By this we know love, because He laid down His life for us. And we also ought to lay down our lives for the brethren. (17) But whoever has this world's goods, and sees his brother in need, and shuts up his heart from him, how does the love of God abide in him? (18) My little children, let us not love in word or in tongue, but in deed and in truth. (19) And by this we know that we are of the truth, and shall assure our hearts before Him. (1 John 3:16-19 NKJV)

The specific, practical way we are to love our enemies is given in the book of Romans.

> Therefore "If your enemy is hungry, feed him; If he is thirsty, give him a drink; For in so doing you will heap coals of fire on his head." (21) Do not be overcome by evil, but overcome evil with good. (Romans 12:20-21 NKJV)

Thus love is not a mere emotion detached from action. It is not a sentiment that we can "have in our hearts" without ever acting on it. Love is a spur to action. Faith working through love moves us to do things of a practical nature

Love is a way of life.

> Therefore be imitators of God as dear children. (2) And walk in love, as Christ also has loved us and given Himself for us, an offering and a sacrifice to God for a

sweet-smelling aroma. (Ephesians 5:1-2 NKJV)

To "walk in love" means to make it our lifestyle. This lifestyle is reflected in Acts chapters 2-7 where the early church is shown living in love, helping widows, healing the sick, preaching the gospel, obeying the commandments and enduring persecution in a noble and forgiving spirit. The lifestyle of the early church was one of constant worship, constant fellowship, unity of soul and spirit and an incredible desire to meet one another's needs (Acts 4:31-37). It was a lifestyle of love, empowered by the Holy Spirit and led by the apostles. This sort of lifestyle love is called "abiding in love" in 1 John and means dwelling from day to day in love so it totally characterizes one's life. The love we are called to, which perfects us, is thus not an occasional spurt of affection. No one is made into the fullness of God by an occasional spurt of affection. Abiding love, that we can walk in and which transforms us, is not the warm gooey feeling you get singing Scripture choruses, though it is slightly related. Real love is a lot more solid and real and ethical and practical than that. Let's keep going and see if we can figure out what this abiding, transforming, love lifestyle is like.

Love is lived out from Christ within us
Love is a Jesus thing. Love is what Jesus in us wants to do. Love flows from Christ within us. The natural man cannot attain to this sort of love; the love that cares for enemies, that abides in the commandments of God and makes us into the fullness of God. If the natural man could do that then God would have kept Jesus in heaven. If the natural man was adequate to become like God then there is no need for a cross, a resurrection, an indwelling Holy Spirit and a new nature. So if we need a new nature to love then the old nature is useless and the Law is useless. Law-keeping does not make us loving, it only makes us defeated and condemned because we are weak and the flesh always wins (Romans 5-8; Galatians 3 and 4). At best the Law is a holy, and righteous and good tutor that brings conviction of sin and leads us to repentance. The natural man under the tutelage of the holy, righteous and just law just ended up a sordid mess. The flesh ran rampant. God got locked out. So He instituted a New Covenant, in Christ, where the Law is written on our hearts by the Holy Spirit and the Christian life is now lived from the inside out, not from the Law books to the inside. Listen! You can only live the Christian life one way – from Jesus in you, out to others and the world. Love is not a feeling that comes into you. Love is living water that flows out of your inmost being because Christ dwells in your hearts by faith. Hear ye! Hear ye!

Hear ye! Christ IN you is THE hope of glory—the only hope, the sole hope. He is all you have got in the fight against sin and the quest for a godly character. Your strength, intellect, cleverness, willpower and rule-keeping cannot avail. They are not a "hope of glory". They are certain and agonizing defeat. It is God who is at work within you! Let the new man live the new life. Let Jesus in you love others through you.

But how? That was my question for years as people would talk about living the new life from Christ within us. How do we get in touch with Christ within us and how do we "do it"? It just seemed like so much theory to me, a bit of swift-handed exegetical fiddling, a holding out of a hope that there was no way to lay hold of. But the early church did know this love. It worked for them and it can work for us. The secret is connection. Forge the connection with God and with others, and maintain that connection like your life depended on it, which it does, and Christ will flow out of your inmost being. No connection, no – flow, deep connection, deep flow. Let's look at this further.

Love involves a common benevolent connection with God

> But he who is joined to the Lord is one spirit with Him. (1 Corinthians 6:17 NKJV)

Many counselling theorists are now exploring the transformational power of love as it flows in direct personal connection to God and to others. Our selfish individuality has led us astray. For too long we have wanted counselling recipes we can work on our own without having to open up to God or man. We are discovering that God has designed His world to be firstly connected to Him and then to one another in a huge inter-connected cascade of love. In this regard I recommend the recent work of Larry Crabb and his book "*Connecting*". I also recommend the work of Dr. Ed Smith in "*Theophostics*". These are just two people in a vast and growing movement trying to explore the transformational aspects of relationship to God and others. We are not islands, we are people and people need connection. This connection is a vital part of our EQ and a key to maturing in Christ.

> "To know the love of Christ that surpasses knowledge that you may be filled." (Ephesians 3:19).

The knowing of the love is vital. It's the connection that is transformational. It's knowing Christ, and the extent of His love, that matures us. It's the experiencing of that relationship, and being rooted and grounded in love, which stabilizes us. I commenced my Christian life believing that I should be "well grounded in the Scripture" and that was good and helpful. However, it was only much later that I saw the need to be rooted and grounded in love and in Christ. You and I are grounded in a personal relationship with our Savior. Now even if my Bible was confiscated I would still have my rock solid foundation in my relationship with God. The Scripture have contributed immensely to that relationship, of course. However, I relate to a Person not a set of Scripture or even a set of elegant doctrines. Now it's God's Spirit within me, and His personal connection to me, that changes me from glory to glory.

> Now the Lord is the Spirit; and where the Spirit of the Lord is, there is liberty. (18) But we all, with unveiled face, beholding as in a mirror the glory of the Lord, are being transformed into the same image from glory to glory, just as by the Spirit of the Lord. (2 Corinthians 3:17-18 NKJV)

The Jews had the Torah but we have Christ and with unveiled faces we behold Him and by the power of the Spirit we are transformed, rooted and grounded and perfected in love, and go from glory to glory until we reach the fullness of God.

Connection is everything and through it we receive the love that truly changes us. God is our greatest and only real need. We do not need to go on eating, or working or breathing, but we do need to stay in connection with God. We establish that connection at our conversion when we repent from sin and place our faith in Christ. We maintain that connection through setting our minds on the Spirit, on things above, and on Christ and the interests of God. We need to make a definite clear commitment to fix our minds in the right place. That's the only thing we can do to keep the connection open. The mind is the only part of our consciousness we can control. Fixing it on God through prayer, meditation and concentrated love in the Spirit is all we can humanly do to maintain our transforming link with God.

Through the transforming work this connection works in us, we gain mastery over the fight-or-flight response, over the flesh and all the wrong impulses it contains. Through this connection we find the power to be obedient in the Spirit, not according to the letter of the law. Over time the Spirit produces His fruit in us and we bear love, joy and peace and become humble, meek, patient, gentle, kind and full of self-control. We begin to love our enemies and pray for those who persecute us. We have the strength in the inner self to refuse to retaliate. We become rooted and grounded in love and our world moves from being self-centered to being God-centered and other-serving. We start communicating with grace and ministering effectively and grasping the height, depth, width, and length of the love of God until we are filled up with all the fullness of God.

This connection seems horribly fragile at first and the devil tries his best to break it. He assails it with doubt, confusion, distraction, lust, and every spiritual attack he can manage. The first part of this book addresses those concerns. Now let's look at what the Scripture says about the nature of our connection to God. As you read the Scripture below (author's emphasis) notice: a.) What God has done to establish the connection with us, and the nature of that connection. b.) What we must do to maintain the connection, c.) How our connection with God also means connection with other Christians.

> Therefore, having **been justified by faith**, we have **peace with God** through our Lord Jesus Christ, (2) through whom also we have **access by faith into this grace in which we stand,** and rejoice in hope of the glory of God. (3) And not only that, but we also glory in tribulations, knowing that tribulation produces perseverance; (4) and perseverance, character; and character, hope. (5) Now hope does not disappoint, because the **love of God has been poured out in our hearts by the Holy Spirit who was given to us.** (Romans 5:1-5 NKJV)

> But he who is **joined to the Lord** is one spirit with Him. (1 Corinthians 6:17 NKJV)

> By which also you are saved, if you **hold fast that word** which I preached to you; unless you believed in vain. (1 Corinthians 15:2 NKJV)

> Now then, we are ambassadors for Christ, as though God were pleading through us: we implore you on Christ's behalf, **be reconciled to God.** (2 Corinthians 5:20 NKJV)

> But now in Christ Jesus you who once were far off have been **brought near by the blood of Christ.** (14) For He Himself is **our peace,** who has made both one, and has broken down the middle wall of separation, (15) having abolished in His flesh the enmity, that is, the law of commandments contained in ordinances, so as to create in Himself one new man from the two, thus making peace, (16) and that He might **reconcile them both to God** in one body through the cross, thereby **putting to death the enmity.** (17)

And He came and **preached peace** to you who were afar off and to those who were near. (18) For through Him we both have **access by one Spirit to the Father.** (19) Now, therefore, you are no longer strangers and foreigners, but **fellow citizens with the saints and members of the household of God,** (20) having been built on the foundation of the apostles and prophets, Jesus Christ Himself being the chief corner stone, (21) in whom the whole building, being **joined together,** grows into a holy temple in the Lord, (22) in whom you also are being **built together for a dwelling place of God in the Spirit.** (Ephesians 2:13-22 NKJV)

Which are a shadow of things to come, but the substance is of Christ. (18) Let no one cheat you of your reward, taking delight in false humility and worship of angels, intruding into those things which he has not seen, vainly puffed up by his fleshly mind, (19) and not **holding fast to the Head,** from whom all the body, nourished and knit together by joints and ligaments, grows with the increase that is from God. (Colossians 2:17-19 NKJV)

For the love of money is a root of all kinds of evil, for which some have strayed from the faith in their greediness, and pierced themselves through with many sorrows. (11) But you, O man of God, flee these things and pursue righteousness, godliness, faith, love, patience, gentleness. (12) Fight the good fight of faith, **lay hold on eternal life,** to which you were also called and have confessed the good confession in the presence of many witnesses. (1 Timothy 6:10-12 NKJV)

Draw near to God and He will draw near to you. Cleanse your hands, you sinners; and purify your hearts, you double-minded. (James 4:8 NKJV)

"I know your works, and where you dwell, where Satan's throne is. And you **hold fast to My name,** and **did not deny My faith** even in the days in which Antipas was My faithful martyr, who was killed among you, where Satan dwells. (Revelation 2:13 NKJV)

God has done an enormous preparatory work. He has brought us near by the blood of Christ, which cleanses us from sin and allows us to approach the throne of grace in time of need (Hebrews 4:14-16). We have access to the Father through the Spirit and this access is so intimate that Paul says we are joined to the Lord and one spirit with Him (1 Corinthians 6:17). We are at peace with God (Romans 5:1-5) and the love of God pours into our hearts through the Holy Spirit who is given to us. Yet as we saw earlier we can grieve and quench and resist the Spirit by sinning. Maintaining the connection means maintaining a good relationship with the Holy Spirit who is our access to God (Ephesians 2:18). To keep that connection wide open and draw near to God we must purify our hearts if we are double-minded and put away sin (James 4:8). We also need to deal with speculative spirituality that can disconnect us from the Head which is Christ (Colossians 2:19). We have to flee greed and worldliness and the love of money and pursue virtue as Timothy did so that we may lay hold of eternal life (1 Timothy 6:10-12). Keeping our connection strong may involve some vigorous effort, in the midst of persecution we may have to hold fast and not deny the faith, an injunction that appears many times in the letters to the seven churches (Revelation 2:13).

What we are doing in all this is not inventing a new law but maintaining an existing relationship we have with God through faith according to His grace. Our relationship started with a faith connection to God and it is maintained by keeping that faith connection so that the Christian life can be said to be "from faith to faith".

> For in it the righteousness of God is revealed from faith to faith; as it is written, "The just shall live by faith." (Romans 1:17 NKJV)

Now the faith connection is kept by intensely loving God, and having our minds fixed on Him so His Spirit can touch our consciousness, which is absolutely staked on things above. Christ in us wants to focus His entire attention on the Father and the things of the Spirit but it requires our minds be set on things above. There is an act of the will before Christ can most fully connect. As the Father communicates with His Son in us, by the Spirit which gives us access to the Father, we experience grace and are transformed.

This grace requires our faith. We must trust God and trust His Word and launch out and rest myself on Him. As we draw near to God by faith we will naturally move away from sin. If we want to stay near to sin, it is very hard to draw near to God. Faith means trusting that God is a rewarder of those who seek Him. Faith is the inner pragmatic calculation that the goodness we will receive through our connection with God far outweighs the goodness we think we will receive through sin. It's a decision that the word of God is reliable, and that the reward He promised will arrive, and that God is utterly trustworthy. God gives us a hint that this is so through the Holy Spirit, which is the guarantee of the inheritance to come. As we make this definite, tough, strong decision to seek our goodness in God and not in sin the Christ life within us is fully released.

This is "holding fast". I do not mean that you need to hold fast or you will fall away. It's not that sort of holding fast. You are not in a precarious relationship with an angry Creator. You stand forgiven in the love of God. The problem is "self", not God. It is we who break the connection not Him. We hold fast in order not to disconnect ourselves from the Head or grieve the Holy Spirit that pours Himself out into our hearts.

Let's look at this another way. The relationship with God is rock solid on His side. I do not have to do anything to please Him. However, sin grieves Him. Sin is disruptive to our relationship so it goes. We are justified by faith alone and not by any works of the Law. We are safe in grace.

It's like a marriage here in the Philippines where there is no possibility of divorce. You can sin all your like in that marriage and theoretically and legally it will never rupture. It is rock solid. But I love my wife and I value our relationship and I have no wish to grieve her so I do not sin against her. Similarly, I am safe with God and legally speaking the relationship is rock solid. I can sin a great deal and still He will be faithful even though I am faithless (2 Timothy 2:13) but if I did so the transforming relationship of agape love would be in tatters. I have no desire to grieve Him so I choose not to sin; not because I "have to" in order to get into heaven but because I want to in order to know Him more fully and because I "want to" be transformed by His love being poured out in my heart through the Holy Spirit. I have decided for the fullness of the Christ-like life.

What incentive do we have to make this tough decision? And what has it got to do with love, which after all is the subject of this chapter? This love that we abide in, and walk in, and which penetrates every corner of our being is the royal highway to the highest reaches of the Christian life and the very ground of all that we will inherit in Christ. As we love, we fulfill the Law (Romans 13:10), become imitators of God (Ephesians 5:1,2), and perfect as our heavenly Father is perfect (Matthew 5:43-48). We attain to all the fullness of God (Ephesians 3:19), we abide in God and He abides in us (1 John 4:16), we become like Him (1 John 3:1-3) and share key aspects of His nature so the apostle can say, "as He is, we are" (1 John 4:17). This is not heresy, it is Scripture. God intends us to be like Jesus, in every aspect and to be full of love. That is, we are to be spiritual, eternal, loving, wise and mature like Jesus. We are the redeemed (Revelation 5:8-10). We are the brands snatched from the fire (Zechariah 3). We are the ones clothed in white standing before the throne of God, and as we stand there we will realize that we are like Him (1 John 3:1-3). Our destiny is to bear his image (Romans 8:28-31) and we will be eternal, and immortal, and clothed in a spiritual body (1 Corinthians 15:42-54). We will be so like

Him that Jesus will not be ashamed to call us brethren (Hebrews 2:11-17). God has done something magnificent in us by grace, and seated us in heavenly realms with Himself, that the succeeding ages may marvel (Ephesians 2:4-7). The inheritance I want is to be so transformed by God's blazing love poured out in my heart that I am made utterly like Jesus Christ. That is something worth focussing on, and it makes leaving sin alone very worthwhile.

Love involves connecting with others

At this point some of you are probably saying something like "John, I thought this was going to be a wonderful, practical book, but you go and ruin it at the end with all that theology". Aha! This is the point, I could have left it as a "wonderful how-to book" and you could have tried to put it into action in your own strength. And you would have done what you have always done and got what you have always got. Unless you learn to tap into the power of Jesus within you, this book will be of little use to you. However, if you get that connection going and God's power working within you and you set your sights on having your emotions redeemed so you can be like Jesus and love people – then, guess what? You will make ten times the progress.

Now let's go to the last part of our definition of love: *Love is a lawful and practical way of life, which we live out from Christ within us, in a common benevolent connection with God and with others.* What's the "and others"? What is so special about the early church? Why did people love each other? Why is my church cold and dead and selfish? Going back to one of the questions I proposed at the beginning of this chapter with: "Why don't we love very well at all; why are we still mainly selfish?"

Selfishness comes from people who believe in preserving themselves, at all costs, and being competitive. The selfish person who pushes into the queue at the ATM is self-preserving (of their time) and competitive (with the others in the queue). Selfishness results in envy, selfish ambition and a whole list of rotten behaviors that cause disorder in churches and communities and are very well described in James 3 and Galatians 5. In direct contrast with this, love of others flows from self-giving via the cross. Let's look at a very famous passage of Scripture:

"For God so loved the world that He gave His only begotten Son, that whoever believes in Him should not perish but have everlasting life. (17) "For God did not send His Son into the world to condemn the world, but that the world through Him might be saved. (18) "He who believes in Him is not condemned; but he who does not believe is condemned already, because he has not believed in the name of the only begotten Son of God. (John 3:16-18 NKJV)

When God wanted to love the world He did not send a poem. He did not send an e-mail with a nice graphic and a catchy tune. He sent His Son, thus He gave Himself. When we love others we send a bit of ourselves to them. When Christ loves others through us, He sends Himself to others through us. Early in my ministry I received a very nice note from a couple in the church who said, among other things "we see God's love shining out through you." I was flabbergasted and humbled. I had no idea that God's love could be seen in me. All I could see was my mistakes. Somehow Jesus had given Himself to others through me. As Paul said, *But we have this treasure in earthen vessels, that the excellence of the power may be of God and not of us (2 Corinthians 4:7 NKJV)*. Thus when I love others I establish a connection and send a bit of myself along that connection to them, at the same time Christ uses that connection to send Himself to them. God is still sending His Son into the world – through you and me.

Just in case you think I have gone all mad and mystical, go over the metaphors for the church in Scripture. Christ is the Head of the church, which is His body, and so when parts of his body love a person He is loving the person. When I hold my wife's hand, it is not just my hand that is loving Minda, it is all of me, including my head and heart. Similarly when a part of Christ's body loves someone it is also Jesus loving someone. I went through a very dark time in my life once that lasted for a few months. Every time I was at my lowest a certain chatty friend would appear from nowhere with some of my favorite junk food and restore my spirits. Anne was like an angel. She was Christ ministering to me. In her I saw and felt God's love. God sent Jesus wrapped up in Anne. This identification is so close that when Jesus revealed Himself to Saul on the Damascus Road , He said "Saul, Saul why are you persecuting Me?" and "I am Jesus who you are persecuting." To persecute the church was to persecute Jesus.

Then he fell to the ground, and heard a voice saying to him, "Saul, Saul, why are you persecuting Me?" (5) And he said, "Who are You, Lord?" Then the Lord said, "I am Jesus, whom you are persecuting. It is hard for you to kick against the goads." (Acts 9:4-5 NKJV)

Christ is in His body. Where His body goes Jesus goes, what His body loves Jesus loves. What His body forgives, Jesus forgives (John 20:23, James 5:15). What His body binds and looses on earth is bound and loosed in heaven. (Matthew 18:15-20). Thus there is a very intimate relationship between the love of Jesus and the love of His church. Jesus still loves the world in the sense of John 3:16, and Jesus wants to love the world through His body the church. He wants to release His incredible love into His body that they in turn may release it to the world. The church in the early chapters of Acts was a community filled with the transformational love of Jesus that then went out and loved people and changed the world. The basic job of the church is not evangelism, it's loving people; loving them into maturity in Christ (Ephesians 4:11-16).

OK why are so many churches cold and selfish or at best only lukewarm in their love? Here are twelve reasons that may apply:

1) They have no idea of the Christ-centered, Spirit-filled life and are struggling along in legalism.
2) They have no idea that the main task of the church is loving people into maturity in Christ.
3) Their concept of love is weak and little more than "being nice to people". It lacks reality or practicality.
4) They have descended into fleshly behavior or worldly behavior and grieved the Spirit.
5) They have opted for control and respectability and quenched the Spirit.
6) They focus on the things of this world such as current events or politics or even good counselling theories rather than on Christ.
7) They have no mastery, no focus, no disciplined mental attitude; they are not steadily connected to Christ but are unstable and are blown here and there by the latest fashions / "winds of doctrine".
8) They have opted for liberal theology or New Age trends and follow the teachings of men, which have the appearance of wisdom and godliness, but lack any real transforming power.
9) They are riddled with disunity; this robs them of power and love.
10) They are spiritually lazy and hard of hearing or they opt for comfort and avoid the cross.
11) They are financially dishonest like Ananias and Sapphira.
12) There is gross sin or immorality in the leadership.

How then can the church be brought back to a place of burning, blazing love where we love Jesus above all and love one another with powerful agape love, so that Jesus is giving Himself away all day long in our midst? How can we get this "connecting with one another in the power of Christ and the love of the Holy Spirit" working effectively?

1) Fix any of the above twelve faults that are wrong.
2) Renew worship so it is absolutely Christ-centered. Teach on the life and ministry of Jesus.
3) Fix our minds on eternity and seek the presence of the Holy Spirit.
4) Give people a vision for real biblical love as described in this chapter and get them thirsty for it.
5) Follow the leadings of the Holy Spirit.
6) Engage in real, helpful practical one-another ministry (see Gene Getz's excellent book on the one-another commands). Love one another in deed and truth, not just word and tongue.
7) Try and build an adventurous, faith-filled learning community as described earlier in this book.

Connect the church to God and get them to release Christ in them to one another, then stand back and watch what happens. In a functioning Christian community the whole community is connected upwards to Jesus Christ who is the Head and then horizontally as Christ in us ministers to one another through an amazing network of interpersonal connections that carry the love of God. If each person is Christ-focused and self-giving then enormous power is present as they become one in the Spirit. I am not talking about the cultish Groupthink or group conformity, but a creative Spirit-filled diversity, where people are one in soul and spirit but as different as can be individually.

> And He Himself gave some to be apostles, some prophets, some evangelists, and some pastors and teachers, (12) for the equipping of the saints for the work of ministry, for the edifying of the body of Christ, (13) till we all come to the unity of the faith and of the knowledge of the Son of God, to a perfect man, to the measure of the stature of the fullness of Christ; (14) that we should no longer be children, tossed to and fro and carried about with every wind of doctrine, by the trickery of men, in the cunning craftiness of deceitful plotting, (15) but, speaking the truth in love, may grow up in all things into Him who is the head; Christ; (16) from whom the whole body, joined and knit together by what every joint supplies, according to the effective working by which every part does its share, causes growth of the body for the edifying of itself in love. (Ephesians 4:11-16 NKJV)

Those who minister should edify the body of Christ into unity of the faith and the knowledge of the Son of God, to a perfect man, to the measure of the stature of the fullness of Christ. We are back to where we began this chapter taking of the fullness of God. This fullness is achieved in community. It's something the body achieves for its members. We don't do it to ourselves. We have to love people and be loved by people if the fullness is going to happen for us. How do we get there? By speaking the truth in love (v.15), and speaking the truth in love is a good definition of what biblical EQ enables us to do.

Discussion Questions

1. What have you got out of this book? Have you changed?

2. Discuss the definition of love given in this chapter. What is a benevolent connection?

3. How does love lead us to the high ground of the spiritual life? Why do you think Jesus says that loving our enemies will make us perfect as our Father in heaven is perfect?

4. What are the communicable and the incommunicable attributes of God? Which one can we participate in? How can we be "like Jesus"?

5. What are the five stages listed in Paul's prayer? What is involved in entering into being filled with all the fullness of God? What does this extraordinary statement mean?

6. How important is Christ in us when it comes to loving effectively?

7. How can a Spirit-filled community be a place of great blessing and love? How did the early church get love right?

Index

Teacher's Guide

I am a counselor and Bible College lecturer not an educator as such though I have done some post-graduate studies in education. The following suggestions are not meant to be prescriptive for the professional educator but are merely a few suggestions which are meant as a help to those of us who are not professional educators but have teaching responsibilities.

Biblical EQ can be used as a textbook on emotional development and I suggest the book be taught in twenty-four hour lectures as follows – one hour introduction, six hours on the first six chapters in the theological section, ten hours on the five chapters in the ontological section and finally eight hours of lectures on the six chapters in the practical section (2 hours each on the first and last chapters in the section.) However, I think twenty hours of lectures would be a minimum for most undergraduate students to grasp and digest the topic.

For in-service courses and extension learning I would recommend pre-reading the book and discussing it chapter by chapter by teleconference or in email discussion groups. The book can also be easily be broken down into three one-day workshops; one for each section, and taught as an intensive over a long weekend.

Small group discussion in groups of three or four is absolutely essential for this sort of material. The aim of this book will be largely defeated if you teach it in a large classroom and use assignments and exams alone as the assessment tool. A bright student could go through such a course largely unchanged. Students need to interact face to face about the issues and to stretch each other, as gently as possible, so that real change and real growth occurs. Considerable guidance and facilitation by the lecturer is needed to ensure these discussion groups achieve their aims. The section on private and public emotion should perhaps be briefly reviewed in class at the commencement of the small groups as some vulnerable students may share too much emotionally while others share very little.

I would encourage students to keep a personal journal of their reflections on the course if this is considered an acceptable form of

assessment and encourage discussion of case studies that they meet
in their ministry experience. The book raises many deep and provocative
questions such as the mind-brain problem and the nature of the human
spirit. If a class is prone to wandering off into less than edifying
arguments over these issues these might be channeled into fifteen
minute formal class debates with a definite conclusion. These debates
could be made part of the "participation" mark that most lecturers give.

While the book has an objective to achieve emotional transformation it
also has an informational purpose and is content rich. Assessing
understanding of the content and the grasp of the concepts involved is
very important so I would encourage some academic form of assessment,
such as a two-hour exam at the end of the course worth around half the
marks. If assignments are to be used instead of an exam I would suggest
three separate assignments – one on each section as I think it would be
very difficult to cover the course content with a single term paper. Even
in the case of in-services and courses where formal assessment is not
used the academic content still needs a little emphasis because it is the
concepts that will stay with the learner perhaps popping into relevance
many years in the future.

May the Lord lead you as you teach both the academic and experiential
aspects of Biblical EQ.

Further References

Addictions
Alcoholic Anonymous World Services; *Twelve Steps and Twelve Traditions*, Sydney 1952 (authors are anonymous of course!)
Anderson, Neil T. *Set Free*, London 1998, Monarch
Anderson, Neil T. & Quarles M& J *Freedom From Addiction*, Ventura 1996, Regal

Agoraphobia
Weekes, Claire; *Peace From Nervous Suffering*, Sydney 1973, Angus and Robertson
Weekes, Claire; *Simple Effective Treatment of Agoraphobia*, Sydney 1977, Angus and Robertson
Weekes, Claire; *The Latest Help For Your Nerves*, Sydney 1989, Angus and Robertson

Behavioral Medicine
Melamed, Barbara G. & Siegel, Lawrence J. *Behavioral Medicine*, New York 1980, Spinger

Boundaries (Personal)
Cloud, Henry; & Townsend John; *Safe People*, Grand Rapids 1995, Zondervan
Cloud, Henry; & Townsend John; *Boundaries*, Sydney 1992, Strand Publishing

Community Building
Banks, Robert; *Life In The New Testament Church* (or a similar title)
Crabb, Larry; *Connecting*, Nashville 1997, Word
Holpp, Lawrence; *Managing Teams*, 1999 McGraw Hill, "A Briefcase Book" imprint.
Limerick, David; & Cunnington, Bert; & Crowther, Frank; *Managing the New Organization* 2nd Edition, Warriewood 1998, Business and Professional Publishing
Peters, Tom; *The Circle of Innovation*, London 1997, Hodder & Stoughton
Senge, Peter; et. al *The Fifth Discipline Fieldbook* , London 1994, Nicholas Brealey

Cognitive Psychotherapy and Depression
Burns, David M.; *Feeling Good a New Mood Therapy*
Seligman, Martin E.P.; *Learned Optimism*, Sydney 1998, Random House
Winter, Richard; *The Roots of Sorrow*, Westchester Illinois 1986, Crossway Books

Emotions and Emotional Intelligence
Cava, Roberta; *Dealing With Difficult People*, Sydney 2000, Pan Macmillan
Cooper, Robert; & Sawaf, Ayman; *Executive EQ*, London 1997, Orion Business
Dobson, James; *Emotions Can You Trust Them*, Ventura 1980, Regal
Goleman, Daniel; *Emotional Intelligence*, London 1996, Bloomsbury

Goleman, Daniel; *Working With Emotional Intelligence*, London 1998, Bloomsbury
Weisenger, Hendrie; *Emotional Intelligence At Work*, San Francisco 1998, Jossey-Bass

Family Therapy (not directly quoted but behind a lot of my ideas on community)
Minuchin, Salvador; *Familes and Family Therapy*, London 1974, Tavistock Publications
Minuchin, Salvador; & Fishman, Charles; *Family Therapy Techniques*, 1981, Harvard College

Inner Child/ Trauma Counseling
Bradshaw, John; *Homecoming*, New York 1990, Bantam Books
Pellaur, Mary D.; Chester, Barbara; Boyajian, Jane; (Eds) *Sexual Assault And Abuse, A Handbook For Clergy and Religious Professionals*, San Francisco 1991, Harper
Smith, Ed; *Theophostics – Beyond Tolerable Recovery* (workshop manuals)

Mid-Life Crisis & Dream Therapy
Kelsey, Morton; *Dreams A Way To Listen To God*, New York 1978, Paulist
Langs, Robert; *Decoding Your Dreams*, New York 1988, Ballantine Books
O'Connor, Peter; *Understanding The Mid-Life Crisis*, Melbourne 1981, Sun Books
O'Connor, Peter; *Dreams and The Search For Meaning*, Sydney 1986, Methuen Haynes

Mind Power
Hill, Napoleon; & Keown, E. Harold; *Succeed and Grow Rich Through Persuasion*, New York 1989, Signet

Nouthetic Counseling (based on biblical exhortation and repentance)
Adams, Jay E.; *Competent To Counsel*, Phillipsburg 1970, Presbyterian and Reformed
Adams, Jay E.; *The Christian Counselor's Casebook*, Phillipsburg 1974, Presbyterian and Reformed

Pastoral Counseling (General approaches to)
Collins, Gary R.; *Christian Counseling*, Waco 1980, Word
Oates, Wayne E.; *The Presence of God In Pastoral Counseling*, Dallas 1986, Word

Southard, Samuel; *Theology and Therapy*, Dallas 1989, Word
Tournier, Paul; *The Strong and The Weak*, 1984, Highland
Tournier, Paul; *Guilt and Grace*, New York 1973, Harper & Row
Tournier, Paul; *The Meaning of Persons*
(anything by Paul Tournier is deep, thoughtful and worth reading)

Solution-Focused Thinking
O'Hanlon, William Hudson; & Weiner-Davis, Michele; *In Search of Solutions*,
London & New York 1989, W.W Norton & Co.

Spiritual Discernment
Israel, Martin; *The Spirit of Counsel*, London 1983, Mowbray

Spiritual Experiences
Wesley, John; Wesley, Charles; Whitfield, George; (abr, by Weakley, Clare G.)
The Nature of Revival, Minneapolis 1987, Bethany House

Spiritual Warfare, Power Ministry, Healing Ministry
Murphy, Ed; *The Handbook For Spiritual Warfare*, Nashville 1992, Thomas
Nelson
Taylor, Harold; *Sent To Heal*, Ringwood Victoria 1997, Order of St. Luke The
Physician
Wimber, John; *Power Healing*, London 1986, Hodder and Stoughton

Stress
Wilkie, Dr. William; *Understanding Psychiatry* , Melbourne, 1987 , Hill of
Content Publishing Company.

Temperaments
Kiersey and Davis, *Please Understand Me*
La Haye, Tim; *Transformed Temperaments*, Wheaton, Illinois 1971, Tyndale
House

Transactional Analysis (*Games, Life Scripts for section on Thoughts and
Intents of the Heart*)
Berne, Eric; *Games People Play*, London 1976, Penguin
James, Muriel; Jongeward, Dorothy; *Born To Win: Transactional Analysis With
Gestatalt Experiments*, Reading Massachusetts 1973, Addison-Wesley

Note: Where references are missing some publishing details, these are books I have loaned and lost but which I have found very useful and which I recommend. Most of the above works are secular and some are even a bit anti-Christian but if you read them with discernment and in the framework Biblical EQ places them in I am sure you will find them very useful.

About The Author

 **John Edmiston** B.Sc. Adv. Dip. Min. B.D. is the Chairman and CEO of Cybermissions, a missionary society that uses computers and the Internet to facilitate the Great Commission. He has served as a missionary in Papua New Guinea and the Philippines and did his theological training at a Baptist seminary in Queensland, Australia. Before becoming a missionary, John worked as a career guidance and workplace-counseling consultant. He desires to see revival come to God's church through the spiritual and emotional renewal of Christian workers and the structures in which they work. John is married to Minda, who is a botanist, and they live in Los Angeles. John can be contacted by e-mail at johned@aibi.ph.